The *Incredible* History of God's True Church

Ivor C. Fletcher

Published by
Living Church of God
Charlotte, North Carolina
May 2014

Manufactured by
United Book Press, Inc.
Baltimore, Maryland

Printed in the United States of America

ISBN-10: 162479999X
ISBN-13: 978-1-62479-999-0

Scriptures in this book are quoted from the *New King James Version* (©Thomas Nelson, Inc., Publishers) unless otherwise noted.

CONTENTS

Contents

The Incredible History of God's True Church

AUTHOR'S NOTE

More than two billion people in today's world consider themselves to be Christians. Most seem very sincere in what they believe. Yet Jesus described His true Church as a "little flock" (Luke 12:32). Is there a contradiction here? Could two billion people really be described as a "little flock?"

An important key to unlocking this apparent mystery is given by Christ Himself: "And Jesus answered and said to them: 'Take heed that no-one deceives you. For many, will come in My name, saying, I am the Christ [paying lip service to Jesus as Messiah], and will deceive many" (Matthew 24:4–5).

Spiritual deception began soon after Christ's crucifixion. Some 20 years later, in the mid 50s, the Apostle Paul, in his second letter to the brethren at Corinth, mentions "false apostles," who were attempting to introduce "another Jesus" and "a different gospel" (2 Corinthians 11:1–15).

By the second century A.D., many of these false ministers had gained positions of great influence and authority within the church. Several of the most important teachings given by Jesus Christ and proclaimed by the first apostles, such as the gospel of the Kingdom of God, were no longer being taught. New teachings, such as the popular pagan belief in immortal souls going to heaven at the time of death, replaced the earlier teachings.

The weekly and annual Sabbaths, or Holy Days, that Jesus and His apostles had always kept, and which reveal God's awesome plan of salvation for humanity, were also rejected on the grounds that they were "Jewish."

Down through the centuries, since that time, the teachings of mainstream Christianity, which in many respects are very different to the actual teachings of Jesus and His first apostles, have dominated the religious life of much of the world.

Despite this, however, the "little flock" that constitutes God's true Church has continued to exist, and to do God's Work, down through the centuries. That Church continues to "live by every word of God" (Matthew 4:4)—the Old Testament as well as the doctrines of Jesus Christ and the apostles found in the New Testament.

In this book, I have tried to lay bare the facts about the Church of God through the centuries based on the characteristics found in the scriptures and from historical sources. I hope you find this as fascinating and enlightening as I have. It has been a privilege to dig out all this information in order to present it in one volume.

Ivor C. Fletcher
Bristol, England
February 2014

PREFACE TO THE SECOND EDITION

As the book that I wrote on Church history was first published in 1984, the question could be asked why a second edition is required. My publisher had printed 3,000 copies that sold out fairly quickly. Since then I have received a steady stream of enquiries from interested readers. It has been somewhat frustrating to be unable to satisfy this demand.

Another reason is that since the death of Mr. Herbert W Armstrong, in 1986, the Church of God has experienced some of the most traumatic and astonishing events in its entire history. Mr. Armstrong's successors, although claiming to be "following in his footsteps," have in reality taken the Church back into orthodox Protestant theology. His distinctive and Bible-based doctrines have been rejected as "unorthodox."

Many have seen a real need for some form of written record of this period in Church history. My hope is that this may be partly achieved by the addition of two new chapters. This book, though surely not the last and final word on its topic, is the result of exhaustive research. Yet I do not intend it merely to be accurate; I hope readers will also find it to be a very readable historical account rather than a dry academic text.

Church history can provide a vehicle through which we as God's people can trace our spiritual family history. It has been said that: "Those who fail to learn the lessons of history, end up making the same mistakes." For us this can have eternal consequences. We are told to beware of those who can lead us astray spiritually and even "take your crown" (Revelation 3:11). I hope that you find this updated version of the book to be of interest.

INTRODUCTION

If ever a man could be said to have lived up to his own "Seven Laws of Success," that man must surely be Herbert W. Armstrong. Already highly successful and prosperous in the field of journalism and advertising whilst still in his twenties, Armstrong went on to establish Ambassador College in order to provide the world with the "missing dimension" in education.

In 1934, thirteen years before the founding of the College, the *World Tomorrow* radio broadcast was started on a radio station in Oregon, at a cost of $2.50 per week. By 1979 the programme had grown in its scope and impact to the point that multiple millions of people worldwide could hear the message, and in some areas watch it on television.

The Plain Truth magazine, also started by Mr. Armstrong, had similar humble beginnings. Its first edition of February 1934 consisted of some 175 copies of a paper that few would have dignified with the title of "magazine." The cost of producing that first issue was probably less than two dollars. Since its modest birth, a staggering 224 million copies of the magazine had been circulated worldwide (up to January, 1979). Many in the publishing field admired the professional expertise used in the production of this "magazine of understanding."

Mr. Armstrong's personal work output was truly amazing. In 45 years he authored over 750 magazine articles, some 50 booklets, several books, and nearly 500 letters to co-workers and members of the Worldwide Church of God, of which he was Pastor General. This was in addition to his duties as a College Chancellor, his work with the Ambassador International Cultural Foundation, radio and television broadcasting, and personal meetings with heads of state and other important political leaders around the world.

Herbert Armstrong's basic philosophy of life was based on the principle that "it is more blessed to give than to receive." He saw the role of the church as preparing the way for the return of Jesus Christ, when the government of God and the "give" philosophy of life will be restored to the world.

His extensive foreign travels and meetings with world leaders earned Mr. Armstrong the title of "ambassador for world peace" and "A builder of bridges between all peoples everywhere." In 1970 King Leopold of Belgium awarded him a special watch. This watch was one of four that had been made from a World War I cannonball. It was the intention of the king's father to present each watch to the four men who had made the most significant contributions to world peace.

In 1973, Mr. Armstrong received the Order of the Sacred Treasure—the highest honour that the Japanese government can bestow on a private citizen of another country. He had a personal meeting with Emperor Hirohito the same year.

Although the Worldwide Church of God, previously known as the Radio Church of God, had only been in existence since the early nineteen thirties, there is evidence to suggest that this body was merely the twentieth-century continuation of the "Church of God" which dates back to apostolic times.

Members of the Church of God were among the early colonists of New England who came to America from England over three centuries ago. Tracing back the spiritual roots of these people we find that the Church of God, holding to the same basic doctrines as the modern Worldwide Church of God up to 1995, existed in Britain through the Middle and Dark Ages—clear back to Roman times.

The true Church, although a "little flock" as Christ described it, has always been "worldwide" in the sense that its message has never been confined to one single nation, but was to be taken to "the very ends of the earth." To trace the history of the true Church in every nation would be a monumental task, and for this reason I propose to confine this work mainly to the Church of God in Britain and America.

So far as I am aware, the history of the Church of God in Britain is a story which has never been told, at least not in any detail, apart from passing references within the context of church history in general.

Considerable research, however, has taken place relating to the Church of God in America. My purpose in writing this book is to tell this story, and in the telling of it, to provide a measure of inspiration and encouragement to the present era of God's Church living in these awesome days of the digital age.

One of the main problems relating to books on church history in the past has been the style in which they have been written. Such books have often been written in a dry and scholarly manner that has proved to be somewhat tedious reading for the average layman.

The work of one Puritan writer of some three centuries ago was described as follows: "This huge volume is the most tedious of all the Puritan productions about the Sabbath. There is not a spark of originality to animate the lump." The critic goes on to state that but for one chapter "its dullness would be without relief."

The story of God's people is not primarily concerned with almost endless debates and discussions over dates or doctrines. It is above all else a story about *people*. In this book I have sought to emphasize what a modern journalist might call the "human interest" side of the story. And why not? The story of God's people through the ages contains all the elements that one might find in a good novel—adventure, romance, tragedy and mystery.

When dealing with a subject that covers nearly two thousand years of human history, one is forced to rely on records and sources of information that are ancient and sometimes obscure. A great deal of controversy among scholars surrounds many of the early writings on church history, regarding authenticity—some such records may well prove to be, as experts have claimed, deliberate forgeries.

In the light of these facts, no absolute guarantee can be given regarding the authenticity of all material quoted in this book; some information given relating to the Church of God in past ages, comes from enemies and persecutors, and as such can hardly be regarded as objective and unbiased material—the reader is advised to exercise a degree of caution. Having said this, however, I would like to point out that great care has been taken in the selection of these data, with a view to presenting a picture which is as accurate, fair and balanced as circumstances allow.

The prophet Daniel foretold "many shall cleave to them (the Church of God) with flatteries." One cannot assume that every individual mentioned within this book who claimed to be a part of God's Church really was a converted member—a great many were little more than friends and sympathizers. It is not my purpose, however, to judge any individual in this regard.

Perhaps the greatest lesson that we can learn from a study of this nature is that history does repeat itself and that the past is indeed the key to the future. Although the political, economic and social climates in which many of the events in this book took place are entirely different from the setting of the pulsating digital age in which we live, problems relating to people and human nature are the same.

The Incredible History of God's True Church

There is much that we can learn from the failings and triumphs of God's people through the ages.

This project would hardly have been possible without the valuable assistance and encouragement of several organisations and individuals.

Among those to whom I wish to express my sincere thanks are Ambassador College Press, the Seventh Day Baptist Historical Society, British Museum Publications, and the Society for Promoting Christian Knowledge.

The staff of the Bristol Public Reference Library, through their expert knowledge, were able to produce and make available much of the research material, some of it centuries old, upon which this work is based. I thank them for their help. I also thank the Covenant Publishing Company for granting me permission to quote from their material.

Richard C. Nickels of Portland, Oregon, made available to me the results of his own research relating to Church history in the United States of America, for which I thank him.

Thanks should also go to Mr. Andrew Rowley for his support and advice; and, finally, to my wife, Susan, for typing the manuscript and providing support for the writing of this book.

ABOUT THE AUTHOR

Ivor C. Fletcher was born in Bristol, England, in 1942. In 1958, as a teenager, he became an aircraft mechanic in the Royal Navy. This gave him the opportunity to travel to many interesting and even exotic parts of the world. Most of the remaining part of his working life was spent in the aerospace industry, at the local factory that built the iconic Concorde aircraft.

In 1969 he married his wife, Susan. Her background in typing and secretarial work provided valuable assistance in preparing the church history book for publication. Both had become members of the Worldwide Church of God in 1968. The church booklet, *A True History of the True Church*, by Dr. Herman L. Hoeh, sparked the author's interest in the subject. The booklet, although a compelling read, was very brief. It motivated him to carry out extensive research into the subject. The material uncovered led to the first edition of the church history book, published in 1984.

Ivor and Susan became members of the Living Church of God in 2009. Several of the leaders of this group had read the book and shared the author's interest in publishing a second, updated edition which would include the events that had taken place since the publication of the first edition in 1984. We hope that you enjoy reading this new edition.

Chapter One

THE SETTING

*"For mountains, bridges, rivers, churches and
fair women, Britain is past compare"*
—Marcus Valerius Martialis (Martial), Roman epigrammatist
(*Lib. I*, Ep. 32; *Lib. III*, Ep. 20).

*"Therefore those who were scattered
went everywhere preaching the word"*
(Acts 8:4).

I have before me a Bible Atlas showing the growth of the early Christian Church to the time of Constantine. In common with other publications of this type, it traces the establishment of the Church in Britain back to about the reign of the Roman Emperor Diocletian, close to the year A.D. 300.

This view is one that is also reflected by many, if not most, modern writers on this subject. Statements by earlier writers, suggesting a first century A.D. apostolic origin of the Church in Britain, have been relegated to the realm of tradition, myth, or plain wishful thinking.

Even the majority of churches at the present time seem to be of this opinion, but this has not always been the case. About 300 years ago a massive work entitled, *The Ecclesiastical History of Great Britain*, by Collier, was produced. The book, published in ten volumes, gave the generally held view of leading theologians and churchmen of that time.

On page 27, Vol. 1, Collier makes the point that: "it is evident Christianity got footing here in the apostolic age: but what progress was made upon the infidels; in what parts the church was settled, and under whom; what successes or discouragements; what revolutions happened in the ecclesiastical history of this island, from the apostles to King Lucius, is altogether uncertain."

It is not surprising that Collier knew nothing of the period between the apostles and the second-century A.D. King Lucius. In Britain, as elsewhere, this represented the incredible "Lost Century" of Church history.

The Incredible History of God's True Church

For many centuries there existed two separate schools of thought regarding Church history in Britain. Many have assumed that prior to the Reformation, the only church in Britain was the Catholic Church.

There existed, however, until Saxon times, the British or Celtic Church, along with the Church of Rome. These two churches often differed in their general approach and also on many doctrinal points. By about the time of King Alfred, however, Catholic influence within the Celtic Church had increased to the point that the British Church as a separate body had virtually ceased to exist.

The British Church for many centuries held the view that the apostolic origin of the Church in Britain was a point of historical fact—not mere tradition. Early Catholic writers such as Bede placed the origin of Christianity in Britain in the second century A.D., under King Lucius.

The Catholic position seems to have been based not so much on theology or history as on political considerations. During the "Holy Roman Empire" period one of the major foundations of papal authority was the antiquity of the Roman Church.

The first-century church at Rome was claimed to have been the "Mother Church" or headquarters church for Europe and the West. Other churches in the West were said to have been established from Rome. The British view, based on the statement by Gildas that Christianity arrived in Britain during the last year of the reign of Tiberius (A.D. 36–37), proved an embarrassment to Catholic writers. This date is more than 20 years before the arrival of the Apostle Paul in Rome.

One of the major problems relating to the history of the Church of God in Britain during the early centuries is an almost total absence of local written records. Prior to about A.D. 542, one is forced to rely on the testimony of foreign writers regarding Christianity in Britain.

In that year, Gildas, often said to have been the first British historian, wrote the amazing statement that "We certainly know that Christ, the True Sun, afforded His light, the knowledge of His precepts, to our island in the last year of the reign of Tiberius Caesar."[1]

The words "we certainly know" are an indication that in the time of Gildas, the date of A.D. 36–37 for the establishment of Christianity in Britain was more than just speculation or tradition; it was the commonly accepted view of the time.

Gildas wrote primarily as a historian rather than a theologian. Although a Catholic, he seems to have had nothing but contempt for the clergy of his day. He describes them in the following terms:

"Britain has priests, but they are foolish; a multitude of ministers, but they are shameless; clergy, nay, crafty ravishers; shepherds as they are called, but they are wolves, ready to slay souls—teaching the people, but showing them the worst examples, vices and wicked manners."

This writer, although probably not the first British historian, was certainly the first that we have any record of to commit his thoughts to paper. He was aware of the British identity, as part of the "ten lost tribes of Israel."

Commenting on the Saxon invasions that were in progress at the time, he stated that the reason why God allowed such events was: "to the end that our Lord might in this land try after His accustomed manner these His Israelites, whether they loved Him or not."

Gildas was personally affected by the troubled times in which he lived. It was said that on one occasion he was forced to seek refuge from pirates on an island in the Bristol Channel, near the site of the modern town of Weston-Super-Mare.

It is important to realize that before the time of Gildas the British language (there was no "English" language prior to Saxon times) was primarily a spoken rather than written language.

Edinburgh University professor Kenneth Jackson, an authority on the subject, mentions that "It would not occur to anyone to write in British, nor would they know how to do so."

Celtic, Pre-Roman Europe and Britain passed on law, genealogy, story, song and myth in oral but not written form. This does not mean that all first-century Britons were uneducated. Oral communication was considered to be superior to the written word. Education was primarily a matter of memorizing a vast accumulation of knowledge.

"They [scholars] are said there to learn by heart a great number of verses; accordingly some remain in the course of training twenty years. Nor do they regard it lawful to commit these to writing." [2]

Some sources state that by the time of graduation students were expected to have committed to memory the staggering total of 20,000 verses. It is probable that such material was arranged in allegorical or poetic form to aid the memory.

The Incredible History of God's True Church

The knowledge of Church history, in common with knowledge in general, was passed on by word of mouth from teacher to student, father to son. In process of time such information as remained extant took the form of traditions.

There must have been a tendency, human nature being what it is, for each generation to add a little "colour" before passing on the story. Someone once described tradition as the "accumulated common sense of centuries."

When the empire-wide persecution of the Christian church under Diocletian reached Britain about A.D. 300, church buildings, Bibles, and other written records were put to the torch. Any records that survived almost certainly perished in the Saxon invasions of the following centuries.

Archaeologists have sometimes been puzzled by the scarcity of remains of church buildings from the Roman occupation of Britain. This might seem strange in the light of the comment by Chrysostom (A.D. 347–407) that: "The British Isles, which are beyond the sea, and which lie in the ocean, have received the power of the Word. Churches are there founded, and altars erected."[3] The answer to this apparent contradiction lies in the building materials used for church buildings at the time.

"The story of Patrick's work in Ireland explains the problem which has sorely puzzled some of our archaeologists, why there are so few remains of churches in the Roman period. St. Martin's, Canterbury, and a few others, none of which are in Wales, contain Roman work, and may have been used for Christian purposes even in the Roman period, by the Roman Christians or the Romanized Britons; but probably the majority of the churches throughout Britain, and almost certainly the majority in Wales, were wooden. Occasionally when wood was scarce, Patrick built a church of earth, as at Foirrgea—he "made a quadrangular church of earth, because there was no forest near at hand!"[4] At this time, churches of stone were rare.

Many modern writers have rejected early evidence of a first-century Church in Britain on the grounds that the Britons living in that age were Gentiles.

Indeed, the apostles (including Paul) were commanded to go to "the lost sheep of the house of Israel." Paul however, could have visited Britain in his special capacity of apostle to the Gentiles, a role he filled in a way unlike the other apostles.

In Chapter Two we will examine the question—were the first-century Britons really Gentiles, or a part of Israel?

Chapter Summary

Where did the apostles go? The limited scope of the book of Acts. Only 30 years out of almost 70 years of New Testament history covered. Main focus is on Peter and Paul, where did the other apostles go? Early writers indicate that the gospel was preached in Western Europe and Britain.

Chapter Two

LAND OF THE CELTS

"They (the Saxons) were a people thought by good writers to be
descendants of the Sacae, a kind of Scythians in the north of Asia, thence
called Sacasons, or sons of Sacae, who with a flood of other northern
nations came into Europe toward the declining of the Roman Empire"
(*History of England*, Milton, Book 3, pp. 406–407).

"So Israel was carried away from their
own land to Assyria, as it is to this day"
(2 Kings 17: 23)

Who were the Celtic peoples that inhabited Britain and much of Europe during the time of Christ? Why did they have Asiatic style war chariots? And why did the Belgae of Southern England have palm trees, of all things, on their coins?

Diodorus Siculus, writing in 60 B.C., stated: "The Britons live in the same manner that the ancients did; they fight in chariots as the ancient heroes of Greece are said to have done in the Trojan Wars—they are plain and upright in their dealings—the island is very populous—the Celts never shut the doors of their houses; they invite strangers to their feasts, and when it is over ask who they are and what is their business."

The Celts were a prosperous and industrious people. Wealth was centered in large flocks of sheep and herds of cattle. Food was often preserved in smoked, cured, or salted form. International trade flourished, wine was imported from the Mediterranean region.

Mixed farming, cereal and livestock, was practiced, and a system of crop rotation with regular manuring sought to avoid land exhaustion.

The Celts were a proud warrior race. After nine long years of bitter warfare, from A.D. 43, the Romans, although employing their finest legions and military generals, had only succeeded in conquering a part of the island.

Even at this point the Roman position was far from secure. Tacitus (A.D. 55–120) lamented that: "In Britain, after the captivity of Caractacus, the Romans were repeatedly conquered and put to the rout by the single state of the Silures alone."[1] But were these people, as Gildas was to claim some four centuries later, "Israelites"?

7

It would be good at this point to trace some of the movements of the "lost ten tribes" of Israel after being taken into captivity by the Assyrians in 721–718 B.C.

The Lost Ten Tribes in Assyria

Scripture gives us this information: "Now the king of Assyria went throughout all the land, and went up to Samaria and besieged it for three years. In the ninth year of Hoshea, the king of Assyria took Samaria and carried Israel away to Assyria, and placed them in Halah and by the Habor, the River of Gozan, and in the cities of the Medes" (2 Kings 17:5–6).

Cuneiform tablets discovered at Khorsabad, to the north of Nineveh, the capital of ancient Assyria, give the Assyrian version of the same event, which as we can see confirms the biblical statement:

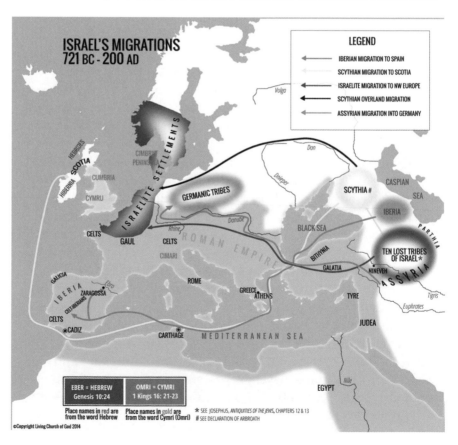

"I besieged and captured Samaria, and carried off 27,290 of its inhabitants as booty."

The Israelites were settled in the regions around Lakes Van and Urmia, which are situated in northern Iran and eastern Turkey.

The name "Israel" took different forms in the various nations that had contact with Israelites. Pre-captivity Assyrian records use "Bit-Khumri" meaning "the sons of Omri." An obelisk held by the British Museum has an illustration of Jehu paying tribute to Assyrian king Shalmaneser and carries the inscription, "This is Iaua [Jehu], the son of Khunui [Omri]."

The Hebrew pronunciation of "Khumri" was "Ghonui," which later became corrupted into Gimera. People having this name began appearing in Assyrian records a mere eleven years after the captivity—and in the very region where the Israelites had settled.

Cuneiform tablets found in the ruins of ancient Nineveh tell of the reports of Assyrian spies who in 707 B.C. witnessed a battle between the Gimera and a tribe known as Urartians.

Assyrian records show that shortly before they settled the Israelite captives in the area around Lake Van, the previous inhabitants were driven out by Assyrian troops. The indications are that these people made an attempt some years later to recapture their territory, being defeated in the process by the Gimera or exiled Israelites.

The Israelites Move on From Assyria

After several decades the power of the Assyrian Empire began to wane and its hold over the Israelite captives weakened. In 679 B.C. some of the tribes broke away and escaped into the mountains of Asia Minor (2 Esdras 13:40–44). At about the same time the Gimera rose in rebellion against their Assyrian captors but were defeated in the upper Euphrates region.

In Media, the other region where the Israelites were settled, one finds in the Assyrian texts reports of roaming bands of hostile Gimera.

In 675 B.C. we find the first report of Scythians in the Assyrian records. In the annals of Esarhaddon we read: "I scattered the Mannaean people, intractable barbarians, and I smote with the sword the armies of Ishpaki, the ISKUZA; alliance with them did not save him."

Within 45 years of Israel's captivity, we find the Gimera and Iskuza in exactly the same regions where the Israelites were settled.

Iskuza is the Assyrian version of Scythian. According to Herodotus the Persians called the Scythians "Sacae" or "Saka." In the days of Amos the Israelites called themselves after Isaac (Amos 7:16), the word probably being "Isaaca." In Hebrew the "I" is not emphasized as it is in English. In time it likely became lost and was pronounced as "Sacca"—almost identical to the Persian "Sacae," the word for Scythians.

Much later in history we read of Saxons or "Saacs Sons." The Babylonian version of the Persian "Sacae" was Gimiri, an almost identical word to the Assyrian Gimera. The clear indications are that all these names, making allowances for different languages, refer to the same people—the Scythians or "ten lost tribes" of Israel.

In 1947 evidence was discovered at Ziwille, about 70 miles south of Lake Urmia, of the close relationship between the Assyrians and Scythians. A royal treasure dating to the end of the seventh century B.C. was unearthed. Among the items uncovered, some were of Assyrian origin, some Scythian and others a mixture of the two cultures. It is believed that at least some of the treasure consisted of wedding presents given on the occasion of the wedding between a Scythian king and an Assyrian princess.

As Assyrian influence declined, that of the Scythians increased. Herodotus relates "A battle was fought in which the Medes were defeated, and lost their power in Asia, which was taken over in its entirety by the Scythians."

About 625 B.C. the Scythians began moving north. Soviet archaeologists have discovered evidence of a Scythian attack on the ancient fortress of Karmir Blur.

Following the defeat of their Assyrian allies in 609 B.C., the Scythians were driven into Southern Russia by the Medes. Others moved towards the West, and moving across Asia Minor, they were known to the Greeks as Cimmerians. How significant it was that the Hebrew meaning of the word Scythian was "wanderer."

For some 300 years, the Scythians prospered in southern Russia, but about 250 B.C. they were driven out by the Sarmatians and made their way into Western Europe and later Britain. About this time they became known as the Celts.

This is why Celtic influence in the third century B.C. is said to have stretched from Southern Russia in the east to Britain and Spain in the west.

The Israelites Arrive in The Isles

Even as late as the time of the church historian Bede, the Scythians were still sometimes known by that name. "Coming from Scythia [i.e. Scandinavia] in their long boats, and, being carried by tempest to the northern parts of Ireland"—Bede relates that the local inhabitants, although related to the newcomers, persuaded them to move on and settle in Scotland. [2] Another writer adds a few further details to the story: "To which end they accustomed themselves to the sea; and so, from thence (Scandinavia), these Scythians came into the northern parts of Britain, whence they had the name Caledonians; and, upon new supplies coming after the Romans had subdued the southern parts of Britain, were then called Picts." Explaining how Scotland received its name, he states: "and Scotia from these Scythae."

And it is of considerable interest that a late Irish antiquary tells us "that a part of their country, [Ireland] in their own language, is called Gaethluighe, i.e. Gothland from the Goths or Scythians who took possession of it." [3]

As the Scythians moved westwards across Asia Minor and Europe, so the territory of "Scythia" moved West with them. This is why by Roman times "Scythia" was located in Scandinavia. This is where the Scythians came from immediately before their arrival in Britain.

The traditional home of the Norse god Odin was at Asgerd near the Euxine (Black) and Caspian Seas. The city is thought to have been located some 30 miles north of Lake Van—the very area where the Assyrians had settled their Israelite captives.

One branch of the Scythian or Israelite group did not reach Britain until after the Roman occupation—they were the Saxons. Along with the Saxons came the Danes and Jutes. In the *Vetus Chronicon Holsatiae*, on page 54, we read that—"the Danes and Jutes are Jews of the tribe of Dan."

The Saxons were not only a branch of the Scythian race, but also traced their own origins to Armenia, a Roman province, which included the territory in which the exiled Israelites were settled.

"The Saxons were a Scythian tribe, and of the various Scythian nations that have been recorded, the Sakai, or Sakae, are the people from whom the descent of the Saxons may be inferred with the least violation of probability. Sakai—Suna or the sons of Sukai, abbreviated into Saksun, which is the same sound as Saxon. The Sukai, who in Latin are called Sacae, were an important branch of the Scythian nation."[4]

"This important fact of a part of Armenia having been named Sukasuna, is mentioned by Strabo in another place," and seems to give a geographical locality to our primeval ancestors, and to account for the Persian words that occur in the Saxon language as they must have come into Armenia from the northern regions of Persia.[5]

Milton too, confirms the relationship between Saxons and Scythians. "They [the Saxons] were a people thought by good writers to be descendants of the Sacae, a kind of Scythians in the north of Asia, thence called Sacasons, or sons of Sacae, who with a flood of other northern nations came into Europe, toward the declining of the Roman Empire."[6]

The Angles who invaded England at the same time were a branch of the Saxon race. Nennius, writing in about A.D. 800, traced the Saxons back to Scythia.

The Saxons recorded that the earlier Celtic inhabitants of Britain, whom they displaced, also came from Armenia. In the opening paragraph of the *Anglo-Saxon Chronicle* we read: "The inhabitants of this land were Britons, they came from Armenia, and first settled in the south of Britain."

Bede recorded that there were "twenty-eight noble cities" in Britain during "former times" and that copper, iron, lead and silver were all mined in ancient times. Vines were cultivated and an abundance of fish, along with salmon, dolphins and whales were found around the coasts.[7]

"It would appear, that at first the aborigines of the country could not have been what we should now call 'barbarians or savages.' Their earliest traditions speak of the pre-existence of letters, arts, and sciences; and all the notices of the arrangements of their policy go to prove, that their original condition was neither ignorant nor barbarous."[8]

The Welsh Triads

Among the earliest of all British records that relate to the origins of the Celtic peoples are the Welsh Triads. These interesting writings contain a mixture of history and tradition. "Yet even in their imperfect state, they give us much intelligence respecting the aborigines of Britain." [9]

Declaration of Arbroath (1320)

After the English invasion of Scotland in 1297, the Scottish lairds appealed to the Pope in Rome to restore their independence. In the document they trace their origins to Greater Scythia between the Caspian and Black seas. They stated that they traveled via Spain and later into Scotland (see Israel's Migrations map, p. 8).

"Whatever opinion therefore may be formed of those Welsh records, it may be safely asserted, that the general scope of their teaching is consistent with itself, and harmonizes with the early traditions of almost every other ancient people." [10]

Several eminent scholars have supported the authenticity of the Welsh Triads. "Their contents furnish, in my opinion, strong evidence of their authenticity. I cannot account for them at all upon other grounds." [11]

The Triads relate that all but two people, of the first inhabitants of Britain were drowned in a great flood. A ship, containing a man and his family, along with a male and female of every living creature were the only ones to survive the flood.

After the flood the Triads mention the arrival of the Cymry or Kymry. This name means "the first race." They were known to the Greeks as Kimmerioi. The Cymry came from ancient Albania (not the modern European state by that name), which was situated to the south of the Caucasus mountains and bordering the western coast of the Caspian Sea.

"There are three pillars of the nation of the Isle of Britain. The first was Hu the Mighty, who brought the nation of the Kymry first to the Isle of Britain; coming from that which is called Defrobani," also rendered, by Thomas Wood, "more correctly Dyffynbanu, or Dyffynalbanu, that is, the deep vales or glens of Albania, a country between the Euxine [Black] and Caspian Seas."

In "The Scottish Declaration of Independence," an important official document drawn up in A.D. 1320, we find that the Scottish people of that period traced their ancestry back to greater Scythia," which included the territory between the Black and Caspian Seas. [12]

The fact that the Saxons, Celts and Scots all traced their origins to the area between the Black and Caspian Seas is of the utmost significance. It was in this precise region that the Assyrians settled their Israelite captives.

"The people of Israel were deported to the lands lying immediately *south of the Caucasus Mountains* and south of the Caspian Sea."[13]

"According to reliable estimates there were somewhere around 7,000,000 or more people in Israel and Judah prior to their captivity. The Northern Kingdom of Israel must have easily contained a population of 5,000,000 or more at the time of the beginning of the overthrow of Israel by Assyria in 741–721 B.C." [14]

What became of this great mass of exiled Israelites? Not a shred of evidence exists to prove that they ever returned to the land of Israel. Even during the time of the Jewish historian Josephus in the late first century A.D., the ten tribes had not returned to Palestine. He mentions "there are but two tribes in Asia and Europe subject to the Romans, while the ten tribes are beyond Euphrates till now, and are an immense multitude and not to be estimated by numbers." [15]

"Yes, just what happened to these teeming millions of prolific Israelites? This is a question which has perplexed countless millions down through the ages and has baffled Catholic, Protestant, and Jewish theologians as well." [16]

In view of the fact that Saxons, Celts and Scots all trace their ancestry back to the Scythians, is it not significant that "The Sacai or Scythians do not appear in history before Israel's captivity, but they do appear in the areas of the Black and Caspian Seas, shortly after Israel was deported to those same general regions." [17]

The Lost Tribes
The Behistun Rock inscription dating to the time of the Persian king Darius the First contains vital keys to the identity of modern European races. This inscription lists 22 provinces, the nineteenth of which was Scythia. The information is given in three languages, Scythia is mentioned in the Persian language, the Babylonian version gives this as "in the land of the CIMMERIANS" (Gi-mi-ri).

"The ethnic name of Gimiri first occurs in the Cuneiform records—as the Semitic equivalent of the Arian name Saka (Sakai)— whether at the same time these Gimiri or Saka are really Cymric Celts we cannot positively say—but the Babylonian title of Gimiri, as applied to the Sakae, is not a vernacular but a foreign title, and may simply mean 'The Tribes.'" [18]

Terms such as "The tribes" or "Lost Tribes" have frequently been employed in relation to the tribes of Israel.

The Behistun Rock inscription classifies the Gimiri (GHOMRI) as the same people as the Sacae or Scythians who were the ancient ancestors of the Saxons, Celts, Cimmerians, Cymri and several other groups.

The Welsh, to this day, still retain the ancient name of Cymry.

"The Cimmerians seeming to be the same people with the Gauls or Celts under a different name, and it is observable that the Welsh, who are descended from the Gauls, still call themselves Cymri or Kymry."[19]

Lysons, quoting a series of ancient authorities, traces the origin of the Cymric Celts to Armenia, adding that "it confirms the traditions of the Welsh, the views of Nennius and the *Anglo-Saxon Chronicle* and all our earliest histories, and to anyone who has studied the question seems most convincing."[20]

According to Sharon Turner, the Cimmerians and Celts shared a common language.[21]

The Welsh Triads mention that the Cymry crossed the Bosphorus on their way out of Asia Minor. Herodotus traces the origin of the Cimmerians to South Russia and the area of the Caucasus during the seventh century B.C. They were driven into Asia Minor and later moved into Western Europe. Strabo also confirmed their settlement in the Western extremities of Europe.

Later writers identify this group with the Cimbri or Cymry. The main body of the Cimmerians later merged with the Scyths.

"The Celts had an unvarying tradition that they came from the east."[22]

Dr. Wylie in his *History of the Scottish Nation*, page 15, identifies the European Celts with the Gimirrai of the Assyrian monuments.

He also states "there exists abundant evidence to show that all the inhabitants of Britain, from this early period onwards, were all sprung from the same stock, though they arrived in our island by different routes and are known by different names."[23]

If the early Britons were indeed descended from the Israelites it would be logical that a measure of similarity should exist between the Hebrew and British languages. This is exactly what we do find. Very few vowels are found in either the Hebrew or Welsh languages, but the affinity between the languages goes even further than this.

"Yet this we gather from the names attaching to the British monuments still remaining among us, when divested of modern corruptions, that there is a strong affinity between these British names and that language of which Hebrew is either the original or one of its earliest off-shoots; and therefore Hebrew, Chaldee or some other very near cognate, must have been the language of the first inhabitants in this island." [24]

"Many have remarked upon the biblical surnames in Wales. Those are often very striking and always belong to truly Welsh families whose origins are lost in the mists of time; obvious examples are Joseph, Israel, Abraham, Mordecai, David and variations of these. Scotland also has its share of biblical surnames, like Adam, Asher, and some combining 'mac' or 'son' in the name, but Scotland tends more to the use of Gaelic place names with a Hebrew content." [25]

Danites in Ireland

The earliest historical records of Ireland abound in references to the Israelites, especially the "Tuatha-de-Danaan" or Tribe of Dan. Some have tried to connect such references to the "pious fables" promoted by Irish monks of the Dark Ages but in reality the monks did not

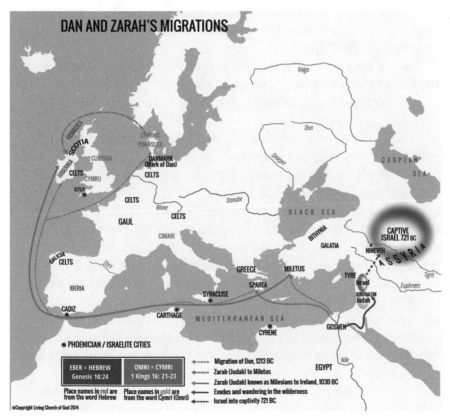

produce these records and denied the Israelite connections with Ireland. [26]

According to the *Domestic Annals* of Ireland the first settlement in Ireland was established by Nin mac Piel, whom some have identified as the Assyrian king Ninus, son of Bel or Belus. For about 300 years after the Flood, Ireland remained uninhabited, but in 2069 B.C. a group of warriors under the leadership of Partholan founded a colony at Inis Saimer, a small island in the river Erne, at Ballyshannon. This group was destroyed by a plague in 1769 B.C. [27]

Moore states (p. 63) that a colony of people called Nemedians came from the Black Sea area and settled in Ireland in 1709 B.C. They were dispersed and destroyed by "African Sea Rovers" or Formorians (who were probably Phoenicians) in 1492 B.C.

The next settlement was established by a group known as "Fir-Bolge." "They were dispossessed by the Tuatha-de-Danaan." [28]

Dr. Robert Gordon Latham, well known nineteenth-century ethnologist, saw a clear relationship between the Danaans and the Israelite tribe of Dan." [29]

The Danites arrived in Ireland in 1213 B.C., during the time of Barak and Deborah when "Dan abode in ships" (Judges 5:17).

Keating gives further details of the Danite adventurers and of their arrival in Ireland.

"The Danaans were a people of great learning, they had overmuch gold and silver—they left Greece after a battle with the Assyrians, and for fear of falling into the hands of the Assyrians, came to Norway and Denmark, and thence... to Ireland." [30]

"In process of time, the Tuatha-de-Danaan were themselves dispossessed of their sway; a successful invasion from the coast of Spain having put an end to the Danaanian dynasty, and transferred the scepter into the hands of that Milesian or Scotic race, which through so long a series of succeeding ages, supplied Ireland with her kings. This celebrated colony, through coming directly from Spain, was originally, we are told, of Scythic race." [31]

The Danites appear to have had an outward looking and adventurous spirit even as early as the time of the Exodus of the Israelites from Egypt.

Diodorus Siculus, writing in 50 B.C., but quoting from a much earlier source (Hetataeus), mentions that a group led by Cadmus and Danaus left Egypt and settled in the southern parts of Greece. He goes on to relate that the greater part of the Israelites left Egypt under the leadership of Moses. Diodorus also mentions that Danaus and his company brought with them from Egypt the custom of circumcising their male children.

Herodotus provides us with the information that the Dorian Greeks had come into Greece from Egypt. The Spartans also claimed a common ancestry with the Jews. In a letter from the Spartan king Arius to the Jewish high priest Onias, he makes the point that "it hath been found in writing concerning the Spartans and Jews, that they are brethren, and that they are of the stock of Abraham." [32]

Josephus records that the Spartan seal affixed to the letter was the Danite symbol of an eagle holding in its claws a dragon or serpent. The Jews returned a message of greeting to "their brethren the Spartans."

The Danites of Greece became a maritime people extending their influence to the islands and coastal regions of Greece, and the Black Sea, where the Danite prefix D-N is found in river names Don, Danube and Dnieper; their ships also carried out raids on the coast of Egypt.

"From the records of Rameses III, as given by Hall in his *Ancient History of the Near East*, it is learned that a collection of marauding peoples, including the Danauna and Pulesti, moved down towards Egypt from the Aegean, through Palestine. Cotterell, in his *Ancient Greeks*, is prepared to accept the Danauna as Danaans. Hall, who dates this movement about 1200 B.C. says that the Pulesti were undoubtedly the Philistines." [33]

"The eponym Dan is found to be a root-name applied to some of the most famous sections of the ancient Greeks and their leaders, the derivations of this name include Danans, Danae, Danaans, Danoi, Danaoi, Danaids." [34]

Dr. R.G. Latham, makes the point that "Neither do I think that the eponymus of the Argive Danai was other than that of the Israelite tribe of Dan; only we are so used to confine ourselves to the soil of Palestine in our consideration of the history of the Israelites that we ignore the share they may have taken in the ordinary history of the world." [35]

St Michael's Mount (Nineteenth-Century Tinted Photo)
This nineteenth-century photo shows the position of the mount at high tide. At low tide, a causeway connects the island to the Cornish coast. From Phoenecian times, this was the "entrance" to England and the tin trade. Joseph of Arimathea would probably have brought the young Jesus here as he visited his uncle's rich tin mines.

In the light of such information can it really be such a mystery why the Danite settlers in Ireland traced their origins to Greece?

The greater part of the tribe of Dan entered the promised land of Israel in the time of Joshua. From the beginning of their settlement there they seemed to have played no major part in the internal affairs of the new nation, but preferred to engage in shipping and international commerce. Deborah complained that the people of Dan remained with their ships rather than taking to the field of battle in order to assist the other Israelites in the defeat of their enemies (Judges 5:17).

Phoenician Influence
Although they had been warned against it, a measure of inter-marriage took place between the tribes of Dan and Naphtali and the Canaanite Phoenicians. [36]

The Danites along with elements of Asher and Naphtali began to share in the maritime enterprises of the Phoenicians. These "ships of Tarshish" were to create what has been termed the "Golden Age of Phoenicia."

During the reign of Solomon the Phoenicians assisted the king in the establishment of an Israelite navy based near Elath on the Red Sea coast. "Then Hiram sent his servants with the fleet, seamen who knew the sea, to work with the servants of Solomon" (1 Kings 9:27).

There are indications that this maritime cooperation between Phoenicians and Israelites continued for centuries. A trading empire of global proportions was to develop, which established trading settlements in Spain (the Tarshish of antiquity), Britain and many other areas. Some have even claimed to have discovered evidence of Phoenician settlements in North and South America.

An entire chapter of the Bible is devoted to listing the trading enterprises of the Phoenicians and the numerous nations that shared in this commerce (Ezekiel 27).

"At a time yet more remote, the Phoenician inhabitants of Tyre, we are informed, visited the western parts of Britain, and purchased of the inhabitants, tin and other productions from the soil. The commence of this traffic is supposed to have been in a year ranging between B.C. 1200, and B.C. 600—these events are considered to be well authenticated." [37]

The chief Phoenician port in Britain and the center of the tin trade was probably St. Michael's Mount in Cornwall, the "Ictis" of Strabo and other writers of antiquity. The Cassiterides or Tin Islands of the Greek records are generally held to be the Scillies.

Many ancient place names in Cornwall are thought to have had a Phoenician or Hebrew origin. Baal Rock brings to mind the infamous god of the Phoenicians. Other examples include Boswidden and Chegwidden, both meaning "house of the Jews." The suffix "Ywedhyon" is found in several place names and means "of the Jews."

Other parts of Britain have also revealed traces of Phoenician influence. A small trading settlement probably existed in the vicinity of the modern port of Avonmouth near Bristol.

In his paternal blessing Jacob said that Dan would be "a serpent by the way." A serpent leaves a trail that can be followed. The Danites fulfilled this curious prophecy by naming cities, towns, rivers and coastal areas "after the name of Dan their father" (Judges 18:29). By this means we may trace the wanderings of the Danites across Europe. Their voyages from Greece to the Black Sea probably led to the naming of such rivers as the Danube. Further west we find a peninsula bearing the name of Denmark, or Danmark (the mark of Dan).

In Britain the D-N prefix is found many times in coastal place names and some inland locations, such as Dungeness, Doncaster, Dundee and Dumbarton. Ireland, too, has its Dunmore, Dundalk, Donegal, and Danslaugh.

Few references to the Danites are found in the Bible after the period of the Judges, a clear indication that most of them migrated to areas outside of Palestine. In the time of Jeroboam, civil war threatened to divide the Israelites. A ninth-century A.D. Jewish writer, Eldud, informs us that "in Jeroboam's time, the tribe of Dan being unwilling to shed their brethren's blood, took a resolve to leave the country."

History clearly shows that they moved into the west, to "the isles afar off" (Jeremiah 31) identified by Jewish scholars such as Dr. Moses Margouliouth and Rabbi Menahem ben Jacob as Britain and Ireland.

The Danite tribal symbol of an eagle with a serpent in its talons has been found on examples of early Danish and Irish jewellery.

According to *The Chronicles of the Kings of Briton* a chieftain named Barthlome along with 30 ships full of people settled in Ireland—they had earlier been driven from Spain. The chief related to Gwrgant, an English king, that his people had originally come from "Israel."

This group may have come to Britain from the Spanish port of Gades or Cadiz. In this area a Hebrew-Phoenician colony was established about 1000 B.C. The Spanish river Guadalquivir got its name from "the river of the Hebrews."

A Royal Dynasty

One of the clearest and strongest promises and guarantees in all the Bible relates to the throne and royal dynasty of King David of ancient Israel. David stated, at the end of his life that "he [God] has made with me an everlasting covenant, ordered in all things and secure" (2

Samuel 23:5). The nature of this covenant was "your house and your kingdom shall be established forever" (2 Samuel 7:16). The promise was repeated, concerning David's son Solomon: "I will set up your seed after you... and I will establish his kingdom" (2 Samuel 7:12).

This throne and royal line were to continue in existence through the centuries and would be taken over by Jesus Christ at His second coming (Luke 1:32).

The last recorded king of David's line to reign in Jerusalem was Zedekiah. He was taken prisoner by the Babylonians in 585 B.C. and died in a dungeon at Babylon. Since that time not one king of David's line has reigned over the Jews in the Holy Land.

Does this mean, as several "higher critics" of the Bible such as Tom Paine and Bob Ingersol claimed, that God has broken His "everlasting and sure" covenant with David, and that the scripture that Christ said "cannot be broken" has indeed proved to be false and unreliable?

Centuries after David had died, God confirmed through Jeremiah that His promise to David was as certain and unshakable as the natural cycle that produced day and night (Jeremiah 33:19–26).

"My covenant will I not break, nor alter the thing that is gone out of my lips. Once have I sworn by my holiness that I will not lie unto David. His seed shall endure forever, and his throne as the sun before me. It shall be established for ever as the moon and as a faithful witness in heaven" (Psalm 89:34–37).

A point generally overlooked by the critics is that the Bible *nowhere* states that David's throne would always be located at Jerusalem. Many assume that David's royal line would have to reign only over the Jews, but the Bible does not say this. "David shall never want a man to sit upon the throne of the House of Israel" (Jeremiah 33:17). The Jews, from the time of Rehoboam, were known as the "House of Judah," not *Israel*.

The "House of Israel," sometimes known as "the ten lost tribes," had left Palestine by 718 B.C. and gone into captivity. It was amongst these people that David's throne was to be located.

The Role of Jeremiah

Jeremiah the prophet had a vital part to play in this mystery. God told him "I have set you this day over nations and kingdoms, to pluck up and break down, to destroy and to overthrow, to build and to plant" (Jeremiah 1:9–10).

The nation of Judah and its king were indeed overthrown by the armies of Nebuchadnezzar, king of Babylon. Zedekiah died in prison, at Babylon, and *all* of his sons were killed. It would seem, to the world, that David's dynasty had come to an end and God's promise to David had been rendered null and void (Jeremiah 19:1–7).

David's line, however, had not been totally extinguished. We read that "Ishmael carried away captive all the residue of the people that were in Mizpah, even the king's daughters" (Jeremiah 41:10). The *king's daughters*, descendants of David, had survived. It was the royal house, represented by these Hebrew princesses, that Jeremiah was to "plant." This is the reason why Jeremiah visited Mizpah—the princesses were there (Jeremiah 40:6).

Jeremiah, along with his scribe Baruch, the royal princesses and some of the people who had survived the invasion, were later taken to Egypt (Jeremiah 43:5–7).

Archaeology has uncovered evidence of "the palace of the Jew's daughter" at Tahpanhes in Egypt, the probable temporary residence of the princesses.

A prophecy of Isaiah mentions "the remnant that is escaped of the house of Judah," probably speaking of the princesses, "shall again take root downward, and bear fruit upward" (Isaiah 37:31).

Other prophecies speak of the throne being overturned three times (Ezekiel 21:25) and of being removed from its former location and planted elsewhere (Ezekiel 17). Jeremiah, it will be recalled, was the one who was given the task of replanting.

The location where Jeremiah "replanted" the Hebrew princess may be identified by a careful study of Irish history. Several references are found relating to a "Royal Sage" or "Saint" by the name of Ollamh Fodhla who arrived in Ireland about 600 B.C. accompanied by "Simon Brach," or "Berach," and an eastern princess.

He was described as a "celebrated personage" and "a being of historical substance and truth," a great legislator and founder of a college at Tara." [38]

The Hebrew princess, known in Irish history as Tea-Tephi, married an Irish prince, Heremon of Ulster who later became king. "Ollam Fodhla distinguished himself by an exquisite talent for

Hill of Tara
Situated in Co. Meath, Ireland, the Hill of Tara is one of the most ancient ceremonial sites in the world. It was here that the High Kings of Ireland were crowned on the Lia Fail stone. The Milesians arrived in Ireland in 1060 B.C. and established themselves as the Royal House since they were descended from Zara (Zerah), half-tribe of Judah.

government. He infused health into the Irish Commonwealth by excellent laws and customs." [39]

Other sources show that a large part of early Irish law was based on "the book of the law" or the first five books of the Bible, an indication that the one who introduced these "excellent laws and customs" was indeed the prophet Jeremiah.

Irish writers were unable to identify the nationality of Ollam Fodhla but were aware that he had not been born in Ireland.

The Chronicles of Eri inform us that he was "brought up amongst the Olam [prophets]" and that "all eyes delight to look upon him, all ears are charmed with the sound of his voice."

According to the *Annals of Clonmacnoise*, Ulster (Ulladh) took its name from him and describes him as "soe well learned and soe much given to the favour of learning." This work states that he was also known as "Cohawyn," which in Hebrew means "The Long-suffering" or "The Patient." How appropriate for a man of Jeremiah's background.

Some of "the laws of Eri, set in order by Ollam Fola" seem to have been taken directly from the Old Testament.

"Let not man slay his fellow.

"Let not man take the belongings of another privily.

"Let not the lips utter what the mind knoweth to be false.

"Man be merciful.

"Let man do even as he would be done by." [40]

Some traditions mention that Jeremiah took the other princess to Spain where she married into the royal family of Zaragossa. Jeremiah is also said to have brought to Ireland two unusual objects, a harp and the "Stone of Destiny" or "lia-fail."

The "harp of Tara" was later to be adopted as the national emblem of Eire.

The princess Tephi is said to have been buried on the hill of Tara. For centuries local Irish people have considered this to be a sacred spot.

"Jeremiah's tomb" is said to be located near the ruins of Devenish Abbey, on the Isle of Devenish in Lower Lough Erne, near Inniskillen, County Fermanagh.

The Stone of Destiny

Few objects in the history of Britain has attracted such an aura of mystery and superstitious awe as the "Stone of Scone" or "lia-fail." For two and a half thousand years the kings and queens of Ireland, Scotland and England have been crowned sitting over this rock.

Several daring attempts have been made to illegally remove the stone from the Coronation Chair in Westminster Abbey; so highly regarded was the stone that in 1940 when enemy invasion threatened, it was placed in a secret hiding place known only to a few in high office; the Prime Minister of Canada was also sent a plan of the hiding place. In 1996 the British government returned custody of the stone to Scotland, when not being used for a coronation.

Why such great interest in a 26-inch long block of dull reddish sandstone?

Stones and rocks play an important part in the symbolism of the Bible. They are often used to represent kings and kingdoms. Jesus Christ, a future "king of kings," is described as a "chief cornerstone" (1 Peter 2:6) and a "rock of offense" (1 Peter 2:8). His kingdom is represented as a "stone" (Daniel 2:34).

The Coronation Chair
Located in Westminster Abbey, London, this ancient chair was made for Edward I in 1300 A.D. It was made to hold the Stone of Scone (also known as the Lia Fail). All but three kings and queens of England have been crowned on the chair since.

Stones or pillars have often been used in coronation ceremonies. In ancient Israel King Jehoash was found "standing by a pillar as the custom was" (2 Kings 11:14).

In England the Saxon kings used a stone in their coronation ceremonies. According to tradition the "Stone of Destiny" was the very one upon which Jacob rested his head at Bethel. "Then Jacob rose early in the morning, and took the stone that he had put at his head, set it up as a pillar, and poured oil on top of it" (Genesis 28:18).

Some skeptics have claimed that the stone consists of "Scottish red sandstone." However, it should be noted that reddish sandstone of this type is found near the Dead Sea, not far from the spot where Jacob had his dream.

Later, if the tradition is correct, Jeremiah brought the stone to Ireland. For about a thousand years the descendants of Tea-Tephi and Heremon of Ireland were crowned sitting over the stone and ruled Ireland. In the fifth century A.D., Fergus MacEarca of the same royal line landed an army on the Mull of Kintyre in Scotland and began a dynasty ruling in Scotland.

Until 1297 the kings of Scotland were crowned sitting over the stone; in that year it was seized by King Edward the First of England and placed beneath the Coronation Chair in Westminster Abbey.

In 1603 the Scottish royal line in the person of James the Sixth of Scotland inherited the English throne and thus the ancient prophecy that the throne of David would be overturned three times was fulfilled (Ezekiel 21:27). It was overturned once when it was transferred from Jerusalem to Ireland during the time of Jeremiah, overturned a second time about a thousand years later when the royal line was moved to Scotland, and then overturned the third time when James the Sixth of Scotland inherited the throne of England in 1603.

It is to be overturned "no more, until he comes whose right it is [speaking of Jesus Christ at His second coming]; and I will give it to him." Yes, God has surely kept His promise to David, his royal line does exist to this very day, ruling over a part of the Israelitish peoples.

The husband of Tea-Tephi was a member of the Milesian Royal House. The Milesians, who conquered Ireland in 1016 B.C. were of Scythian stock and were related to the Danites who controlled Ireland prior to the arrival of the Milesians. Keating in his *History of Ireland* provides a comprehensive coverage of this subject.

Tea-Tephi was of the Pharez line and her husband was of the Zarah branch of the "Scepter" family of Judah (Genesis 38:27–30). This marriage healed the "breach" between the two branches of this line.

The symbolic "Red Hand" of Ulster could well represent the red or scarlet thread tied around the wrist of Zarah (Genesis 38:29–30). The traditional flag of Northern Ireland included both the red hand and a six pointed "star of David."

Several marked similarities exist between the ancient coronation ceremony used in the crowning of British monarchs and that used for the kings of Old Testament Israel. Some have considered the twelve jewels in the crown of St. Edward symbolic of the twelve tribes of Israel.

A further proof of the relationship between the people of Britain and the Israelites is that a host of tribal symbols used by the "ten lost tribes" are found in British heraldry, and some are even found in the national symbols of the United States of America. A detailed study of this subject, though quite worthwhile, is well beyond the scope of this present work, but an adequate coverage, with many illustrations, is given in the book *Symbols of Our Celto-Saxon Heritage* by W.H. Bennett.

Many have admired English law and some nations have attempted to adapt it to their own use. In its earliest form, dating back to about the time of Alfred the Great, it was based upon the Mosaic "Book of the Law"—the first five books of the Bible. This civil legal code incorporated more "Mosaic" legal principles than any other national code. Through the centuries, however, this early system became greatly overlaid with a mass of man-made, non-biblical ordinances, which in many cases contradicted the early, but simple and effective legal system.

Our Scythian Ancestry

One of the most important keys in tracing the ethnic origins of the early Britons is found in the Cephalic Index. This is an accurate scientific method for determining race by examination of skeletal remains, including the shape of the head.

"The origin of the peoples of Northwestern Europe has occasioned much controversy! As a result, a considerable amount of confusion has been generated over the question of the racial affinities of the various branches of those people who inhabit primarily the coastlands, islands and peninsulas of Northwestern Europe."[41]

"It can further be proved beyond question that the longheaded Scythian [or Sacae] skulls which were formerly found on the Steppes all across South Russia and Northern Europe from the Danube to the

The Red Hand of Ulster
Ulster's (Northern Ireland) flag shows the crown of Queen Elizabeth II on top of the six-pointed "Star of David." Within the star is a red hand. This is understood by many Ulstermen to be the symbol of the half-tribe of Judah named after Zara (Zerah). The Queen's lineage also traces back through this line to King David and Judah.

Don River [and even further east] are today found in type only among North-West Europeans." [42]

Most authorities agree that the Scythians were of the "Nordic" racial type. They are distinguished from the Mediterranean races of Southern Europe by their longer limbs and larger skulls.

The modern Nordics are the English, Flemings, Dutch, North Germans and Scandinavians. The English are of the long headed type. Nordics produce the adventurers, explorers, sailors and above all rulers and organizers.

Considerable evidence exists to link the Scythians with the Celtic and Saxon peoples of Britain. Nennius, in his account of the arrival of the Saxon leaders Hengist and Horsa in Thanet mentions that "messengers were sent to Scythia" for reinforcements.

Several Scythian customs reveal intriguing traces of an Israelite ancestry: "The migrating Hebrews, wherever they are found, though usually tainted by the paganism of neighboring nations, always show some custom or almost forgotten religious rite that is a memory of their early history. The Scythians are no exception. Herodotus tells us that they never sacrifice swine, nor indeed is it their wont to breed them in any part of their country. They may have forgotten why they were to regard the pig as 'unclean,' but the custom remained." [43]

One of the reasons why Israel was driven into captivity was the excessive use of "wine and new wine" (Hosea 4:11). The prophets spoke of the "drunkards of the tribe of Ephraim." Herodotus records that the Scythians too, had the same reputation; other nations he mentions used the proverb "pour out like a Scythian," which seems to have been the equivalent of our saying "as drunk as a lord."

"The many references to the Scythian horses, during Alexander's invasion of Asia, combined with the fact that the Scythians were so frequently on the move that their enemies seldom caught up with them, shows that the greatest migratory movement took place on horseback, or with the use of wheeled vehicles. The Scythians used 'scores of chariots equipped with scythe blades' the same type of chariot as that used by Boadicea in her battles against the invading Romans, a strange fact if there were no connection between the Scythians and Britons." [44]

The Scythians were skilled in the use of cavalry and excellent archers. Even the Persians found them a difficult enemy to defeat. They sometimes adopted a "scorched earth" policy as they retreated into their vast plains beyond the reach of an invading army. They were a prosperous people and conducted an extensive trade with Greece in such commodities as grains, furs, hides, meat, honey, salt, fish and even slaves.

Scythian kings were often buried with their horses and various objects, some of which were made of gold and silver. From time to time a tomb is discovered in Siberia, where deep freeze conditions have preserved even perishable items such as carpets.

Scyths wore baggy trousers, belts and pointed caps. They, in common with the early Britons had a fondness for tattooing themselves. The great majority of Scyths were long headed, a very small number however, due to intermarriage were Mongoloid. Evidence taken from Saxon cemeteries in Britain shows that the Saxons were of the same long-headed ethnic type as the Scythians.

As a separate race the Scythians seem to have almost vanished by about the time of Christ. In Europe they were then known by a variety of other names.

The Apostle Paul, when listing four ethnic groups (Colossians 3:11), mentions the Scythians as being distinct and separate from the Greeks, Jews and Barbarians. As descendants of the ten lost tribes of Israel this is precisely what we would expect.

Scythians and Celts mixed freely with each other, giving rise to the term "Celto-Scythians." Ancient writers always described the Celts as being very tall, fair-haired with blue or grey eyes.

According to Dinan, one Celtic tribe was called "Ombri." Could there be any connection with "the land of Onui," the Assyrian term for ancient Israel?

Scythian art was very similar to that of the Celts and Saxons: "Soon after a schoolboy discovered, on St. Ninian's Island, a rich hoard of objects inlaid with gold, silver and enamel, with typical Celtic Zoomorphic decoration, a cache of equally wonderful work, carried out in the very same style, was discovered in a remote spot west of the Caspian Sea.

"It is surely more than coincidence that metal workers in places thousands of miles apart should have been using identical methods; apart from the remote possibility of British craftsmen sending such a quantity of goldwork to that distant region in the Middle East, the only conclusion is that the craftsmen themselves migrated from east to west, bringing the skills and practicing them in all the regions of their settlement." [45]

British Nordic Origins

Some have assumed that because many different groups of people have settled in Britain under different circumstances and at different times that the people of Britain are a mixed or mongrel race. But is this really so?

"Although this mixed race theory has long prevailed, ethnologists declare that the various peoples who settled in the British Isles were branches of a common stock. Thus Professor Grunther, in *The Racial Element of European History* (pp. 222–29), remarks: 'The racial composition of England is worthy of special mention, for the common and wrong opinion exists about the English people that it owes its capacity to much racial admixture—Whatever peoples, whatever individual Viking bands may have trodden English ground—Kelts, Angles, Saxons, Jutes, Danes, Norwegian and Icelandic Vikings, Normans—they were always predominantly Nordic peoples... English history is rich in movements of peoples; in movements of races it has little to show.'" [46]

Great confusion exists among both Jewish and Gentile historians over the question of exactly what happened to the ten "lost" tribes of the Israelites, although it is generally agreed that the descendants of these people do still exist—somewhere.

Israel was to be sifted among all nations, yet not to be destroyed (Amos 9:8–9). Although the kingdom was to be destroyed, the people were to continue in existence because of God's promise to Abraham. The lost tribes were to ultimately return to the Holy Land (Ezekiel 11:15–17).

The Israelites were prophesied to multiply rapidly (Genesis 22:17, 24:16). By the time of Joshua (1450 B.C.) two to three million of them entered the promised land.

The children of Jacob or Israel were, according to the prophecy, to become "a nation and a company of nations" (Genesis 35:9–12). Other prophecies speak of them spreading around the world, becoming prosperous and of playing a dominant economic and military role in world affairs. The Jews, who were only one (Judah) of the twelve tribes, never fulfilled these prophecies. The United States of America and the British Commonwealth on the other hand have very clearly fulfilled all such prophecies.

The Bible speaks not just of the Jews but of *Israel* and *Judah* (Ezekiel 37:15–22; Jeremiah 3:17–18). Israel was to be "scattered among the heathen" and "dispersed through the countries" (Ezekiel 36:16–20).

The Apostle James, in the first century A.D., addressed his epistle to "the twelve tribes scattered abroad."

Evidence exists that traces the westward migration of the Israelites towards Europe. Many gravestones have been discovered in the Crimea, including one belonging to a member "of the tribe of Naphthali." The inscription mentioned that he "went into exile with the exiles, who were driven away with Hosea, the king of Israel." [47]

Within a few generations the exiles seemed to have lost the knowledge of their early history and had begun to develop a new culture.

What of the physical appearance of the early Israelites? How did this compare with the appearance of the modern day West European or North American?

The early Israelites did not necessarily look like the average Jews of today. They were more Nordic than Jewish. Sarah was described as a "fair" woman (Genesis 12:11). The meaning of the Hebrew word used in this case is "to be bright" or a fair skinned person. A description of Sarah is given in the seventh of the Dead Sea Scrolls: "Her skin was pure white; her hair was long and lovely; her hands were long and slim."

Although some of the Jews are of swarthy appearance due to intermarriage with Canaanites, others are of Nordic appearance.

"The famous traveller, Lady Burton, in *The Inner Life of Syria*, speaks of visiting a prominent Jewish family in Damascus and finding that 'they were white with blue eyes and fair hair, like any English people.'" [48]

The meaning of the name Laban, a close relative of Abraham, is "white." David was "ruddy and of a fair countenance," (1 Samuel 17:42, *KJV*), like many a modern Western European. The subject of the Song of Solomon is described as "white and ruddy" with black hair. This description is very much like that of a modern Sephardic Jew.

Nazarites of Israel were described as "purer than snow" and "whiter than milk," "more ruddy in body than rubies" (Lamentations 4:7).

The ancient Israelites were not dark or olive skinned people, but light skinned—many were blonds, others were black or brown haired. They were "Nordic" in racial type. Some intermarried with other races.

Pictures of Israelite prisoners have been found engraved on the walls of the temple of Karnak in Egypt. These people are of the blond Nordic type. A tomb painting at Thebes also shows an Israelite (described by some authorities as "Jewish" or "Amorite"), having white skin and light, reddish brown eyes and hair.

The word "Amorite" was used by the Babylonians, and in their language means "Westerner." It was used to describe the inhabitants of Palestine. Some of the latest research indicates that the Amorites were a long-headed race with blue eyes, straight noses and thin lips much like the Northern Europeans of today.

The much earlier Biblical Amorites were dark Canaanite people whose land the Israelites later occupied. Several sources mention that the Amorites were Caucasian in physique and appearance, closely related to the Celtic peoples.

Some scholars have noted similarities between the beliefs of the Amorites and those of the early inhabitants of Europe, i.e, including the Druids.

The religion practiced by the early population of Britain gives a clear indication of the ethnic origins of the people.

"We cannot avoid the conclusion that our British ancestors were devoted to that kind of worship which they brought with them from the East, even close upon the Patriarchal times of Holy Writ." [49]

Several early authorities mention "the remarkable similarity which the practices of the Hebrew patriarchs bore to those of our forefathers... the first inhabitants of our island brought with them the religion of Noah and Abraham; they knew and worshipped the one living and true God... and this continued, subject to various alterations and additions, through many ages. It would be very interesting and highly instructive, to follow the history of these additions and corruptions." [50]

Who Were the Druids?

This early form of religious worship is often classified by observers as being Druidic. Although the word "Druid" does not appear in Greek and Roman records until some three to four centuries before Christ, it is clearly evident that the form of religion from which Druidism emerged had arrived in Britain some 1,500 years before this time.

Regarding the Druids, Smith writes that "they believed that the Deity was the source of life, and giver of good; they defined his duration as eternal, and attributed to him omnipotence as the measure of his power. And as they found nothing in the animal creation or in man, which had any proportion or resemblance to God, they had neither statues nor pictures to represent him. From which we infer, that they regarded God as a pure Spirit." [51]

The Druidic definition of wisdom is almost identical to the Biblical precepts on the subject.

"Obedience to the laws of God, concern for the welfare of mankind, and suffering with fortitude all the accidents of life." [52]

The first Britons seemed to have been keenly aware of the Creation story as given in Genesis. Early sites where worship was conducted had marked similarities to the picture given of the Garden of Eden.

"Hence we find everywhere, in the description of the first sacred places, some allusions to the scene of man's temptation and fall: a garden or grove, with one or two trees in the midst, watered by a river, and enclosed to prevent unhallowed intrusion. This was evidently the case with our ancestors." [53]

Pillars, oaks and altars of uncut stone played a significant part in early British worship, as they had done in the form of worship employed by Abraham, Moses, Joshua and other Old Testament figures.

The oak tree was used as a symbol of Israel (Isaiah 6:13). It often marked a place of worship, both in the true religion (Joshua 24:26) and also the false (Isaiah 1:29; Ezekiel 6:13).

Druidic altars in Britain were of uncut or uncarved stone, as was the case in ancient Israel (Exodus 20:25–26).

Excavations conducted at Stonehenge and other places of worship in Britain have uncovered the remains of animal sacrifices, mostly of bullocks, sheep and goats; the animals sacrificed in Britain were the same "clean" beasts as are found listed in the Levitical regulations of the Old Testament.

Except for a few brief periods, the religion of the Israelites consisted of a mixture of Mosaic precepts and the paganism of the various Canaanite cults of the surrounding nations. They were warned in the strongest terms that such compromise would lead to the ultimate horror—ritualistic human sacrifice (Deuteronomy 12:30–31).

By Roman times the Druids had largely exchanged the simple sacrifices of an earlier era for the gruesome and abominable sacrifice of living people.

Caesar described great wickerwork figures, the limbs of which were filled with human victims and then set on fire. Tacitus records that the British Druids "deemed it indeed a duty to cover their altars with the blood of captives and to consult their deities through human entrails."

The practices of the early Britons were mirrored by the later Israelite tendency to mix the religion of the true God with the rites of pagan worship. The "Golden Calf" incident is an excellent example of this.

This calf is supposed to have represented Tammuz, the false messiah of the Babylonian Mystery Religion. The mother of Tammuz was Semiramis the so-called "queen of heaven" (Jeremiah 44:17–19). In Egypt this calf or bull was known as Apis that was worshipped by the Egyptians and mummified and buried with great pomp. In 1851, Mariette discovered a huge sarcophagus containing no less than 64 such mummified bulls.

This Apis or golden calf was worshipped by the Israelites in what they called "a feast to the Lord" (Exodus 32:1–6). Centuries later Jeroboam gave the Israelites "two calves of gold" to worship (1 Kings 12:28). God strongly condemned this false system of worship that included kissing "the calves" (Hosea 13:1–3).

Those calves were taken by the Israelites into captivity at the time the people were to become "vagabonds or wanderers among the nations" (Hosea 9:17; 10:5–6). The calves or Apis were introduced into Britain in the form of "a spotted cow" and "astral bull."

"The cow of Athor, however, the female divinity corresponding to Apis, is well known as a spotted cow, and it is singular that the Druids of Britain also worshipped a spotted cow." [54]

"The astral bull of milk-white hue, its horns crowned with golden stars, became the symbol, or visible sacrament of Druidism." [55]

In Celtic Britain and Western Europe the Druids appear to have held a position that was almost identical in many respects to that of the Levites in Israel.

Caesar states, "the former [Druids] are engaged in things sacred, conduct the public and private sacrifices, and interpret all matters of religion. To these a large number of the young men resort for the purpose of instruction, and they [the Druids] are in great honour among them.

"For they determine respecting almost all controversies, public and private; and if any crime has been perpetrated, if murder has been committed, if there be any dispute about an inheritance, if any about boundaries, these same persons decide it... The Druids do not go to war." [56]

They believed in repentance, purification and observed one day in seven as peculiarly sanctified and made holy by the Great Creator." One tenth of their income was dedicated to religious purposes. [57]

Good health and public hygiene seems to have been of particular interest to the Druids.

"Druidic physicians were skilled in the treatment of the sick; their practice was far removed from the medicine-man cult. They prayed to God to grant a blessing on His gifts, conscious that it should always be remembered that no medicine could be effective nor any physician successful without Divine help. The chief care of the physicians was to prevent rather than to cure disease. Their recipe for health was cheerfulness, temperance and exercise. Human bones which had been fractured and re-set by art have been found in Druidic tumuli." [58]

"The supposed magic of the Druids consisted in a more thorough knowledge of some of the sciences than was common—astronomy, for instance. Diodorus Siculus states that the Druids used tele-scopes—this evidently is the origin of the story that the Druids could by magic bring the moon down to the earth." [59]

Druids also looked forward to a coming Messiah to pay the price of human sins.

There is a darker side to the picture of the Druids—a side that has received by far the most publicity through the centuries. They became deeply influenced by paganism, particularly the Baal worship so strongly condemned by Jeremiah and other Old Testament prophets.

They believed in a pagan trinity, the immortal soul concept, and took part in the worship of "Baal and Astarte." "The Pagan festival of the 24th of June was celebrated among the Druids by blazing fires in honour of... Baal." In common with some of the Israelites the Druids probably caused human victims "to pass through the fire unto Molech" (Jeremiah 32:35). [60]

When all the facts are clearly examined it becomes very clear that the early Britons were indeed a part of the "lost sheep of the house of Israel" to whom Christ sent some of His apostles.

Land of the Celts

Chapter Summary

What really happened to the "lost ten tribes" of Israel? Israelite captives taken to Southern Russia. The slow migration into Western Europe and Britain. What was the background and history of the various tribal groups, such as the Celts, Scythians, Danites, Angles, Saxons and Jutes that settled in Britain? Were they a part of Israel?

Chapter Three

DID JESUS VISIT BRITAIN?

"And did those feet in ancient time walk
upon England's mountains green?"
(William Blake, from the hymn *"Jerusalem"*).

"And the Child grew and became strong in the spirit, filled
with wisdom; and the grace of God was upon Him"
(Luke 2:40).

A t least four entirely separate traditions exist in the West of England relating to Jesus as a boy or young man having visited this part of Britain prior to His ministry.
This tradition has even been set to music in Blake's famous hymn *Jerusalem*:

> *And did those feet in ancient time*
> *Walk upon England's mountains green?*
> *And was the Holy Lamb of God*
> *On England's pleasant pastures seen?*

The question is, did He really visit England—and, if so, for what purpose?

One cannot be dogmatic about this subject because the Bible is silent concerning the matter.

At the end of John's gospel, however, we find the intriguing remark that most of the activities of Jesus Christ were never recorded in the Gospels (John 21:25). This included all of His activities between the ages of 12 and 30.

There is nothing in the entire Bible to suggest that Jesus could not have visited foreign parts prior to His ministry. Indeed, it plainly states that He spent time in Egypt with His family shortly after His birth (Matthew 2:13).

Many assume that Jesus became a world famous figure only after His death, that His human life was lived out in obscurity, that He was known only by a handful of followers and local officials.

The Incredible History of God's True Church

History records, however, that the "historical Jesus" was well known even in the more remote regions of the known world of His day. Eusebius, writing in the early fourth century A.D., records that the fame of Jesus and the knowledge of His healing miracles spread far beyond the borders of His own nation.

Jesus Christ's Fame Spreads Far and Wide

Being a bishop and historian of considerable reputation, Eusebius had access to official archives and written records. He was writing some 150 years before the fall of the Roman Empire and during his day many original first-century documents were still extant.

He records two letters from the official archives of Edessa, a city state in Mesopotamia. The king or ruler of the area had heard of the healing miracles of Jesus, and being afflicted by a disease, wrote a letter to Him requesting that Jesus should visit him and heal the disease. Eusebius quotes the letter as follows: "Agbarus [some editions read Abgar], prince of Edessa, sends greeting to Jesus the excellent Saviour, who has appeared in the borders of Jerusalem. I have heard the reports respecting thee and thy cures, as performed by thee without medicines and without the use of herbs. For as it is said, thou causest the blind to see again, the lame to walk, and thou cleansest the lepers, and thou castest out impure spirits and demons, and thou healest those that are tormented by long disease, and thou raisest the dead. And hearing all these things of thee, I concluded in my mind one of two things: either that thou art God, and having descended from heaven, doest these things, or else doing them thou art the Son of God. Therefore, now I have written and besought thee to visit me, and to heal the disease with which I am afflicted. I have, also, heard that the Jews murmur against thee, and are plotting to injure thee; I have, however, a very small but noble state, which is sufficient for us both."

The letter was delivered to Jesus by the courier Ananias who also took back to the king the letter written by Jesus in reply to the king's request. Eusebius quotes this as follows: "Blessed art thou, O Agbarus, who, without seeing, hast believed in me. For it is written concerning me, that they who have seen me will not believe, that they who have not seen may believe and live. But in regard to what you hast written that I should come to thee, it is necessary that I should fulfill all things here, for which I have been sent. And after this fulfillment, thus to be received again by Him that sent me. And after I have been received up, I will send to thee a certain one of my disciples, that he may heal thy affliction, and give life to thee and to those who are with thee."[1]

Eusebius, who it seems examined the original documents, adds the following points:

"To these letters there was, also, subjoined in the Syriac language: 'After the ascension of Jesus, Judas, who is also called Thomas, sent him Thaddeus, the Apostle, one of the seventy."

Eusebius then proceeds to relate the various miracles and other works of Thaddeus, including the healing of King Agbarus. Following this the king assembled all the citizens together that they might hear the preaching of the apostle.

Although Eusebius considered this material authentic, the view of some later scholars is that the letters were third-century forgeries. Although this could well be the case, it is far from impossible that the publicity Jesus' miracles aroused could have spread far from the borders of His own country.

Later in his history, Eusebius relates the fact that the resurrection of Jesus Christ was not just an obscure event mentioned only by the Gospel writers. He records that the event was well known to the Roman Emperor Tiberius and the Senate.

"The fame of our Lord's remarkable resurrection and ascension being now spread abroad, according to an ancient custom prevalent among the rulers of the nations, to communicate novel occurrences to the emperor, that nothing might escape him, Pontius Pilate transmits to Tiberius an account of the circumstances concerning the resurrection of our Lord from the dead, the report of which had already been spread throughout all Palestine.

"In this account he also intimated that he ascertained other miracles respecting him, and that having now risen from the dead, he was believed to be a God by the great mass of the people."[2]

It was said that Tiberius was so impressed with the report that he tried to have Jesus ranked among the Roman gods. The Senate, however, rejected his proposition.

It must be remembered that the Roman Empire was still in existence when Eusebius wrote. Had he been in error in his writings the facts would have been exposed by reference to the official Roman archives. The Romans took great care over the preservation of official records.

At the time of the crucifixion we read that "there was a darkness over all the earth until the ninth hour" (Luke 23:44).

Extent of the Druid Religion

In far off Ireland, Conor Macnessa, king of Ulster, who died in A.D. 48, is said to have inquired of his Chief Druid as to the meaning of the event. The Druid, after consulting the Druidic prophecies relating to the Messiah, then gave the king a correct explanation for the darkness.[3]

It might seem strange that the Irish Druids should have prophetic knowledge of Christ until we realize that the Druids were closely related to the "Magi" or "wise men" who visited Jesus shortly after His birth.

The word "Magi" is merely the Latin equivalent of "Druid." In many Celtic records the word Magi is used instead of Druid. In some early Irish histories Simon Magus (Acts 8:9) is known as "Simon the Druid."

The impact that Druidism had on the ancient world is often not fully realized. Because of the influence that this religion had on the early generations of the Church of God in Britain, it will be dealt with in some detail in a later chapter. It would be good at this point, however, to note the following point concerning Druidism.

"Westward of Italy, embracing Hispania, Gallia, the Rhenish frontiers, portions of Germany and Scandinavia, with its headquarters and great seats of learning fixed in Britain, extended the Druidic religion. There can be no question that this was the primitive religion of mankind, covering at one period in various forms the whole surface of the ancient world."[4]

Other sources show that the Druidic religion stretched from India in the East to Britain in the West, including the territory of the "wise men" of Matthew chapter 2. Interestingly, one of the meanings for the word "Druid" is "wise men."

Some have speculated that when they "departed into their own country another way" (Matthew 2:12), they returned via Britain.

The mid-day darkness that occurred at the time of Christ's crucifixion was not only observed in Britain; the third-century "Church Father" Tertullian, a native of North Africa, in addressing his pagan adversaries, makes the point that "at the moment of Christ's death, the light departed from the sun, and the land was darkened at noonday; which wonder is related in your own annals, and is preserved in your archives to this day."[5]

Traditions of Where Christ Travelled
West Country traditions associate several sites with a visit from Jesus. Among these are St. Michael's Mount, St. Just-in-Roseland, Redruth, Glastonbury, and Priddy. The tradition appears to have been the inspiration for naming districts as "Jesus' Well" in Cornwall, and "Paradise" in Somerset.

Across the English Channel in Brittany the same tradition has lingered for many years. The source of the French version is not difficult to trace. Following the Saxon invasions of Britain from the fifth century onwards, many Britons fled from the Western parts of Britain to nearby Brittany, taking much of their history in written and spoken form with them. The stories relating to Jesus appear to be of considerable antiquity.

As Jesus spent most of His early life in Galilee, one would expect that the people of that area would have retained some information relating to a local man who later became famous.

Indeed, this is exactly what has happened. Among the Marionite and Catluei villagers of Upper Galilee lingers the tradition that Jesus as a youth became a shipwright on a trading vessel from Tyre, one of the biblical "ships of Tarshish."

According to the story, He was storm-bound on the Western coasts of England throughout the winter. The location of the visit is given as "the summerland," a name often used in ancient times for the modern county of Somerset. A district associated with this visit to Somerset is known as "Paradise." This place is sometimes found on old maps of the area.

In the book of Isaiah from chapter 41 onwards, one of the major themes is the first and second comings of Christ. An interesting point relating to this section is that no fewer than seven references are made to "the isles" and "the isles afar off."

Ancient Indian writers employed similar terminology when

writing of Britain. They used terms such as "isles of the West" and "isles of the sea."

During Roman times, at least some of the Jews believed that Isaiah was referring not to "isles" in general but a specific group of islands, i.e. Britain.

In the *Sonnini Manuscript*, an ancient document translated from the Greek, we read that "certain of the children of Israel, about the time of the Assyrian captivity, had escaped by sea to 'the isles afar off,' as spoken by the prophet, and called by the Romans Britain."

On one occasion Isaiah links "the isles" with "the ships of Tarshish."

Jeremiah also mentioned "the isles afar off" in his writings.

The Jewish scholar, Dr. Margouliouth, made the point in his *History of the Jews* that:

"It may not be out of place to state that the isles afar off mentioned in the 31st Chapter of Jeremiah were supposed by the ancients to be Britannia, Scotia and Hibernia."

That Jeremiah had these areas in mind when he wrote seems likely, as early Irish records indicate that he probably visited Ireland—the ancient name for this country being Hibernia—towards the end of his life.

The gospels relate that Jesus followed the profession of his legal father Joseph and became a carpenter. Nowhere are we informed of the exact nature and extent of such training. It is entirely possible that at least a part of that training could have involved work as a shipwright or ship's carpenter.

The fact that Phoenician trading vessels visited Britain in ancient times is beyond question. The existence of the tin trade between Britain and Phoenicia is often mentioned by classical writers such as Diodorus Siculus and Julius Caesar.

Herodotus, writing about 445 B.C., speaks of Britain as the Tin Islands or Cassiterides. Some authorities believe that this trade existed as early as 1500 B.C. Creasy, in his *History of England*, writes: "The British mines mainly supplied the glorious adornment of Solomon's Temple."

Ancient ingots of lead bearing official Roman seals have been discovered in the West of England dating from the time of the first-century emperors Claudius and Nero.

Pilton Flag
*Flag in St. John the Baptist Church, Pilton,
Somerset. Notice the imagery of Joseph of
Arimathea and the boy Jesus.*

An interesting point indicated by the gospel writers is that Jesus was more relaxed and confident at sea, in the Sea of Galilee incident, than the disciples who were trained fishermen (Mark 4:35–41).

This could be a further indication of his experience at sea if He had been to sea prior to His ministry.

A man who, according to the traditions, had experienced sailing in the Mediterranean Sea and Bay of Biscay, would have considered a storm on a mere "lake" to be a matter of no great consequence.

Joseph of Arimathea

In many of the traditions relating to Jesus coming to Britain, He is brought by Joseph of Arimathea. According to Eastern tradition, Joseph was an uncle of Mary and thus a relative of Jesus.

The gospel record of Joseph burying the body of Jesus in his own sepulchre strongly supports this tradition. A casual reading of the account would lead one to assume that Joseph claimed the body from Pilate on the grounds of being a friend or follower of the dead man.

This is far from being the case, however. The chief priests, with the permission of Pilate, had made special arrangements regarding the security of the body of Jesus for the express purpose of keeping it out of the hands of His followers (Matthew 27:62–66).

We are told that Joseph did not reveal at that time that he was a follower of Jesus. He was a disciple "secretly for fear of the Jews" (John 19:38).

If Joseph did not approach Pilate on the grounds of being a disciple, what exactly was his status?

The only grounds he could have had that would be in agreement with Jewish and Roman law, and at the same time avoid giving offence to the chief priests, would be as the nearest relative of the dead man.

Under both Jewish and Roman law it was the responsibility of the nearest relatives to dispose of the dead, regardless of the circumstances of death.

Mary, the mother of Jesus, would clearly be in no fit emotional state for such a task, which would have been considered "man's work" anyway. The brothers of Jesus as young men or teenagers would have lacked the maturity to perform such a duty, leaving Joseph (according to tradition the uncle of Mary) the next in line.

Unless Joseph had had strong legal grounds, as described, for claiming the body, the Jews would have resisted the idea of a man whom they hated and had caused to be executed given the honour of being buried in a private sepulchre, instead of the official burial place for criminals.

The last time that Joseph, the legal father of Jesus, is mentioned in scripture is when Jesus is twelve years old (Luke 2:44–52). From then on the Bible speaks only of His mother and brothers. The clear implication is that Joseph died when Jesus was a young man or teenager. The people of His hometown of Nazareth asked the question, "Is not this the carpenter, the son of Mary?" (Mark 6:3). A son would only be spoken of in this way if the father were dead.

Under Jewish law the nearest male relative would have the clear responsibility to assist the widow and her children. As we saw earlier, this role would almost certainly be taken up by Joseph of Arimathea.

Luke records of Joseph that "he was a good and just man" (Luke 23:50). Someone who was likely to go far beyond the letter of the law in this matter, especially as he was also rich (Matthew 27:57), and in a strong position to aid the bereaved family.

In the Latin Vulgate version of the gospels Joseph is described as "Decurio," and in Jerome's translation as "Nobilis Decurio"—the noble decurio.

The term "decurio" was commonly used to designate an official, under Roman authority, who was in charge of metal mining. The office seems to have been a lucrative and much coveted one. Cicero remarked that it was easier to become a Senator of Rome than a Decurio in Pompeii. The office is also known to have existed under the Roman administration in Britain.

In the Greek, Mark 15:43 reads "Joseph—of rank a senator;" a further indication of him holding office under the Romans.

To go "boldly" (Mark 15:43) to Pilate, the highest authority in the land, and to obtain immediate access and agreement to the request put forward is further proof of the man's position and influence.

Virtually all early records and traditions concerning Joseph associate him with the mining activities of Cornwall and the Mendips. Is it really so incredible that he may have had commercial interests in this part of the world?

For centuries the Hebrews and Phoenicians were trading partners, and in Solomon's time shared the same navy (1 Kings 10:22). Among the merchandise imported by these traders was tin and lead (Ezekiel 27:12).

Cornish Tin Mines

The British mines were a major source of these metals, and in Roman times, because tin was used in the making of alloys, the metal was in great demand. It is entirely possible that Joseph obtained his wealth from this trade.

A large community of Jews existed in Cornwall during ancient times, called by the local people "Saracens." They were engaged in the trade of extracting and exporting metals.

In a work published in 1790 by Dr. Pryce on the origin of the Cornish language, he states that "Cornish and Breton were almost the same dialect of a Syrian or Phoenician root."[6]

Modern historians who tend to be sceptical of the origin of the tradition relating to Joseph, will readily admit that a wealthy Jewish merchant could more easily have traveled from "Palestine to Glastonbury" during the 30 years following the Crucifixion than at any later time until well into the nineteenth century. It should also be noted that trading links between the two areas existed long before the Roman invasion of Britain in A.D. 43.

According to local tradition, Joseph taught the boy Jesus how to extract Cornish tin and purge it of its impurities. Is it not perhaps significant that in his prophecy and analogy of Jesus, the prophet Malachi casts Him in the role of a refiner of metals (Malachi 3:2–3)? The prophet mentions silver, and interestingly enough silver was often extracted from Mendip lead during the time of Christ.

The common factor, it seems, in almost all the West Country sites tied to the tradition is the metal mining industry. Priddy, for example, with its quaint proverb "as sure as our Lord was at Priddy," was the centre of the Mendip mining district in Roman times and even before.

A point not commonly realized is the extensive use that was made of metal in its various forms in the construction of both buildings and ships during the time of Christ.

Tin Ingot circa First Century
This ingot of tin was discovered in the sea off the coast of Looe Island, Cornwall. It has been dated to the first century and is typical of smelted tin from the mines in the area. Joseph of Arimathea is believed to have become wealthy from mines that he owned there.

In the houses of the wealthy, plumbing involving the use of pipes and valves was commonplace.

If Joseph had assisted the family of Jesus after the death of His legal father, the education of the eldest son of the family would have been a point of great importance.

A man with Joseph's wealth could have provided a fine education for the young man, including foreign travel.

The gospels make it very plain that Jesus did not begin His ministry as a penniless vagabond. He conducted His ministry on a full-time basis for three-and-a-half years. His disciples too were, for the most part, full-time students.

The cost of maintaining 13 people for this period of time must have been considerable. Although the disciples and probably some of His other followers contributed to the common fund from time to time, it is likely that the bulk of this fund was provided by Jesus. Although Judas was treasurer for the group, Jesus was the one who determined how the money was to be spent.

He paid taxes, contributed to the poor, may have owned His own house, and attended banquets along with the social elite of His day. One of His own parables showed the necessity of wearing clothing appropriate to the occasion. His wardrobe must have been an adequate one.

In order to do all these things, Jesus must have been a successful and prosperous young man. He must surely have been more than just an ordinary tradesman. The occupation of "carpenter" given in the gospels probably obscures the fact that He was closer to the modern equivalent of a general contractor, involved in the total construction of buildings.

Britain, during the first century A.D., would have been an ideal place to study and develop skills in various aspects of the building industry.

Eumenius states that British architects were in great demand on the Continent during his day. Several writers mention the skills of British craftsmen, especially in the metal working industries.

The enameling process was invented in Britain. A superb example of the local "La Tene" art is the famous Glastonbury bowl, which was produced about the time of Christ. There is little doubt that Jesus could have developed many skills from British craftsmen.

Was Christ Educated in Britain?

As a public speaker Jesus had a tremendous impact on the crowds that gathered around Him. The primary reason for this was clearly His teaching, which was utterly unlike anything that the people had heard before. Another important factor was His style of public speaking. In the Greek, Mark 1:22 reads: "And they were struck with awe at His mode of instruction."

He was also an educated speaker. It is recorded that the people of His hometown of Nazareth were astonished at His preaching. "And all bare Him witness and wondered at the gracious words which proceeded out of His mouth" (Luke 4:22).

This statement very clearly implies that not all of His formal education, nor His training as a public speaker, had been received at Nazareth. If His training had been merely the product of a local school or college, the people would not have been so astonished.

It is unlikely that higher education of that calibre was even available in a provincial town such as Nazareth. Nathaniel implied this in his remark: "Can any good thing proceed from Nazareth?" (John 1:46).

Jerusalem was the academic headquarters of the nation, yet Jesus had not trained among the professional public speakers there, either. Mark relates that: "He taught them, as possessing authority, and not as the scribes" (Mark 1:22).

The Jews were deeply puzzled by this very fact. They asked the question: "How does this man know letters, having never studied?" (John 7:15).

The Weymouth translation renders this: "How does this man know anything of books," they said, "although He has never been at any of the schools?"

Here was an educated man and superb public speaker who had not received any such training within any college of Galilee or Judea. If Jesus had received such training, they would have known about it and not remarked: "having never studied."

Although such training may not readily have been obtained in Palestine, it most certainly could have been in Britain. If Jesus had visited Britain, according to the traditions, as part of His education He would have found 40 colleges or universities. The educational standards there were such that students came not only from the

British nobility but also from several foreign nations. It is said that even Pontius Pilate, as a young man, studied in Britain.

A very high standard in oratory or public speaking was often attained by first-century Britons. Tacitus records on a word-by-word basis the speeches of several high-ranking Britons of his day.

Such speeches were often colourful, stirring and inspiring, much like, in some ways, the speeches of Jesus.

A few hundred years before the time of Christ, the Greek writer Strabo described the character of an educated Briton of his day, Abaris, as follows: "He was easy in his address; agreeable in his conversation; active in his dispatch and secret in his management of great affairs; diligent in the quest of wisdom; fond of friendship; trusting very little to fortune; yet having the entire confidence of others, and trusted with everything for his prudence. He spoke Greek with a fluency that you would have thought that he had been brought up in the Lyceum."[7]

It may be mere coincidence, but Jesus is described as having qualities and talents far more like those of an educated Briton, than one would have expected from an educated Jew of the same period.

One might wonder if Jesus would have had a language problem in Britain. He almost certainly spoke Greek in addition to His local Aramaic. The Greek renders John 7:35 "is He about to go to the *dispersion of the Greeks*? and to teach the *Greeks*?"

The Jews would obviously not have made this remark unless they were aware that He spoke the language.

Mark relates a conversation that Jesus had with a woman in the region of Tyre and Sidon, adding the point that "the woman was a Greek" (Mark 7:26).

The disciples or students of Jesus when writing the New Testament wrote in Greek, a clear indication that their "teacher" also understood the language.

Julius Caesar stated that the Britons used Greek in their commercial transactions. Many of the educated classes in Britain spoke the language fluently. A few, such as Pomponia Graecina, were among Europe's leading scholars in the language.

If Jesus had visited Britain He would have had no language barrier to overcome.

A final indication that Jesus may well have been abroad for some years prior to His ministry is the curious relationship that He had with John the Baptist.

In comparison to the intimate rapport that Jesus had with His own disciples, His relationship with John was somewhat formal and distant. A clue to the reason for this is given by John when he mentioned: "And I did not know Him" (John 1:33).

Although the two men were related and their mothers seem to have been close friends (Luke 1:36–45), they appear to have had little or no contact as adults. Is this an indication that Jesus had been absent from the area for several years prior to His ministry?

Having related the traditions of Jesus' visit to Britain to the considerable circumstantial evidence from the gospels and other sources, one could well say that there may indeed be a grain of truth in the idea that those feet in ancient times did "walk upon England's mountains green."

Chapter Summary

The mysterious lost years, from age 12 to 30 in the life of Jesus Christ. Did He travel to foreign parts during this time? International trading voyages during the time of Jesus. An examination of West Country traditions that relate to Jesus Christ.

Chapter Four

THE GLASTONBURY STORY

"It is certain that Britain received the Faith in the first age from the first sowers of the Word. Of all the churches whose origin I have investigated in Britain, the Church of Glastonbury is the most ancient"
(Sir Henry Spelman, *"Concilia"*).

"After this, Joseph of Arimathea, being a disciple of Jesus, but secretly, for fear of the Jews, asked Pilate that he might take away the body of Jesus; and Pilate gave him permission"
(John 19:38).

T here can be few places in the whole of Britain so steeped in folklore, superstition and mystery as the little town of Glastonbury, tucked away in the heart of rural Somerset.
A place of pilgrimage for thousands even in this scientific age of the early twenty-first century, a strange magnetic attraction seems to draw people to this spot, be they Christian, mystic, or wandering tourist.

Through the centuries some have regarded Glastonbury as none other than the fabled "Avalon" of antiquity, the "many-towered Camelot" where King Arthur and his beautiful Queen Guinevere held court.

Although many modern writers regard the story of Joseph of Arimathea coming to Glastonbury as mere pious fables fabricated by the local monks, some of the most eminent early authorities consider this in an entirely different light.

The Mother Church at Glastonbury

According to Archbishop Ussher: "The Mother Church of the British Isles is the Church in Insula Avallonia, called by the Saxons 'Glaston.'"

Sir Henry Spelman in his *Concilia* writes: "It is certain that Britain received the Faith in the first age from the first sowers of the Word. Of all the churches whose origin I have investigated in Britain, the Church of Glastonbury is the most ancient."

Fuller, in his evaluation of the testimony of early writers on the subject, states: "If credit be given to ancient authors, this Church of Glastonbury is the senior church of the world."

The Incredible History of God's True Church

It should be mentioned that Fuller, in this context, was talking of the church building known as "the old church" made of wattle and daub that survived until destroyed by fire in 1184.

Although Christian converts met together at Jerusalem and elsewhere in Palestine from an earlier date than that given for the construction of the wattle church at Glastonbury, those meetings took place in private houses or the synagogue.

If the construction of the wattle church was begun in the last year of the reign of the Roman Emperor Tiberius (A.D. 36–37), as ancient writers claim, then it would indeed be "the first above-ground church in the world."

The fact that the story of Joseph at Glastonbury was regarded as historical fact from the earliest times is evident by the enormous importance and prestige that the Abbey attracted.

The Abbey was built on the site of the wattle church but bore no resemblance in size or design to the earlier structure that measured 60 ft. by 26 ft.

The "old church" was sometimes also called the "church of boughs," by virtue of its construction, which was of timber pillars and framework doubly wattled inside and out with clay, and thatched with straw.

It was probably more than coincidence that the measurements of the church agreed almost exactly with those of the Tabernacle erected by Moses in the wilderness. Christianity was brought to Britain by men of Hebrew rather than Roman extraction.

The Catholic writer Robert Parsons, in his *Three Conversions of England*, admits, as do many other early Catholic writers, that:

"It seems nearest the truth that the British Church was originally planted by Grecian teachers, such as came from the East, and not by Romans."[1]

The fact that for centuries the British churches followed Eastern rather than Roman usages confirms this point. Even as late as the time of Augustine the British bishops were reluctant to change the customs they had received from the churches in Asia. When confronted with demands brought by Augustine from the Pope, they replied: "We cannot depart from our ancient customs without the consent and leave of our people."[2]

In a book published by William Camden in 1674 we read: "The true Christian Religion was planted here most anciently by Joseph of

Glastonbury Abbey
The ruins of Glastonbury Abbey, which was built in the seventh century, supposedly on the original site of the "wattle and daub" church built by Joseph of Arimathea in 37 A.D.

Arimathea, Simon Zelotes, Aristobulous, by St. Peter, and St. Paul, as may be proved by Dorotheus, Theodoretus and Sophronius."[3]

The fact that many other historians shared this view is evident by noting the comment of Stillingfleet that: "It is the opinion generally received among our later writers, as one of them tells the world, 'That the conversion of the British nation to the Christian faith was performed towards the latter end of the reign of Tiberius Caesar,' i.e. about thirty-seven years after Christ's nativity."[4]

The same writer mentioned the general view of British church historians concerning the Glastonbury story: "Who took it for granted, and believed that it is grounded on the testimony of ancient records."

Glastonbury Fables

Why, it might be asked, in the light of such records, do modern authorities relegate the story of Glastonbury to the realm of "pious fables" having little if any historical validity?

One reason is that few such "ancient records" are still extant. For centuries the church library at Glastonbury housed what was probably the finest collection of material on church history in Britain. This unique collection of rare documents was totally consumed by the fire of 1184. As this was the era of handwritten books and documents, prior to the invention of printing, it is probable that in many cases only single copies existed and thus vital evidence was destroyed.

There is some evidence to suggest that the monks, in order to raise funds for the rebuilding of their Abbey, attempted to reproduce some of these documents from memory; passing them off to the gullible pilgrims as the ancient originals.

It is likely that the monks, many of whom were poorly educated, had only a hazy understanding of the exact content of much of the material they were reproducing, or as some would put it, "forging."

An example of this is *St. Patrick's Charter*. Although Patrick could well have visited the Glastonbury church in the mid-fifth century, the charter that bears his name was very clearly written some seven to eight centuries after his death.

The language and terminology used in the charter is beyond doubt mediaeval. Indulgences are also mentioned, which were not used in the context of the charter until the eleventh century.

In spite of the fact that so much mediaeval superstition has clouded the true history of the Glastonbury church, it would be simply untrue to claim that no genuine records of great antiquity existed prior to the fire of 1184.

William of Malmesbury, possibly the leading historian of his day, visited Glastonbury in about 1125 and after examining the early records, mentions his findings: "Since this is the point at which I must bring in the monastery of Glastonbury, let me trace from its very beginning the rise and progress of that church so far as I can discover it from the mass of source material."

Concluding his evidence of a second-century Work in the area he continues the narrative: "As a result, missionaries sent by Eleutherius came to Britain, whose labours will bear fruit for evermore, even though the rust of ages has eroded their names. These men built the ancient church of St. Mary of Glastonbury, as faithful tradition has handed the story down through decaying time.

"However, there are documents of no meagre credit, which have been found in certain places, saying thus: 'No other hands than those of the disciples of Christ erected the church of Glastonbury.' Nor is this totally irreconcilable with truth, for if the Apostle Philip did preach to the Gauls (as Freculfus says in the fourth chapter of his second book), then it is possible to believe that he broadcast the seed of the Word across the sea also."[5]

For a hundred years and more after William wrote this, various "revised" versions of his work were produced by the monks.

Five years after the fire, which destroyed the old church and all the later buildings in the vicinity, Richard I came to the throne and all available funds were diverted to his crusade. The monks, in common with advertising men in later ages, decided to add colour to the product that William had provided.

The scholarly though cautious work of William needed something extra that would appeal to the superstitious pilgrims and visitors, and induce them to donate generously to the ambitious new building project.

To his simple statement that the Glastonbury church was "the first church in the kingdom of Britain, and the source and fountain of all religion," the monks added miracles, visions and a personal visit by no less a personage than the angel Gabriel who instructed the builders of the old church to dedicate it to "the Blessed Virgin."

In 1191 the monks proclaimed to an astonished nation that they had uncovered the remains of King Arthur and Queen Guinevere in the vicinity of the old church. Visitors flocked to Glastonbury and the building fund swelled—the age of the Glastonbury legends had begun.

In their day the legends were more popular that many a Hollywood film epic of our present age. In time stories about the "Holy Grail," the "Holy Thorn" and the thrilling adventures of Arthur's Knights of the Round Table were added to the earlier stories.

To come to a more realistic study of the subject one needs to go back beyond the time of William of Malmesbury and look at the known history of the area.

Glastonbury Facts

The fact that "the old church" did indeed exist is clear historical fact and no fable. Direct references to this building, many made by writers who visited and examined the structure, are numerous.

There is also clear evidence that the building was erected in antiquity and was pre-Saxon in construction.

Even a writer who was unconvinced of its association with the first-century Church admitted that: "I do not, then, deny that there was an ancient church before Ina's time, which after the Western Saxons became Christians, grew into mighty reputation...."[6]

The *Domesday Book*, published in 1088, from existing Saxon records provides information of the "Domus Dei, in the great monastery of Glastonbury, called the Secret of the Lord. This Glastonbury church possesses, in its own villa, twelve hides of land which have never paid tax."

The land grant, according to tradition, was made by the local ruler to Joseph of Arimathea and his companions. Further grants of land were made to the church by Saxon kings. The exact extent of a "hide" of land is now unknown but is thought to have represented a plot of land sufficient to support one family.

This grant was obviously made at a very early period, as it is clear that even in 1088 the exact circumstances relating to the grant were no longer known.

By the time of the Saxon king Ina, who erected a church building of stone near the wattle church in 725 A.D., the earlier structure had already become "a thing of untouchable mystery and holiness."

One of the reasons for the superstitious awe that surrounded the old church was that during the Dark Ages, prior to the conversion of the Saxons to the Catholic faith, the Glastonbury church was one of the very few, perhaps even the only church building, to survive from the Roman period.

A belief developed that the church was under some form of divine protection, and the history of the period would seem to bear this out. Time and again the violent tide of war seemed about to engulf the wattle church but always it came through intact.

In 577 A.D. the invading Saxons reached Glastonbury after looting and slaughtering their way across England. Within sight of the Tor, however, they halted, for some unknown reason, and the old church was preserved.

In 658 A.D. the church was the location chosen for the signing of a peace treaty between the Britons and Saxons. "Here, for the first time, the English treated the Britons with respect as potential members of a larger fraternity," commented the historian Robinson.

The Danes attacked Glastonbury in 878 A.D. They set fire to several of the later buildings surrounding the old church, but the ancient wattle structure escaped unscathed.

Great stress was placed on the preservation of the original fabric of the building. In 630 A.D. the entire structure was encased in lead.

About a hundred years before this a pillar was erected bearing a brass tablet, the purpose being to define the exact limits of the church. As several other buildings had been erected over the years in the vicinity of the church this precaution was taken in order to prevent future possible confusion.

The pillar survived for about a thousand years—its base was discovered in 1921. The brass tablet bore the inscription: "The first ground of God, the first ground of the saints in Britain, and the burial place of the Saints."[7]

Traces of monastic buildings and military encampments have been discovered in the vicinity of Glastonbury dating to the "Dark Ages" period, following the withdrawal of the Roman legions from Britain in 410 A.D.

St. Patrick is said to have established the first monastic community in the area and to have been buried there in 472 A.D. The location of his burial is given in one work as "by the right side of the altar in the 'old church.'"

Other authorities, as one might have expected, deny this and claim that he was buried in Ireland. Regardless of the identification of the personalities involved, the evidence of archaeology is that a community of Irish monks did settle in the area either during or shortly after the lifetime of Patrick.

Fragments of the buildings erected during this period may be inspected at the museum that has been set up near the site of the old church. It should be noted that the monks never claimed to have erected the old church, indeed the presence of this structure seems to have been the primary reason for their settlement in this area.

The monks, in addition to erecting several buildings of their own, seem to have carried out some restoration work on the old church. The first Saxons to reach the area reported that by their day the church was in a state of decay, patched up with boards and having a lead roof, replacing the earlier thatch. Four windows had also been made in the side and end of the building.

William of Malmesbury makes it clear in his *A Life of St. Dunstan* that "Glastonbury had already passed under ecclesiastical authority long before the time of St. Patrick, who had died in A.D. 472."

In 1966, excavations carried out at Cadbury Castle and the nearby Glastonbury Tor established the existence of the "historical Arthur" or an "Arthur type figure." The former site seems to have been his base camp and the latter a military look-out post.

Arthur and Lucius

The real or historic Arthur was a far cry indeed from the King Arthur of mediaeval legend. Recent evidence indicates that the Glastonbury Arthur (even this name is by no means clearly established) was a local Romano-British warrior king, or even a country gentleman turned soldier, who led his forces against the invading Saxons.

Several of the final last-ditch battles of the Britons against the Saxons took place in Somerset. The evidence of recent archaeological findings strongly point to Cadbury Castle as the headquarters of the real King Arthur.

Over the centuries the story of Arthur's desperate struggles with his enemies developed into a make-believe fantasy world of intrepid knights engaged in seemingly hopeless struggles against not only human military foes, but an impressive array of giants, monsters and wizards; a romantic world of knights in shining armour setting off to rescue beautiful damsels in distress.

The history of the Glastonbury church is almost a total blank during the third and fourth centuries—the site could well have been abandoned during this period.

William of Malmesbury picks up the story again with the visit to Glastonbury of the second-century bishops sent out by King Lucius. William believed that they were the builders of the wattle church.

Other sources, however, indicate that they did not build the church but merely carried out restoration work to an already existing structure.

"The church dedicated to St. Mary at Glastonbury repaired and raised out of the ruins by Faganus and Davianus, where they lived with twelve associates A.D. 187."[8]

Churches are also said to have been established by Lucius in London (A.D. 179), Gloucester and Winchester (A.D. 180) and Bangor, Dover and Canterbury.

Traces of buildings, thought to have been churches and dating from the Roman period, have been discovered at Dover and Canterbury.

Although some later writers have doubted the very existence of Lucius, the fact remains that for many centuries the establishment of churches at these sites during the second century was treated as historical fact. As the dates given for these churches are earlier than the visit of the bishops to Glastonbury, it is evident that the building work carried out there involved the restoration of an already existing structure.

There is no record that any of the second-century British churches challenged the greater antiquity of the Glastonbury church.

There was a foreign challenge to this claim, however, and R.W. Morgan, the Victorian author, mentions the outcome of this: "This priority of antiquity was only once questioned, and that on political grounds, by the ambassadors of France and Spain, at the Council of Pisa, A.D. 1417. The Council however, affirmed it."

A further Council at Sena reached the same decision: "This decision laid down that the Churches of France and Spain were bound to give way in the points of antiquity and precedency to the Church of Britain, which was founded by Joseph of Arimathea immediately after the passion of Christ."[9]

Elvanus and Aristobulus

Traces are found in the early records of a college or school that existed at Glastonbury during the first half of the second century for the training of ministers and others involved in preaching the gospel.

There can be little doubt that the work being done by these people, about which very little is known, was a small scale operation. As a noted archaeologist has recently pointed out, Christianity in Britain during the second century represented a "minority sect."

The most noted scholar of the college, and indeed the only one of whom any record has survived was Elvanus Avalonius (Elvanus of Avalon or Glastonbury). He was also known as Elfan in Welsh sources.

The Incredible History of God's True Church

The Church of Saint Laurence, Priddy

Welcome to our Church, dedicated in 1352 but which has an earlier C13th tower.

There are Bronze Age barrows to the N and SW, close by the Churchyard, so this must be very ancient sacred ground.

There is a legend that Jesus came to Priddy on a trading expedition with Joseph of Arimathea and the hymn 'Jerusalem' has special meaning here. We know there were local mines from which lead was sent to the Roman Empire. Two roads from Priddy were named Pilton Drove and Axbridge Street and led to small ports.

The main body of the Church, the nave, has a Victorian pine roof, open timbered with arch braces and collars. Wall posts are supported on medieval carved stone corbel heads.

In 1896, during internal restoration, plain oak benches were replaced by these pine pews, possibly the rood loft was removed then and parts of the screen were renovated. Estimates of the age of the central section vary from C14th to C17th. The newest part of the screen is in the single-bay south aisle, with a plaque recording that it was given by Mr. Henry John Rossiter. Beside it is the Jacobean chest which would once have held all the parish records. The stained glass window nearby was given by Mr. and Mrs. Ivor Gibbons in memory of their daughter Catherine, who enjoyed a healthy and energetic childhood at Eastwater Farm, until a severe illness in her teens led to operations and much time in London hospitals. She sadly died whilst convalescing at home. Her pony is pictured here.

On one side of the chancel steps are the lectern and remains of a stone stair to the rood loft and on the other is the Jacobean pulpit with restored legs.

The chancel has a Victorian oak ceiling, barrel vaulted with moulded ribs and carved oak base and carved oak crosses. By 1880 the Church was in great disrepair and roof renewal dates from the £2000 restoration of 1890. On the sill of the C14th lancet window is a piscina and at its head a C13th re-used grave cover with a foliated cross.

The prayer desk and serving table were given by Church Wardens and the lighting is in memory of Phillip Sherrell, tragically killed whilst on holiday abroad.

Tradition of Jesus in England Lives On

Located in the Mendips in Somerset, England is the town of Priddy. Here in the local church is a reference to the tradition. The Mendip Hills produced lead from at least 1000 B.C. till the early twentieth century A.D. The lead produced from this area was mixed with tin from Cornwall to produce pewter, a vital metal for daily use by the Romans. Locals still believe that Jesus walked these hills.

"Bale saith that Elvanus Avalonius was a disciple to those who were the disciples of the Apostles, and that he preached the Gospel in Britain with good success...."[10]

It is significant that Glastonbury seems to have been the headquarters, within a generation or two of the apostolic age of "the disciples of the Apostles."

Welsh authorities mention that Elfan presided over a congregation of Christians at Glastonbury. This, one would assume, must have taken place after the generation that had known the apostles had died out.

The Book of Llandaff records that Elfan was appointed second Bishop of London in A.D. 185. About this time he wrote a book on the origin of the British church.

One of the "disciples of the Apostles" may have been Aristobulus (Romans 16:10). According to Cressy: "St. Aristobulus, a disciple of St. Peter or St. Paul in Rome, was sent as an apostle to the Britons, and was the first Bishop in Britain, he died in Glastonbury, A.D. 99."

The *Greek Martyrologies* mention that: "Aristobulus was one of the seventy disciples, and a follower of St. Paul the Apostle, along with whom he preached the Gospel to the whole world, and ministered to him. He was chosen by St. Paul to be the missionary bishop to the land of Britain, inhabited by a very warlike and fierce race. By them he was often scourged, and repeatedly dragged as a criminal through their towns, yet he converted many of them to Christianity. He was there martyred, after he had built churches and ordained deacons and priests for the island."

Glastonbury Architecture

The style of building and method of construction employed by the builders of the Glastonbury church reflects the general building styles used in Britain during the first century of the Christian era; this is particularly true of buildings erected prior to the Roman invasion of A.D. 43.

The church had little if anything to distinguish it from other buildings of the period used as public meeting places. Architecture of a distinctly ecclesiastical style is not known to have existed earlier than the third or fourth centuries.

"There is no clear example of a separate building set apart for

The Incredible History of God's True Church

Christian worship within the limits of the Roman Empire before the third century," wrote Lightfoot.

Churches erected by Constantine in the early fourth century and later were said to have been styled after the plain basilical halls of pagan antiquity. As early as the second century anti-Jewish feeling within the professing Christian church had become so intense that it is unlikely that a church building such as the one erected at Glastonbury could have been permitted, whose measurements coincided with those of the Hebrew tabernacle set up by Moses.

The Glastonbury church lacked even a baptistry, at its original construction, although this feature was one of the earliest to find its way into church architecture. It seems probable that the first converts were baptized in a local river or other natural water source.

This building, in common with other very early churches, faced towards the west. The builders could well have had in mind the strong warning given in Ezekiel 8:16 against pagan worshippers carrying out their devotions with "their faces toward the east."

In 1957–58 the remains of a wattle and daub structure with thatched roof, similar in construction to the Glastonbury church, was discovered near the site of the Roman town of Calleva Atrebatum (Silchester) in Hampshire. It has been dated to A.D. 25–43, the same period given by ancient writers for the construction of the church.

Since the Second World War, excavators have uncovered the remains of much of the first stages of construction of the Roman City of London dating from the time of the destruction of the city by Boadicea in A.D. 61. Evidence has come to light that most of the buildings from the period were of daub and wattle construction. The clear indications from this and other Roman sites are that stone buildings of Roman building styles began to rapidly replace the earlier daub and wattle structures during the second century. By the latter part of this century few buildings of the earlier type were being erected.

Fuller, in his *Church History of Britain*, mentions the Glastonbury church as a place "where at one view, we may behold the simplicity of primitive devotion, and the native fashion of British buildings in that age, and some hundred years after, it had a thatched covering."

During the sixth and seventh centuries the native Britons, along with the incoming Saxons, no longer having the advanced building techniques of the Romans available to them, reverted to wattle and daub construction methods. There can be little doubt, however, that the erection of the Glastonbury church took place during the earlier period. By the second phase of this style of building the church was already surrounded by mystery and superstitious awe, and was of such great antiquity that major restoration work was required to preserve the original fabric of the structure.

Non-British Testimony
Moving on to non-British sources, we are able to pick up the story of Joseph in the *Ecclesiastical Annals* of the sixteenth-century Vatican librarian, Cardinal Baronius. A historian of great integrity, Baronius relates how he discovered a document of considerable antiquity in the Vatican archives. The manuscript related that in the year A.D. 35 a group of Christians including Lazarus, Mary Magdalene, Martha, Joseph of Arimathea, and several others were cast adrift in a boat from the coast of the Holy Land by persecuting Jews.

"In that year the party mentioned was exposed to the sea in a vessel without sails or oars. The vessel drifted finally to Marseilles and they were saved. From Marseilles Joseph and his company passed into Britain and after preaching the Gospel there, died."

According to the *Recognitions of Clement,* which is thought to have been written ca. A.D. 150–200, the group lived for a time at Caesarea prior to their voyage. This work has been described as a "kind of religious novel" containing a vast amount of theological speculation. Much of the historical framework in which it is set, however, bears a close relationship to known facts of the period.

Caesarea was the major port in Palestine. It was a cosmopolitan city and a home for many foreign seamen and merchants. As such, a much greater measure of religious freedom existed there than at Jerusalem. It would have proved an ideal place of temporary refuge for those fleeing from the persecutions recorded in the Acts of the Apostles.[11]

It is recorded in Acts 11:19 that many Christians were driven by persecution into Phoenicia. Caesarea lies on the route between Jerusalem and Phoenicia. As the city is mentioned several times in the book of Acts the indications are that a Christian community of some size existed there.

This city was also the home of Philip the evangelist (Acts 21:8), a man closely associated with Joseph in the early records. According to tradition he was the man who ordained Joseph and supervised much of his later work.

According to Isidorus Hispalensis, this Philip who was formerly "one of the seven deacons" carried the Gospel first to the Samaritans and later to Gaul (France).[12]

Elsewhere he states: "St. Philip preached to the Gauls, and persuaded the neighbouring and savage tribes on the borders of the ocean to the light of knowledge and of faith."[13]

No trace of Joseph in Palestine is found after about A.D. 35, no record of any martyrdom and no reference to his movements outside of the areas of Britain and France. The information given by Baronius relating to the enforced voyage to Marseilles of Joseph and his companions seems the most likely and logical account of his movements.

The French Connection

A great many local traditions have been handed down in the Marseilles area relating to the arrival and later work of Joseph and his companions. It is a clear historical fact that Southern France was one of the first areas in the West to receive the gospel message.

It was here that some of the earliest and most severe persecutions took place.

The earliest records relate a simple narrative rather similar in style to that of the book of Acts; stories of incredible miracles associated with the group seem to have been added at a later date.

One local tradition mentions the boat drifting to the coast of Provence, and after following the Rhone, arriving at Arles. The first Jewish settlers in the area are said to have "come in a boat which had been deserted by its captain."

A Spanish version of the story leaves the group in Aquitaine "as the histories of the Gauls and the local traditions plainly teach."

Several of the Rhone Valley churches traced their origins back to Lazarus and other fellow travelers of Joseph. In the annals of the mediaeval writer Roger de Horedon we read: "Marseilles is an episcopal city under the domination of the King of Arragon. Here are the relics of St. Lazarus, the brother of St. Mary Magdalene and

Coat of Arms of East and West Looe Council
On the Cornish coast of England are the towns of East and West Looe. Their council has chosen for its coat of arms the legend of Joseph of Arimathea and the boy Jesus.

Martha, who held the bishopric here for seven years after Jesus had restored him from the dead."

Recognized trade and military routes existed during the first century A.D. from Marseilles, across France to the Channel ports and from these into Britain. The Emperor Claudius for example traveled from Marseilles to Boulogne and from there to Colchester in Britain, returning by the same route to Rome.

Joseph of Arimathea

Traces of Joseph of Arimathea are found in the local traditions of Limoges and Morlaix, both located on the trade route to Britain. The first bishop of Treginer is said to have been Drennalus, a disciple of Joseph. It is significant that even critics of the Glastonbury legends admit that Christianity came into Somerset "via Brittany."

One objection that has been raised to the point of Joseph arriving in Britain as early as the last year of the reign of Tiberius (a mere five to six years after the crucifixion of Christ) is that Eusebius records an ancient tradition "that our Saviour commanded His Apostles not to depart from Jerusalem within twelve years after his ascension."

Even if this tradition reflected an accurate point of historical fact, as it could well have done, the evidence is considerable that the instructions applied to the apostles—and only the apostles.

Other members of the Church driven by persecution traveled to Phoenicia, Cyprus and Antioch (Acts 11:19). The restrictions put on the movements of the apostles do not appear to have applied to the Church in general, nor on the activities of Joseph of Arimathea.

Some have mentioned that the Christian message, at this early period, was taken only to the Jews, or as Rabanus, the eighth-century writer, puts it, to "the twelve tribes of the Hebrews."

The West of England about this time, however, supported many who were of Hebrew or Eastern Mediterranean extraction. Several artifacts originating in that area have been discovered in Somerset.

Many involved in the Cornish mining operations had a Jewish background. "The Jews appear to have called themselves or were called by the Britons of Cornwall 'Saracens.'"[14]

Joseph, if he restricted his preaching to those of his own race, would have found many of his fellow countrymen trading in the West of England.

Archbishop Ussher records that "from Juvenal indeed it appears that Arviragus became king of the Britons while Domitian was Emperor, since our Joseph is said to have died under Vespasian in the year 76."

Cressy in his *Church History of Brittany* writes: "Joseph was buried near the little wattle church he built. The lid of the sarcophagus said to have contained his remains bore the simple inscription: "To the Britons I came after I buried the Christ. I taught, I have entered my rest."

John Bloom of London, conducting excavations under a license granted by Edward the Third, claimed to have discovered Joseph's body at Glastonbury in 1345.

The point made by Bishop Godwin in his *Catalogue of Bishops* seems to adequately sum up the story of Joseph: "The testimonies of Joseph of Arimathea's coming here are so many, so clear, and so pregnant, as an indifferent man cannot but discern there is something in it."

Chapter Summary

The iconic ruined Abbey of Glastonbury in Somerset was built on the site of a much earlier pre-Catholic structure known as "the old church." According to local tradition and many early written records, this ancient structure was erected by Joseph of Arimathea during the first century. This chapter delves into the fascinating details of this subject.

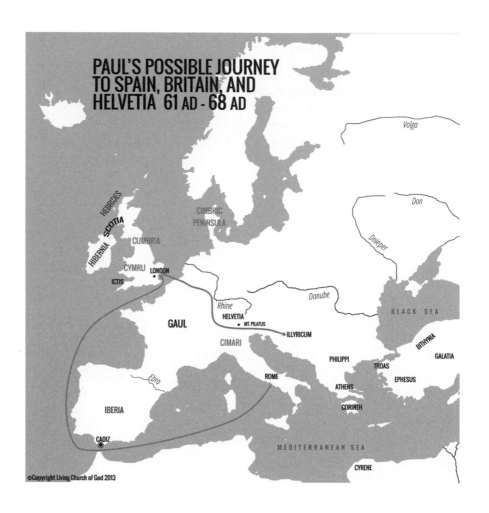

PAUL'S POSSIBLE JOURNEY TO SPAIN, BRITAIN, AND HELVETIA 61 AD - 68 AD

©Copyright Living Church of God 2013

Chapter Five

THE UTMOST BOUNDS OF THE WEST

*"And so having taught the whole world righteousness, and for that
end travelled even to the utmost bounds of the West; he (the Apostle
Paul) at last suffered martyrdom by the command of the governors"*
(Clement of Rome, "Epistle to the Church of God at Corinth," A.D. 96).

*"...and you shall be witnesses to me in Jerusalem, and in all
Judea and Samaria, and to the end of the earth."*
(Acts 1: 8).

O f St. Paul's journey to Britain, a point of great importance
in the history of the Gospel, and of the Protestant church,
we are blessed to possess as substantial evidence as any
historical fact can require.

"Some of our most valuable Ecclesiastical historians have no
scruple in acceding to the general testimony of the Fathers that the
Gospel was preached in Britain by some of the Apostles soon after
the middle of the first century."

So wrote Bishop T. Burges in 1815.[1] Burges was not alone in his
view; many other authorities could be cited who upheld this position.

Even the most cautious of writers feels compelled to admit
that "whether any apostle or companion of an apostle, ever visited
Britain, cannot be determined; yet the balance of probability rather
inclines towards the affirmative."[2]

St. Paul in Britain
William Cave presents the case in more positive terms when he
relates that "Theodoret and others tell us that he [the Apostle Paul]
preached not only in Spain, but that he went to other nations, and
brought the gospel into the isles of the sea, by which he undoubtedly
means Britain; and therefore elsewhere reckons the Gauls and
Britons among the nations which the apostles, and particularly the
tent-maker, persuaded to embrace the law of Christ."[3]

The actual statement of Theodoret made in A.D. 435 is as follows:
"Paul, liberated from his first captivity at Rome, preached the Gospel
to the Britons and Others in the West. Our fishermen and publicans

not only persuaded the Romans and their tributaries to acknowledge the Crucified and His laws, but the Britons also and the Cimbri [Cymry, i.e. Welsh].

"When Paul was sent by Festus on his appeal to Rome, he traveled, after being acquitted, into Spain, and thence extended his excursions into other countries, and to the islands surrounded by the sea."[4]

Venantius Fortunatus in A.D. 560 mentions that "St. Paul passed over the ocean to the Island of Britain, and to Thule, the extremity of the earth."

It is significant to note that almost all early authorities relating to Paul's visit to Britain are non-British in origin, largely coming from a Greek or Latin background. There can be no possibility that the visit was a mere fabrication of British writers who were seeking an apostolic foundation for the British church on patriotic or political grounds.

Clement's Testimony

Perhaps the most important of all sources concerning Paul's movements after leaving Rome is Clement's *Epistle to the Corinthians*.

In an attempt to encourage the Christians at Corinth to remain firmly established in the true faith, he relates firstly how Peter, and then Paul met their deaths: "Let us set before our eyes the Holy Apostles: Peter by unjust envy underwent not one, or two but many sufferings; till at last being martyred, he went to the place of glory that was due to him. For the same cause, did Paul in like manner receive the reward of his patience. Seven times he was in bonds; he was whipped, was stoned; he preached both in the East and in the West; leaving behind him the glorious report of his faith.

"And so having taught the whole world righteousness, and for that end traveled even to the utmost bounds of the West; he at last suffered martyrdom by the command of the governors."[5]

This epistle was written in A.D. 95–96. Clement was not writing centuries after the events described, but was in fact a contemporary of Paul, writing less than 30 years after Paul's martyrdom.

Irenaeus in the second century speaks of Clement, "who also has seen the blessed Apostles and conversed with them and had the preaching of the Apostles still ringing in his ears and their tradition before his eyes." Origen in the third century mentions "Clement the disciple of the Apostles" and "the faithful Clement to whom Paul bears testimony."

Not only Origen, but Eusebius and many other early writers identify Clement with "Clement also, and with other my fellow helpers, whose names are in the book of life" (Philippians 4:3).

"The tradition that he [Clement] was the disciple of one or both of these Apostles [Peter and Paul] is early, constant, and definite; and it is borne out by the character and contents of the epistle itself."[6]

Some controversy has surrounded the question of what precisely Clement meant by his statement "the utmost bounds of the West." Was he thinking of Spain or Britain?

In ancient times the term was used to define both Spain and Britain. The Greeks considered Spain to be the western extremity of the known world. When Clement was writing, Britain was commonly known as the western extremity or boundary of the Roman empire.

According to T. Burges, "This is not a rhetorical expression, but the usual designation of Britain. Theodoret speaks of the inhabitants of Spain, Gaul and Britain as dwelling in the utmost bounds of the west.

"Nicephorus says, that the Britons inhabited the utmost parts of the West. St. Paul therefore in going to the utmost bounds of the West went to Britain.

According to Jerome, "Between Spain and Britain there was a frequent intercourse."[7]

The most logical conclusion must surely be that had Clement wished to specify one particular country, and one alone, he would have named it. By using a more general term, however, he could include Spain, Gaul (France) and Britain.

A work conducted in these regions would have been quite in keeping with Christ's command to His apostles to take the Gospel to "the uttermost part of the earth" (Acts 1:8).

Paul spoke of those, including himself, who would spread glad tidings "unto the ends of the world" (Romans 10:18).

Non-Canon Sources
The warning given in Revelation that nothing should be added to, or taken from, "the things which are written in this book" (Revelation 22:19) might lead some to assume that all of the inspired writings of the New Testament Church are included in the canon of the Bible.

Internal evidence from the New Testament itself, however, clearly disproves any such assumption. Luke records that many accurate and authentic accounts of the life of Jesus Christ were in circulation at the time that he began his narrative (Luke 1:1–2).

Paul mentions in his "first" epistle to the Corinthians that "I wrote to you in that letter" proving that at least one other epistle had been written to the Corinthian Christians before his so-called "first" epistle (1 Corinthians 5:9).

An epistle was also sent to the Laodiceans (Colossians 4:16), which is not included in the canon of the New Testament.

Several commentators have expressed their surprise at the obviously "unfinished" state of the book of Acts. It stops in the middle of the story, with some seven years of Paul's life yet to be covered. Luke, although an experienced and polished writer, does not even end with the usual "Amen."

Some scholars feel that Luke had intended writing a third volume covering the remaining years of Paul's life. Perhaps a more logical view would be that he would write a continuation and conclusion to Acts.

Paul mentions that Luke was still with him about A.D. 67, shortly before Paul was martyred (2 Timothy 4:11). The clear implication is that Luke remained with Paul for at least a part, if not all, of the remaining years between the conclusion of Acts in A.D. 61 and Paul's martyrdom in A.D. 68.

It would hardly seem logical that Luke would fail to complete his narrative. So, the question should perhaps be asked, "If the book of Acts was completed, what became of the final section? And why was it left out of the New Testament canon?"

Daniel records that some information relating to the history of the nation of Israel and the "holy people" or Church of God was to be "closed up and sealed"—that is, kept secret—until "the time of the end" or our modern generation. The concluding section of Acts could well have been deliberately omitted, under God's inspiration, from the New Testament canon only to be "discovered" at a later time in history, near the time of the end of this age.

The Lost Chapters of Acts

A Greek manuscript has indeed been discovered, in the archives of Constantinople, which purports to be a concluding portion of Acts, and reads like a continuation of it. Its origin is uncertain but it was translated into English in 1801 by C.S. Sonnini.

The fact that the manuscript was discovered at Constantinople could well be significant. Jerome records that Luke's remains were brought to this city in A.D. 357 and buried there. *The Monarchian Prologue* also seems to imply that Luke spent the later part of his life in this general vicinity. "He never had a wife or children, and died at the age of seventy-four in Bithnia full of the Holy Spirit."

Constantinople, also known at times as Byzantium and Istanbul, lay at the border between the provinces of Thrace and Bithynia (sometimes spelled Bithnia).

It was also at Constantinople that a great many New Testament manuscripts were preserved, at least from the fourth century onwards. It was upon this Byzantine text that the later English versions were largely based.

Although one cannot be dogmatic regarding the authorship of Sonnini's translation of what has been called "The long lost chapter of the Acts of the Apostles," it should be said that a great deal of information contained in this manuscript can be verified by reference to other independent sources.

The terminology and style of writing in the manuscript is very similar, if not identical, to that used by Luke in Acts.

The text of the manuscript begins at the point that Acts finishes, and reads as follows: "And Paul, full of the blessings of Christ, and abounding in the spirit, departed out of Rome, determining to go into Spain, for he had a long time purposed to journey thitherward, and was minded also to go from thence into Britain.

"For he had heard in Phoenicia that certain of the children of Israel, about the time of the Assyrian captivity, had escaped by sea to 'the isles afar off,' as spoken by the prophet, and called by the Romans Britain.

"And the Lord commanded the gospel to be preached far hence to the Gentiles, and to the lost sheep of the House of Israel.

"And no man hindered Paul; for he testified boldly of Jesus before the tribunes and among the people; and he took with him certain of the brethren which abode with him at Rome, and they took shipping at Ostium, and having the winds fair were brought safely into a haven of Spain.

"And much people were gathered together from the towns and villages and the hill country; for they had heard of the conversion of the apostle, and the many miracles which he had wrought.

"And Paul preached mightily in Spain, and great multitudes believed and were converted, for they perceived he was an apostle sent from God."

Commentators have noted with interest the special attention that Luke, in Acts, gives to sea-itineraries and ports of arrival and departure. A similar tendency is found in the text of the manuscript: Ostium was the port used by sea travelers from Rome during the first century.

Paul Visits Spain

It was Paul's stated intention to visit Spain after leaving Rome (Romans 15:24, 28), and not only Spanish tradition but also the testimonies of many early writers confirm that Paul did indeed visit that area after leaving Rome.

The "haven of Spain" mentioned in the manuscript was almost certainly the port of Gades or Cadiz. A colony of Israelite and Phoenician peoples was established here from very ancient times. This was probably the port of Tarshish (Spain) that Jonah was heading for centuries earlier, when he tried to escape from God.

"Cadiz was the commercial centre of Western Europe, and was no doubt the place St. Paul had in mind when, writing to the Romans, he spoke of his 'journey into Spain.'"

"His journey into Spain is mentioned, as if it were a well known historical fact by Jerome, Chrysostom and Theodoret... There was ample opportunity for St. Paul to visit Cadiz, and to found a church there, during the six years that elapsed between his first and second imprisonment at Rome; and among his Spanish converts there could hardly fail to be some who traded with the British Isles."[8]

There was nothing in the least unusual about a sea voyage between Rome and Cadiz during the first century; "the commercial and passenger traffic with Gades was intimate and constant."[9]

Anyone who visits Cadiz and the surrounding countryside can readily equate this area with the "haven of Spain" and its nearby "hill country" described in the manuscript

The commission given by Christ to Paul was to take the gospel to "the Gentiles, and kings, and the children of Israel" (Acts 9:15). When Paul left Rome the first two parts of this task had already been completed, the people of Cadiz and the surrounding area were largely of Israelite and Phoenician stock who had settled in the region for commercial reasons over a period of centuries. They (the Israelite element) represented a small part of the "lost ten tribes" of Israel.

The Muratorian Fragment, which is part of a document dating back to the second century, mentions Paul's work in Spain but gives few of the details.

A generation later, in about A.D. 200, Tertullian mentions that "the extremities of Spain, the various parts of Gaul, the regions of Britain which have never been penetrated by the Roman armies, have received the religion of Christ."[10]

Paul in France

The manuscript continues the story of Paul's travels: "And they departed out of Spain, and Paul and his company finding a ship in Armorica sailing into Britain, they went therein, and passing along the South coast they reached a port called Raphinus.

Armorica (in Brittany) is identified as follows: "In Caesar's time, the whole district lying along the north-western coast of Gaul, till afterwards narrowed down to modern Brittany."[11]

Several writers affirm that the gospel came into Britain by way of Brittany. Dr. Mosheim's *Ecclesiastical History* relates: "The independence of the ancient British churches from the see of Rome, and their observing the same rites with the Gallic churches, which were planted by Asiatics, and particularly in regard to the time of Easter, show that they received the Gospel from Gaul, and not from Rome."

A number of early writers mention that churches were established in France, known anciently as Gaul, during apostolic times. Not only Paul but also Luke and Crescens are said to have had a part in this work.

"In the second century [A.D. 179] Irenaeus speaks of Christianity as propagated to the utmost bounds of the earth, by the Apostles, and their disciples; and particularly specifies the churches planted in Spain and the Celtic nations. By the Celts were meant the people of Germany, Gaul and Britain."[12]

Trophimus is said to have preached and established a church at Arles; a cathedral was later built over the site of his tomb.

Epiphanius (A.D. 315–407) relates: "The ministry of the divine word having been entrusted to St. Luke, he exercised it by passing into Dalmatia, into Gaul, into Italy, into Macedonia, but principally into Gaul, so that St. Paul assures him in his epistles about some of his disciples—'Crescens,' said he, 'is in Gaul.' In it must not be read in Galatia as some have falsely thought, but in Gaul."

Several other authorities support this interpretation of 2 Timothy 4:10, including the Codex Sinaiticus, which translates Galatia as "Gallia."

Paul in London

The exact location of the port of Raphinus, mentioned in the *Sonnini Manuscript* is uncertain. Some identify this as the Roman name of Sandwich in Kent. A port in this vicinity is known to have been used by the Romans during the first century A.D. An old house there, said to have existed at Sandwich until Saxon times, was known as "The House of the Apostles."

Roman roads linked this part of the coast with London. The text of the manuscript continues as follows: "Now when it was noised abroad that the apostle had landed on their coast, great multitudes of the inhabitants met him, and they treated Paul courteously, and he entered in at the east gate of their city, and lodged in the house of an Hebrew and one of his own nation.

"And on the morrow he came and stood upon Mount Lud; and the people thronged at the gate, and assembled in the Broadway, and he preached Christ unto them, and many believed the word and the testimony of Jesus.

"And at even the Holy Ghost fell upon Paul, and he prophesied, saying, Behold in the last days the God of Peace shall dwell in the cities, and the inhabitants thereof shall be numbered; and in the seventh numbering of the people, their eyes shall be opened, and the glory of their inheritance shine forth before them. And nations shall come up to worship on the Mount that testifieth of the patience and long suffering of a servant of the Lord.

"And in the latter days new tidings of the Gospel shall issue forth out of Jerusalem, and the hearts of the people shall rejoice, and behold, fountains shall be opened, and there shall be no more plague.

"In those days there shall be wars and rumours of wars; and a king shall rise up, and his sword shall be for the healing of the nations, and his peacemaking shall abide, and the glory of his kingdom a wonder among princes.

"And it came to pass that certain of the Druids came unto Paul privately, and showed by their rites and ceremonies they were descended from the Jews which escaped from bondage in the land of Egypt, and the apostle believed these things, and he gave them the kiss of peace.

"And Paul abode in his lodgings three months, confirming in the faith and preaching Christ continually.

"And after these things Paul and his brethren departed from Raphinus, and sailed unto Antiurn in Gaul."

The "Mount Lud" mentioned in the manuscript can probably be identified as the modern day Ludgate Hill, located in the City of London. A variety of objects dating to the first century have been unearthed in this area showing that it was a spot used by Romans and the local Britons during Paul's day.

According to Geoffrey of Monmouth, Lud-Gate was built by King Lud in 66 B.C. Several early writers confirm the existence of this ruler of pre-Roman Britain.

Holinshed states that "Lud began to reign in 72 B.C. He made a strong wall of lime and stone and fortified it with divers fair towers, and in the west part of the same wall he erected a strong gate which he commanded to be called after his name, 'Ludgate,' and so unto this day, it is called Ludgate."[13]

St Paul's Cathedral

Another spot where Paul, according to tradition, is said to have preached is the district of Gospel Oak, a part of Hampstead Heath.

A charter given by King Canute in 1030 would also seem to confirm the story of Paul's visit. It reads: "I, Cnut, king of the English, grant lands for the enlargement of the Monastery of the blessed Apostle Paul, teacher of the peoples, and situated in the City of London."

Critics of the manuscript, however, have seen as "too good to be true" the charter's obvious reference to St. Paul's Cathedral, and to a

St. Paul's Cathedral and Churchyard, from Ludgate Hill.

St Paul's Cathedral, London

Designed by Sir Christopher Wren to replace the old St. Paul's, which was destroyed in the Great Fire of London in 1666. All previous churches here as well as the present St. Paul's were built on Ludgate Hill, the highest point in London. It was on this hill that the Apostle Paul was said to have preached when he visited England, somewhere between 63–67 A.D.

prophecy that was said to have been made by Paul under inspiration of the Holy Spirit.

It should be said that the prophecy, if genuine, does not relate to the history of the Church of God, but to a place of national worship, the exact nature of which is not specified; the entire context is one of national history rather than church history.

It can hardly be denied that the former Mount Lud did become the site of a national place of worship. One only has to witness a state occasion such as the Queen's Jubilee celebrations to realize that the representatives of several nations do come to worship on this spot. This great cathedral does indeed bear Paul's name and in a sense testifies of his visit and preaching.

The reference to Paul's meeting with the Druids is probable enough. Although they suffered persecution at the hands of the Romans, it is likely that at this early stage in the Roman occupation they still had great influence with the people and by means of their very efficient system of communications were made aware of Paul's arrival.

It was Paul's policy to establish friendly relationships with civil and religious leaders, whenever this was possible, in order that the progress of the gospel would not be hindered. Although he probably noted with interest the similarities between the Druidic and Jewish religions, he would certainly not have approved of or condoned the many elements of paganism that had influenced the religion of the Druids by this period.

The mention of a visit to Britain by Paul lasting three months is a point of some interest as it seems to have been Paul's policy on several occasions to visit an area for this period of time (Acts 19:8, 20:3, 28:11).

Paul in Southern Britain

It is also quite possible that he paid more than one visit to Britain. The six years that elapsed before his final arrest and death would allow adequate time for two or more visits.

An old history of the Isle of Wight speaks of Paul arriving "with several other Christians, some of whom had been in personal contact with our blessed Lord Himself. He landed at Bonefon in the Isle of Wight. The exact spot is now Sandown Bay, which was a mouth of the harbour of Brading. He passed to the mainland from Rhydd, the ferry or passage now called Ryde, to Aber Deo, the port of God, or Godsport—Gosport."

"This is not so fantastic as it may seem, for nearby Paulsgrove, north of Portsmouth, is said to be named because St. Paul visited there."[14]

The exact dates for these visits cannot be determined but, if they did take place, would almost certainly have been made between Paul's release from Roman captivity in A.D. 61 (some authorities place this event a year later, in A.D. 62), and his arrest in A.D. 67.

Some early writers insist that his first visit must have taken place before the war between Boadicea and the Romans (A.D. 60–61). In the absence of any conclusive evidence, however, one can only admit that our knowledge of chronology relating to first-century Britain is incomplete.

The final section of the *Sonnini Manuscript* concludes the story of Paul's travels as follows: "And Paul preached in the Roman garrisons and among the people, exhorting all men to repent and confess their sins.

Paul in Switzerland

"And there came to him certain of the Belgae to enquire of him of the new doctrine, and of the man Jesus; and Paul opened his heart unto them, and told them all things that had befallen him, how be it that Christ Jesus came into the world to save sinners; and they departed, pondering among themselves upon the things which they had heard.

"And after much preaching and toil Paul and his fellow labourers passed into Helvetia, and came unto Mount Pontius Pilate, where he who condemned the Lord Jesus dashed himself down headlong, and so miserably perished.

"And immediately a torrent gushed out of the mountain and washed his body broken to pieces into a lake.

"And Paul stretched forth his hands upon the water and prayed unto the Lord, saying, O Lord God, give a sign unto all nations that here Pontius Pilate, which condemned thine only-begotten Son, plunged down headlong into the pit.

"And while Paul was yet speaking, behold there came a great earthquake, and the face of the waters was changed, and the form of the Lake like unto the Son of Man hanging in an agony upon the cross.

"And a voice came out of heaven saying, Even Pilate hath escaped the wrath to come, for he washed his hands before the multitude at the blood shedding of the Lord Jesus.

"When, therefore, Paul and those that were with him saw the earthquake, and heard the voice of the angel, they glorified God, and were mightily strengthened in the Spirit.

"And they journeyed and came to Mount Julius, where stood two pillars, one on the right hand and one on the left hand, erected by Caesar Augustus.

"And Paul, filled with the Holy Ghost, stood up between the two pillars, saying, Men and brethren, these stones which ye see this day shall testify of my journey hence; and verily I say, they shall remain until the outpouring of the spirit upon all nations, neither shall the way be hindered throughout all generations.

"And they went forth and came unto Illyricum, intending to go by Macedonia into Asia, and grace was found in all the churches; and they prospered and had peace. Amen."[15]

Eusebius confirms the suicide of Pilate, although he does not record where this event took place.

"It is also worthy of notice that tradition relates that that same Pilate, he of the Saviour's time, in the days of Caius... fell into such great calamity that he was forced to become his own slayer and to punish himself with his own hand. These who record the Olympiads of the Greeks with the annals of events relate this."[16]

There is one tradition, perhaps the one to which Eusebius referred, telling that Pilate, falling out of political favour during the reign of Caligula (Caius) went to Helvetia (Switzerland) where he spent his remaining days in great sorrow on Mount Pilatus (called Mount Pontius Pilate in the manuscript). He is said to have taken his own life by plunging into the dismal lake at the base of the mountain—Lake Lucerne.

Some of the Waldenses, a church of the Middle Ages that probably can be identified as the Thyatira era of the Church of God (Revelation 2:18), traced their origin to the Apostle Paul's preaching in the Alps.

Eusebius also confirms Paul's journey through Illyricum. "Why should we speak of Paul, spreading the gospel of Christ from Jerusalem to Illyricum, and finally suffering martyrdom at Rome, under Nero?"[17]

Did Paul Know About Britain?

As Paul was a citizen of Tarsus and spent most of his life in the eastern Mediterranean, one is tempted to speculate that the material relating to his visit to Britain could perhaps be categorized as nothing more than legend and mere wishful thinking. Was Paul even aware of the existence of Britain?

The apostle was an educated man, having read widely, even taking in the writings of foreign poets. He knew as much, if not more, of world affairs as the average educated man of his day.

The bulk of Paul's ministry took place during the reigns of the Roman emperors Claudius and Nero (A.D. 41–68). During this period, one of the major concerns of the empire was the invasion and conquest of Britain.

This war, which dragged on for decades (Wales was not subdued until about A.D. 79, some 36 years after the initial invasion), absorbed some of Rome's finest legions and most competent military leaders.

Tacitus relates that "When Britain, with the rest of the Roman world, fell to the lot of Vespasian, the ablest officers were sent to reduce the island; powerful armies were set in motion...."[18]

So important was the campaign in Britain to the Romans that Claudius named a son Britannicus in recognition of his victories. News of the progress of the war spread throughout the empire; Josephus relates that during the battle that led to the fall of Jerusalem in A.D. 70 the Romans, in an effort to discourage the Jews, boasted of their victories in Britain.

Who can doubt that if the Jews in Jerusalem were aware of events in Britain, Paul, who spent at least two years in Rome, would have been even more aware of these things? The Romans gave great publicity to their military campaigns, especially those in Britain.

Christianity a "Superstition"
It is probable that Paul had personal contact with at least one British Christian during his visit to Rome.

Plautius, the commander of the Roman forces in Britain, married the sister of Caractacus, the famous warrior king of the Britons, at the time of the first peace treaty about A.D. 45. Some two years later, his military service in Britain completed, he returned to Rome with his wife.

Tacitus records that an unusual thing happened following their arrival at Rome: "Pomponia Graccina, a woman of illustrious birth, and the wife of Plautius, who, on his return from Britain, entered the city with the pomp of an ovation, was accused of embracing the rites of a foreign superstition. The matter was referred to the jurisdiction of her husband. Plautius, in conformity to ancient usage, called together a number of her relations, and in her presence, sat in judgment on the conduct of his wife. He pronounced her innocent."[19]

There is general agreement among scholars that the "foreign superstition" mentioned by Tacitus is a direct reference to Christianity. Suetonius, another Roman writer of the period, mentions the Christians as holding a "novel and mischievous superstition."

The charges could well have been brought by a political enemy of Plautius, in order to damage his political career.

"As Judaism was a religion recognized by Roman law, and as Christianity was not yet distinguished from Judaism Pomponia was entitled to an acquittal on the purely religious grounds. But rumours were already abroad which accused the Christians of flagitious and impure orgies in secret, and the participation in these was the matter referred to the domestic tribunal. The domestic court was charged with the cognizance of this very class of crimes, more especially of the violation of the marriage vow."[20]

The charge of taking part in orgies was commonly leveled at the Christians in Roman times; although true Christians were well aware of God's law relating to sexual sins, many references can be found to prove that Simon Magus and his followers did indeed indulge in such activities; as these people, although not true Christians, called themselves "Christians" it is easy to see how such rumours began.

E. Guest in his *Origines Celticae* adds another important point relating to Pomponia: "For all are agreed that by the 'foreign superstition' was meant Christianity... Moreover, as Pomponia had been charged with the crime of Christianity, and acquitted only by her husband's verdict, she would naturally live in the strictest seclusion, if it were merely to save her husband from dishonour, and we can thus explain the fact that she is never mentioned in St. Paul's epistles."[21]

Pomponia could well have been a member of Paul's congregation during his visit to Rome. As one of the very few Christians of noble or royal birth, she could well have been one of those that Paul was thinking of when he wrote that "not many mighty, not many noble, are called" (1 Corinthians 1:26).

It is possible that Pomponia gave Paul some encouragement to preach in Britain. She had been, prior to her marriage, a princess in Siluria (South Wales), her former name being Gladys. Theodoret wrote that Paul preached, not only to the Britons, but also to the Cymry or Welsh.

"And St. Paul might have some particular encouragement at Rome to come hither from Pomponia Graecina, wife of A. Plautius, the Roman lieutenant under Claudius in Britain; for that she was a Christian, appears very probable from the account Tacitus gives of her."[22]

In 1867 the noted archaeologist, De Rossi, discovered amazing proof of the existence of Pomponia. He uncovered in the catacomb of Callistus at Rome a sepulchral inscription to "Pomponius Graecinus" who was probably a male relative of Pomponia.

J.B. Lightfoot gives more details of the discovery: "The earliest portion of the catacombs of Callistus, the so-called crypt of Lucina, shows by the character and construction that it must have been built in the first century of the Christian Church. In this crypt a sepulchral inscription has been found belonging to the close of the second or beginning of the third century, unquestioningly bearing the name Pomponius Graecinus...

"It is clear therefore that this burial place was constructed by some Christian lady of rank, probably before the close of the first century... among her fellow-religionists within a generation or two a descendant or near kinsman of Pomponia Graecina was buried."[23]

She is thought to have died in about A.D. 83.

Claudia and Pudens

Perhaps the strangest and most interesting story to come from the records of the early British Church concerns Claudia and Pudens.

The tale of this enigmatic pair has been classified as legend by some but thought by others, noted scholars among them, to have been based on historical fact.

Their story has all the elements of a fairy tale romance. Claudia, the beautiful and talented British princess, meets and falls in love with Pudens, wealthy young Roman aristocrat and officer in the Roman army, during the invasion of Britain. The happy couple marry and move to Rome where they become Christians and close friends of the Apostle Paul. Sadly, the story ends with their children all dying as Christian martyrs.

In 1723 a remarkable inscription was discovered at Chichester mentioning one "Pudens." The inscription, which dated to about A.D. 50, was at one time part of a Roman building, and later became known as "the Chichester stone." It reads as follows: "The College of Engineers, and ministers of religion attached to it, by permission of Tiberius Claudius Cogidunus, the king, legate of Augustus in Britain, have dedicated at their own expense, in honour of the divine family this temple to Neptune and Minerva. The site was given by Pudens, Son of Pudentinus."

This Pudens has been identified as the second in command of the Roman forces in Britain, under Aulus Plautius. It was quite a common occurrence for high-ranking officers to be present at the dedication of public buildings, including, as in this case, a pagan temple.

"Here, then, we have a Pudens connected with Britain and joining with a Romanized British prince in forwarding the erection of a public building in that province, and at the same time a British prince, whose Roman name of Claudius would, according to Roman custom, necessitate the adoption of the name Claudia by his daughter."[24]

Other sources indicate the more probable view that Claudia was the daughter not of Claudius Cogidunus, but of Caractacus. As these two British princes were probably related it is likely that she at least knew Cogidunus, even if not being directly related to him.

Pudens could well have been present at the wedding of his commanding officer Plautius and Pomponia Graecina. Claudia, as daughter of Caractacus and niece of Pomponia, was most likely present at the same event; although probably being no more than a young girl or teenager at the time.

Tacitus, although mentioning this event, gives no details regarding the location of the wedding. This marriage, which took place around A.D. 45, could well have had some political significance. Pomponia was a princess of the Silures, a tribe that controlled a part of South Wales. A peace treaty was signed at about the time of the wedding between the Silures and the Romans; peace treaties in ancient times were often accompanied by a marriage between the leader of one side in the conflict (Plautius) and the daughter, or in this case, the sister, of the opposing military leader.

Gloucester, which stood at the border between Siluria and Roman occupied Britain, could well have been the location where the wedding took place.

"While much has been said of Claudius founding Gloucester, it has been confirmed by the discoveries made of recent years at that town, and the greater abundance of the coins of Claudius discovered there, than at almost any other town in Britain."[25]

Lysons speculates that the Apostle Paul visited Gloucester and preached there. Although there is no clear evidence of this, it is reasonable to assume that because of the political and military significance of the town during the reigns of Claudius and Nero, Paul could well have at least heard of it.

Pomponia and Claudia

Pomponia has been seen by some as the source of Claudia's introduction to Christianity.

Several writers on the subject of British history have seen Pomponia and Claudia as the first Christian converts in Britain. It should be noted that these names came from their associations with the Romans; among their own people both ladies were known by the name of Gladys; this was quite appropriate as the name, in the Celtic or Welsh language, means princess and both were indeed princesses in the royal family of Siluria. In a trip to Cwmbran this writer noticed that a modern road has been named "Caradoc's Way" after the famous Caradoc (known to Tacitus and other Roman writers as Caractacus), of the first century A.D.

These people were probably the remote ancestors of the Tudor kings of England who also came from Wales, and as such are distantly related to Queen Elizabeth II.

"Whether it was by the piety of these ladies, or other individuals, that the doctrine of Christianity was first introduced among the Britons, it proceeded with a silent but steady pace towards the extremity of the island."[26]

During this period the Christian Church in Britain was small, consisting of scattered individuals and perhaps a few congregations.

"But though the name of Christ was not altogether unknown in Britain, in this very early period, yet the number of Christians in this island was then certainly very small."[27]

Although the Roman writers Tacitus and Martial mention that these ladies both went to Rome, and as the chronology of the period would place their arrival shortly before Paul's arrival, as recorded in Acts, the Welsh records imply that they could well have been converted to Christianity prior to leaving Britain.

Llan Ilid in Glamorganshire (Gwent) is the site, according to the Welsh Triads, of the first Christian church in Wales. This place name means "consecrated enclosure" or "church of Ilid." It is located within the ancient territory of Sauria where Pomponia and Claudia spent the early years of their lives.

It was said that Princess Eurgain, known in some sources as the eldest daughter of Caractacus (which would make her a sister of Claudia, or perhaps this is simply another name for Claudia), "founded and endowed the first Christian Cor," or choir in Britain. From this Cor-Eurgain issued many of the most eminent teachers and missionaries of Christianity down to the tenth century. Of the saints of this Cor, from Ilid in succession, there are catalogues in the *Genealogies of the Saints of Britain.*[28]

Claudia was a woman of considerable literary ability and culture, several volumes of her poetry and hymns were still extant as late as the thirteenth century. The Iolo manuscript describes Ilid as a man "of the land of Israel." "This Ilid is called in the lections of his life Joseph. He became principal teacher of the Christian faith to the Welsh, and introduced good order into Cor-Eurgain, which Eurgain had established for twelve Saints near the church now called Llantwit."

Some identify Ilid as Joseph of Arimathea. The manuscript relates that after working in Wales for a time he went to Glastonbury "where he died and was buried, and Ina, king of that country raised a large church over his grave."[29]

As intimate contact existed at this time between Somerset, where Glastonbury is located, and South Wales, it does seem probable that the first churches in Wales were established by men from Glastonbury.

The family records of the eleventh-century Prince of Glamorgan, Jestyn ap Gwrgant, referring to this period, mention: "Cyllin ab Caradog, a wise and just king. In his days many of the Cymry embraced the faith in Christ through the teaching of the saints of Cor-Eurgain, and many godly men from the countries of Greece and Rome were in Cambria."[30]

One of these "godly men... from Rome" was almost certainly the

Apostle Paul; Theodoret in the fifth century mentions his association with Wales: "There are six years of St. Paul's life to be accounted for, between his liberation from his first imprisonment and his martyrdom at Aquae Salviae in the Ostian Road, near Rome. Part certainly, the greater part perhaps, of this period, was spent in Britain—in Siluria or Cambria, beyond the bounds of the Roman Empire; and hence the silence of the Greek and Latin writers upon it."[31]

The Triads of Paul

A collection of writings in the ancient British language have been handed down that may relate to Paul's preaching in Britain and have always been known as "the Triads of Paul the Apostle."

A Triad was the traditional style of writing and public speaking in Britain in ancient times and probably could be defined as "three main points."

Ministers and other speakers in the British Churches of God to this day often arrange their sermons or other lectures around three main points. Perhaps Paul, wishing to be "all things to all men" used the traditional style of public speaking in Britain, and that form has been handed down through the generations since that time.

These Triads of Paul are based almost entirely upon the principles that are expounded in his New Testament epistles. A few, taken at random, are reproduced as follows: "Three kinds of men are the delights of God: the meek; the lovers of peace; the lovers of mercy."

"The three chief considerations of a Christian: lest he should displease God; lest he should be a stumbling block to man; lest his love to all that is good should wax cold."

"Three persons have the claims and privileges of brothers and sisters: the widow; the orphan; the stranger."

As there is no attempt made to introduce false doctrine or superstition in these writings and the style is simple and direct, they could well be what the title suggests: "the Triads of Paul the Apostle."

Caractacus in Rome

Tacitus relates that for nine years, the Britons, under the leadership of Caractacus (Caradoc), bravely resisted the Roman advance in Britain. One Roman division that penetrated as far west as Caerleon was cut to pieces. In A.D. 52, however, the British leader was betrayed and along with his family (including Claudia) was captured by the Romans in Shropshire.

Some three million citizens of Rome thronged the streets of the capital when this great warrior king was brought in chains to appear before the emperor Claudius. Perhaps in recognition of his outstanding military leadership Caractacus was pardoned by the emperor, although he was required to remain in Rome, under a sort of "house arrest," in order that he would cause the Romans no further trouble.

Summing up the situation following the arrest of Caractacus and his family, Tacitus records that: "In Britain, after the captivity of Caractacus, the Romans were repeatedly conquered and put to the rout by the single state of the Silures alone."[32]

Had the various tribes in Britain set aside their own differences and presented a united front against the Romans, there can be little doubt that the Roman occupation would have been very short lived.

Caractacus and his family took up residence in the Palatium Britannicum (Palace of the British) at Rome. As a hostage of the state he was required to remain at Rome for seven years.

Pudens, the Roman Senator and former aide-de-camp to Aulus Plautius, commander of the Roman forces in Britain, completed his army service at about this time and returned to Rome.

It seems that Pudens and Claudia had met in Britain, as Claudia's aunt Pomponia had married Pudens' commanding officer Plautius. They, Pudens and Claudia, married in about A.D. 53.

The Witness of Martial
The Roman poet Martial, a friend of the couple, wrote some poetry on the occasion of the wedding. He also makes it evident that Pudens had served in Britain prior to his marriage. He speaks of Pudens suffering from the cold of "the Scythian [North] pole." A clear indication of his army service in Britain.

The poetry also strongly suggests that the couple were both converted Christians at the time of their marriage. Martial describes Pudens as the "sainted husband" of Claudia whom he writes of as having "sprung from the painted Britons."[33] Elsewhere he asks, "Since Claudia wife of Rufus [Pudens] comes from the blue-set Britons, how is it that she has won the hearts of the Latin people?"

The bright blue eyes of the Britons is also noted by Seneca. "The British lady, Claudia, to whom Martial addressed two or three of his epigrams, and others to Linus and Pudens, is supposed to be the very Claudia mentioned with Pudens and Linus, in Paul's second epistle to Timothy. She is believed by Cambrian writers to be of the family of Caractacus, and, perhaps the first British Christian."[34]

Llin, described in Welsh records as a son of Caractacus, is thought by some to be the Linus mentioned by Martial and Paul, the brother of Claudia.

Roman writers mention the fact that Linus was ordained by Paul as the first bishop of Rome in A.D. 68. The significance of this event will be discussed in a later chapter.

"And he [Martial] addresses two or three of his epigrams to Linus, proving the connection of the three."[35]

The connection between the Pudens, Linus and Claudia mentioned by Martial, with their links with Britain, and a group of three related individuals having the same names described by Paul (2 Timothy 4:21) has been noted by several authorities on the subject of Church history.

"That there was a Pudens and Claudia living at Rome, both Christians we have it from... St. Paul himself. That this Claudia mentioned by St. Paul, then living at Rome, was the same Claudia, a Briton born, mentioned by Martial is the opinion and probable conjecture of many modern writers."[36]

We learn from Monocaxius: "That Claudia, mentioned by St. Paul, was Caractacus's daughter, and turned Christian, and after married to Pudens, a Roman Senator; whose marriage is celebrated by Martial in his noted epigrams to that purpose."[37]

There are several indications in the epigrams of Martial that the lifestyles of Pudens and Claudia were Christian rather than pagan. The poet, who seems to have been a family friend of the couple, does not mention their religion directly, and with good reason; during the later part of Nero's reign a Christian could be arrested and executed as an enemy of the state.

Roman poets often used the occasion of a wedding as an excuse for coarse jesting but Martial's poems relating to this couple are lacking in this type of humour.

'Claudia, the fair one from a foreign shore,
Is with my Pudens joined in wedlock's band.'[38]
O Concord, bless their couch for evermore,
Be with them in thy snow-white purity.
Let Venus grant, from her choicest store,
All gifts that suit their married unity,
When he is old may she be fond and true,
And she in age the charms of youth renew.'[39]

A little later, when children had been born to Claudia, he wrote:

'Grant, O ye gods, that she may ever prove
The bliss of mother over girl and boy,
Still gladdened by her pious husband's love,
And in her children find perpetual joy.'[40]

Martial, although perhaps having several friends amongst the Christians of Rome, was not himself of this faith, as is clearly demonstrated by his use of pagan terminology in his writings.

"But without insisting strongly on this argument, we may be able to infer, that the Claudia of Martial was connected with a circle at Rome, the members of which were imbued with Christian, rather than Roman principles."[41]

The epithet "Sanctus" or "sainted" applied by Martial to Pudens is much more likely to have been used in relation to a Christian than a non-Christian. The Apostle Paul uses similar terminology in his epistle to the Romans, written only a short time before Martial's epigrams, when he speaks of Christians at Rome "called to be saints" (Romans 1:7).

Some have objected that because the epigrams were published during the reign of Domitian, who became emperor in A.D. 83, they could not have been related to individuals who were prominent during Nero's time some 20 to 30 years earlier.

"There is however reason to believe, as was remarked by Ussher, Collier and others, that many of the epigrams were written long before they were published, and consequently that the publication of the book was no test, of the age of the epigrams."[42]

Martial took up residence in Rome in A.D. 49 and left the city for Spain in A.D. 86. He would have been about 38 years old when Paul wrote his second epistle to Timothy. There is nothing in the chronology of the period to indicate that the Claudia, Pudens and Linus of Martial were not the same individuals mentioned by Paul in his epistle.

Both writers were writing at about the same time, of individuals living in the same city. It is hardly likely that more than one group of three individuals having a close relationship with each other and having these names would have been living in the same city at the same time.

J. Williams in his comprehensive thesis on this subject remarks that: "It is therefore possible that the first Epigram to which I have alluded might have been written by Martial in the year 67, eighteen years after his arrival in Rome; being the same year in which the Apostle is generally supposed to have written the second epistle to Timothy. And a broad margin of two or three years, on either side, may be allowed without interfering with the argument."[43]

Bale, and later Camden, identify Pudens and Claudia of 2 Timothy with the writings of Martial. The writings of the poet reveal that he had an intimate knowledge of events that took place in Nero's reign.

Williams also makes the point that: "If the Pudens of St. Paul was the Pudens of Martial, and since the Pudens of Martial had married a British maiden, also called Claudia, it seems to me something more than probable that the Pudens of the inscription [Chichester Stone] was also the same identical person."[44]

"...there is no doubt that Pudens the husband of Claudia is mentioned in the Scriptures, for both are there, together with Linus, the brother of Claudia, in one sentence in 2 Timothy 4:21. The odds against the three being mentioned together, if they were not the members of the exiled family of Caractacus, must be very great."[45]

The House Of The British
The residence of the couple at Rome, known as the Palatium Britannicum, seems to have been a regular meeting place for Christians. The high political and social status of Pudens and Claudia seems to have given them, for a time at least, a measure of freedom from persecution.

A series of Christian churches later occupied this site. The first was known as Titulus, the next Hospitium Aposolorum and finally St. Pudentiana, so named in honour of the martyred daughter of Claudia.

According to Cardinal Baronius: "It is delivered to us by the firm tradition of our forefathers that the house of Pudens was the first that entertained St. Peter at Rome, and that the Christians assembling formed the Church, and that of all our churches the oldest is that which is called after the name Pudens."[46]

The Jesuit Robert Parsons in *The Three Conversions of England* mentions that "Claudia was the first hostess or harbourer both of St. Peter and St. Paul at the time of their coming to Rome."

Roman tradition also relates that Pudens and Claudia retrieved the body of the Apostle Paul following his martyrdom in about A.D. 68 and buried it in what was perhaps a family cemetery in the Via Ostiensis.

In later years the lives of this couple and their four children were clouded by sorrow. Claudia seems to have been the only member of the family to have died a natural death, in A.D. 97. Pudens and all of the children died as martyrs at various times during the closing years of the first century or the first half of the second.

A manuscript entitled *The Acts of Pastor and Timotheus*, probably dating to the second century, describes some of the sad details: "Pudens went to his Saviour leaving his daughters strengthened with chastity and learned in all the divine law. These sold their goods and distributed the produce to the poor and persevered strictly in the love of Christ... They desired to have a baptistry in their house. Many pagans came thither to find the faith and receive baptism." The record mentions that their house "night and day resounded with hymns of praise."

When one of the young women was martyred, probably along with several other Christians, the manuscript relates: "Then Pudentiana went to God. Her sister and I wrapped her in perfumes, and kept her concealed in the oratory. Then after 28 days we carried her to the Cemetery of Priscilla and laid her near her father Pudens." Some sources give the date of her death as A.D. 107.

Several years later, a further wave of persecution claimed many more lives. The manuscript mentions "That blessed Prassedis collected their bodies by night and buried them in the Cemetery of Priscilla... then the virgin of the Saviour, worn out with sorrow, only asked for death. Her tears and her prayers reached to heaven, and fifty-four days after her brethren had suffered she passed to God. And I, Pastor, the priest have buried her body near that of her father Pudens."

The two sons of Pudens and Claudia also died as martyrs during the first half of the second century. Timotheus is said to have been named after the evangelist Timothy, to whom Paul wrote two of his epistles.

Other Apostles in Britain

There are indications that other apostles and members of the New Testament Church, apart from Paul, also preached in Britain, and possibly Ireland, too.

Eusebius recorded that "Some of the Apostles"—not just one single apostle—"preached the Gospel in the British Isles."[47]

Church leaders from Britain attended several of the church councils convened during the fourth century. Eusebius, himself a Catholic Bishop, probably found opportunities to obtain information from such men on matters relating to church history.

Much of the detail concerning the early British church does not appear in the records until quite a late date, the early Middle Ages and later, and for this reason modern scholars often reject the material as being unreliable. A fact all too often overlooked, however, is that these writers probably had access to much earlier material now no longer extant.

William Cave, quoting from the writings of Nicophorus and Dorotheus, mentions that Simon the Zealot (one of the Twelve Apostles) "directed his journey toward Egypt, then to Cyrene and Africa... and throughout Mauritania and all Libya, preaching the gospel... Nor could the coldness of the climate benumb his zeal, or hinder him from whipping himself and the Christian doctrine over to the Western Islands, yea, even to Britain itself. Here he preached and wrought many miracles...."[48]

Dorotheus is said to have written that "At length he was crucified at Brittania, slain and buried."[49]

The traditional site of his martyrdom is Caistor in Lincolnshire, where he is said to have been condemned to death in A.D. 61 during the prefecture of Catus Decianus whose atrocities were largely responsible for the Boadicean war.

A number of authorities, Roman, Greek and British, record that Aristobulus, who is mentioned by Paul in his epistle to the Romans, preached and eventually died in Britain. Hyppolytus describes him as "Bishop of the Britons." *The Greek Martyrologies* speak of him converting many of the Britons to Christianity and add that "He was there martyred after he had built churches and ordained deacons and priests for the island."

An alternative version to this is given by Cressy, who states that he died of natural causes at Glastonbury in A.D. 99.

Apostles in Scotland and Ireland

Scotland too seems to have received the gospel at an early date.

"The antiquity of the Irish and Scottish churches is without question. The Scottish church claims an Apostolic foundation which would account for that branch of the Celtic Church possessing eastern traditions. In an old Scottish history entitled *History of Paganism in Caledonia* is the passage, 'During the reign of Domitian, disciples of the Apostle John visited Caledonia and there preached the word of life.'"[50]

Some have linked this reference to a strong local tradition relating that "the three wise men" came to Sutherland. A fact of perhaps greater significance is that the first Catholic monks to reach the islands to the North of Scotland, including Iceland and the Faroes, reported that a much earlier generation of Christians had at one time settled in those parts and that books that had been abandoned revealed that they had adhered to "Judaism," almost certainly a direct reference to the seventh-day Sabbath.

James, son of Alphaeus, another of the twelve, is sometimes associated with Ireland. "The Spanish writers generally contend, after the death of Stephen he came to these Western parts, and particularly into Spain (some add Britain and Ireland) where he planted Christianity."[51]

As regular commercial traffic passed between Spain and Ireland in ancient times, a visit to Ireland from Spain by James is not an improbable possibility.

Although little is known of the church in Ireland during the Roman period there seems to be general acceptance among scholars that a church was established there long before the arrival of Patrick, the "Apostle of Ireland." According to Ussher the church in Ireland was established soon after the death of Christ by disciples from the Asian churches.

Chapter Summary

The apostles of Jesus were commanded to preach the true gospel "to the end of the earth" (Acts 1:8). What does this actually mean? Written records from the Roman period indicate that several apostles did reach the western limits of the Roman Empire, areas such as France, Spain and Britain.

Chapter Six

THE GREAT CONSPIRACY

*"But we meet together on Sunday, because it was the first day, in which
God, having wrought the necessary changes in darkness and matter made
the world; and on this day Jesus Christ our Saviour rose from the dead"*
(Justin Martyr, A.D. 145).

*"For I know this, that after my departure savage wolves will come in
among you, not sparing the flock"*
(Acts 20:29).

I t was said of the first Christians that they were people who
"turned the world upside down." The respected Roman writer
Tacitus records that within a mere 33 years of the execution of
its founder, the new religion had spread like wildfire through much of
the civilized world.

Even at Rome, the capital city of the empire, "vast multitudes" had
embraced the new faith, and were even ready to die in Nero's reign of
terror rather than renounce their newly discovered Saviour.

There were several reasons for the phenomenal success of the
new movement. Firstly, it offered the adherent a reason for living,
beyond mere physical survival into old age. It added a new dimension
in living that transcended the "bread and circuses" concept of the
Roman "man in the street."

Apart from providing practical, living principles for success in this
present life, which would promote bodily health and peace of mind,
material prosperity and happy family relationships, the new faith
offered the prospect that an individual could attain the age-old goal
of overcoming man's final enemy—death, and of living forever.

It offered human beings something no other religion had come
remotely near to offering—the possibility that flesh and blood people
could become children of God (Genesis 1:26; Romans 8:14–17; 1 John
3:1–3), and that through the means of a resurrection from the dead,
the human body, subject to weakness, decay and death, could be
transformed into a glorified spirit body, like that of the resurrected
Christ (Philippians 3:20–21).

As a member of the God Family, an actual brother of Jesus Christ

(Romans 8:29), the "born again" Christian is given the opportunity of rulership not only on this earth (Revelation 2:26) but ultimately over a part of the vast universe (Hebrews 2:5–8).

It is small wonder that the early Christians, faced with the prospect of such an awesome future, were more than willing to pay the price necessary to qualify; that price being the faith to accept Jesus Christ as their Saviour and High Priest, their willingness to obey the laws of God and, with the assistance of His Holy Spirit, develop the very mind and character of God.

The plan of salvation that was revealed to the early Church was universal in its scope and application; it was not confined to one race or religious sect or group. The plan was open to all people of all races, including all who had lived in the past, and will live in the future; although not all people were granted the opportunity to understand the plan at the same time. Gentiles could be grafted into the promises made to Israel (Romans 11:16–32).

Keeping God's Holy Days

In order to keep the true Church constantly aware and reminded of God's plan, the first Christians observed the Old Testament Holy Days or Sabbaths; but in a new spirit and with an expanded level of understanding (Mark 2:27–28).

Many people have assumed that the weekly and annual Sabbaths (Feast Days) of Israel were done away by Christ and perhaps "nailed to the cross"—that new days such as Sunday, Easter and Christmas were introduced to take their place.

History clearly reveals, however, that these days, classified by some as "Jewish," were observed by the true Church of God for centuries, not only in Palestine and Asia Minor but even in remote Britain and Ireland.

Paul, the apostle to the Gentiles, kept these days and instructed his Gentile converts to do likewise. He even refused valuable opportunities to preach the gospel at times saying that "I must by all means keep this feast that cometh in Jerusalem: but I will return again unto you, if God will" (Acts 18:21).

Luke speaks of sailing from Philippi "after the days of unleavened bread" (Acts 20:6), and of Paul making haste to be at Jerusalem to observe Pentecost (Acts 20:16).

Gentile Christians at Corinth were urged, "Therefore purge out the old leaven, that you may be a new lump, since you truly are unleavened. For indeed Christ, our Passover, was sacrificed for us. Therefore let us keep the feast, not with old leaven, nor with the leaven of malice and wickedness, but with the unleavened bread of sincerity and truth" (1 Corinthians 5:7–8). The annual Sabbaths were never part of the temporary ritualistic ordinances that looked forward to Jesus Christ's sacrifice.

Formerly pagan, Christian converts at Colosse were criticized by false teachers in respect of their observance of these days (Colossians 2:16). Paul makes the point that it is the leaders within the Church of God, not unauthorized outsiders, who should determine how these days should be kept.

There is no mention of the abolition of these days but simply guidance as to how they should be kept.

During the first three centuries of the Christian era a controversy raged, sometimes leading to bloodshed and death, about the day on which Christians should rest and worship together. Should they keep the Sabbath (Friday sunset to Saturday sunset) or Sunday?

Keeping the Weekly Sabbath

There is no shred of evidence to show that the first-century Church of God kept any other day than the Sabbath as a day for rest and weekly church meetings. Even some leading theologians of Sunday-keeping churches have agreed that not one single verse in the entire Bible authorizes Sunday observance.

A few New Testament passages have been used as giving sanction for church services on Sunday; but an examination of the context of these passages gives an entirely different picture.

In Acts 20:7 we read: "And upon the first day of the week, when the disciples came together to break bread, Paul preached unto them, ready to depart on the morrow; and continued his speech until midnight."

Some have imagined this to have been a Sunday morning communion service, but it was no such thing. At the time that this was written, each day was counted from sunset to sunset. A meeting that ended at midnight on the first day of the week must have started Saturday evening. The first day of the week ended at sunset on

Sunday. This was a Saturday evening meeting (See *New English Bible* translation). On the Sunday morning Paul set off to walk to Assos, where a ship was waiting for him.

A second important point regarding this verse is that the term "break bread" is used here to denote the taking of a communal meal, not the Sunday communion service. The New Testament church observed the Passover or "Lord's Supper" once a year, not every week on Sunday morning. Verse six of this passage plainly states that this service had already been held about two weeks earlier.

1 Corinthians 16:2 is also sometimes used as an example of a Sunday service. It reads: "Upon the first day of the week let every one of you lay by him in store, as God has prospered him, that there be no gatherings when I come."

Even a casual reading of the earlier verses of this chapter indicates that this instruction, given by Paul, has nothing whatever to do with church services, but rather a gathering of farm produce and other foodstuffs, which was to be sent to the church members at Jerusalem who were suffering from a severe food shortage.

The *Weymouth* translation adds the important point that this collection of food, which certainly was to take place on a Sunday, was to be done by each individual Christian "at his home." These people were not meeting together for a church service on this day but rather gathering food in their own individual homes.

A reference in Revelation 1:10 to "the Lord's day" is also taken to promote Sunday observance. At least one translation renders this "the day of the Lord," and as the entire context of the book of Revelation is one of revealing future world events, including the prophesied "day of the Lord" (the time of God's direct intervention in world affairs), this is clearly the true meaning of the verse. Yet again we find that this has nothing to do with religious services on a Sunday.

Jesus Christ, the ultimate authority on which day is the true "Lord's day," made the revealing statement that "the Son of Man is Lord even of the Sabbath" (Mark 2:28).

Quite late in the New Testament period when the book of Hebrews was written, the entire Church of God was still observing the seventh-day Sabbath, in anticipation of the coming millennial rest that would be ushered in at Christ's return: "Therefore a Sabbath rest remains for the people of God" (Hebrews 4:9).

Christ's Death and Resurrection

From a very early date it was claimed by some that Sunday obser-vance was introduced in recognition of the resurrection of Christ, which they said took place on a Sunday. But is this really correct?

In John 19:31 we read that "The Jews therefore, because it was the preparation, that the bodies should not remain upon the cross on the Sabbath day" obtained permission from Pilate to hasten the deaths of the two men who were crucified with Jesus.

It would seem from the first part of this verse that Christ really did die on "Good Friday." John, however, adds vital additional infor-mation, proving that the "Sabbath" following the crucifixion was not the weekly Sabbath (Saturday) but an annual Holy Day Sabbath ("for that Sabbath was a high day").

This particular high day Sabbath was called by the Jews "the great Sabbath" and is also known as the first day of the Feast of Unleavened Bread in which a "holy convocation" (Leviticus 23:7) was held.

Eusebius relates that Polycarp, a leader of the true Church of God in Asia Minor, was taken for trial and execution on a great Sabbath day." The marginal notes explain that "The great Sabbath was the feast of unleavened bread...."[1]

John 19:14 explains that the crucifixion took place on a "prepa-ration" day. Not the preparation for the weekly Sabbath, but "the preparation for the Passover."

The Jews always killed the Passover lambs on the day before "the great Sabbath." This was the very day on which Christ was crucified. Jesus Christ, "the lamb of God," was sacrificed as "our Passover... sacrificed for us," as Paul puts it, at about the time that the Jews killed the physical lambs.

In A.D. 31, the year of the crucifixion, this day fell on a Wednesday, not a Friday.

The only sign that Jesus ever gave of His Messiahship was that He would be in the grave for "three days and three nights" (Matthew 12:39–40). He died shortly after "the ninth hour" (Luke 23:44) be-tween 3:00 p.m. and sunset. The resurrection took place at the same time of day, three days later. This brings us to a Saturday afternoon.

Mark records that at about dawn on the following Sunday, the next morning, the angel informed the women who had come to the sepulchre that "he is risen." He did not say, "he is rising." The resurrection took place at the same time of the day as the death—the late afternoon. This is why at dawn the next day (Sunday) He was already risen.

The resurrection took place on the Sabbath—not Sunday. There were two Sabbaths in the week that Christ died. The annual Holy Day Sabbath on the Thursday and the weekly Sabbath on the Saturday; the women prepared their spices on the day between, the Friday.

Meaning of God's Holy Days

The true Church continued to observe the *Passover* on the 14th day of the first month (Nisan) as a memorial of the death of Christ for several centuries. The church historian, Bede, records that Christians in Scotland were still keeping the Passover as late as the seventh century A.D.[2]

This day pictures the shedding of Christ's blood, the Lamb of God without spot or blemish, to pay the penalty for human sins. He who never sinned was able, as God in human form, to fully pay the price of all human sins, and to take on Himself the death penalty we have incurred. This sacrifice wipes the slate clean and gives those who repent of sin and wish to accept His sacrifice access to God.

The seven *Days of Unleavened Bread* which follow the Passover picture the newly converted Christian coming out of sin (leaven is used as a type of sin), as the Israelites in the Exodus came out of Egypt immediately after the first Passover. The Christian, like the Israelites coming out of Egypt, has to learn how to keep the Commandments of God. Sin, the thing he has to come out of, is defined as the breaking or transgression of those very same laws (1 John 3:4).

The next Holy Day, *Pentecost*, symbolizes the coming of the Holy Spirit (Acts 2), which gives a fleshly human being the spiritual power to keep a spiritual law—the law of God. It pictures the firstfruits, a small called-out body of Christians, called to do the work of preaching the gospel to the world as a witness (Matthew 24:14), and to qualify as individuals by overcoming "the world, the flesh and the devil" in order to have a part in the world-ruling Kingdom of God, to be set up at the return of Christ.

This group of Holy Days, kept during the early part of the year, portrays the calling and training of the "Firstfruits" of God's Plan of

Salvation. The true Church of God, called by Christ a "little flock" (Luke 12:32), is invited to an understanding of God's plan in advance of the broad majority of the earth's population, in order to prepare to assist Christ in the administration of God's government on earth (Revelation 2:26).

The later group of festivals held in the autumn (fall) of the year picture God's dealings with the world as a whole.

The first festival in this second group is the *"Feast of Trumpets"* defined as "a Sabbath, a memorial of blowing of trumpets, a holy convocation" (Leviticus 23:23–25).

It pictures the historical event, yet future, of the return of Christ to earth as a King and Ruler, to take over the government of the entire world, and set up the Kingdom of God on earth (Revelation 11:15).

It is the time when true Christians who died in the past will be resurrected to glorified spirit life, and those still living at that time will be changed or transformed into the same form (1 Corinthians 15:51–52).

The next Holy Day, *the Day of Atonement*, is observed as a day of fasting. It looks forward to the time when Satan, the devil "who deceives the whole world" (Revelation 12:9) is bound and imprisoned for a thousand years (Revelation 20:1–3). As the live goat in the Old Testament observance of this festival, in a symbolic sense, took the sins of the Israelites into the wilderness (Leviticus 16:20–26), so Satan will carry away with him his part in all human sins (Christ has already paid the penalty for our part in our sins when we repent).

With our human sins now paid for and forgiven, and Satan no longer able to deceive human beings, those who desire God's salvation are now At-one with God. Atonement means At-one-ment—human beings finally "at one" with God.

Christians were still keeping this festival in A.D. 58 when Paul took his sea voyage to Rome. In Acts 27:9 it is recorded that "when sailing was now dangerous, because the fast was now already past...." The "fast" mentioned here was the Day of Atonement.

Shortly after this festival, Christians observed the seven-day long *Feast of Tabernacles*. This pictures the thousand-year reign of Christ on earth, also known as the Millennium (Revelation 20:1–4). This doctrine of the Millennium was believed, as looking forward to a literal thousand-year reign of Christ on earth, for centuries.

During the second century Papias of Hierapolis stated "There will be a period of some thousand years after the first resurrection of the dead, and the kingdom of Christ will be set up in material form on this very earth."[3]

Other "church fathers" of the second and third centuries such as Irenaeus and Tertullian held similar views relating to this doctrine.

This amazing and yet future period of human history will be the time when "all Israel shall be saved" (Romans 11:26). At this time spiritual understanding will be available to all, and human beings, no longer having their minds confused by Satan's deceptions, will become converted in large numbers. It will also be a time of great material prosperity and abundance.

A prophecy relating to a time, after the second coming of Christ, gives clear evidence that the observance of this Festival was not something that was "nailed to the cross" and done away with.

"And it shall come to pass that every one that is left of all the nations which came against Jerusalem shall even go up from year to year to worship the king, the LORD of hosts and to keep the Feast of Tabernacles" (Zechariah 14:16).

Immediately following this festival the seventh and final Holy Day, *The Last Great Day*, was observed. This is called "the last day, that great day of the feast" (John 7:37). On this day Jesus preached that "If any man thirst, let him come unto me, and drink" (*ibid.*).

This Holy Day pictures the event, yet in the future, which is sometimes termed the "White Throne Judgment" (Revelation 20:12) when "the dead, small and great, stand before God." It is the time when the vast majority of human beings who lived and died without having any understanding of salvation will be resurrected to human life and given their first opportunity to grasp the true gospel and plan of salvation.

It is only those who knowingly reject God's ways and plan of salvation, probably a tiny minority of the earth's population, who will be destroyed in the lake of fire (Revelation 20:15). This is the second death, from which there is to be no resurrection.

The people who repent of their own ways and accept God's plan of salvation will all ultimately be changed from human to glorified spirit form, as the very children of God. They shall witness the creation of "a new heaven and a new earth" where "there shall be no more death, neither sorrow, nor crying, neither shall there be any more pain: for the former things are passed away" (Revelation 21:1–4).

The newly born sons of God, no longer restricted by the limitations of the human body, but now sharing the very power of God, will assist God in the development and rulership of the universe for all eternity.

When one considers the awesome magnitude and wonder of God's plan for human beings, it becomes plain why the early church continued the physical observance of the Holy Days, which picture these events on a year-by-year basis.

Truth Corrupted

It was only when people began turning away from "the faith once delivered to the saints" to "another Jesus" and "another gospel" (2 Corinthians 11:2–15), that the concept came into being that these Holy Days had been done away with or "nailed to the cross." Colossians 2:14 is not a reference to God's Law, but to humanly devised ordinances, as verses 21 and 22 make clear.

From the very beginning of human life on earth, Satan, the devil, had opposed God and His plan for human beings. He offered Eve (Genesis 3:4) and all other humans an alternative to God's plan of salvation, a counterfeit of the real thing.

The one thing that would disqualify people from receiving salvation was sin—disobedience to the laws of God. Satan "sold" the idea to Eve that a person could sin, live in whatever manner he wished, contrary to God's law, and yet still receive the gift of eternal life.

The city of Babylon became the headquarters of Satan's counterfeit religion. Nimrod, "a mighty one in the earth" (Genesis 10:8), built the city and exerted an immense influence over the early descendants of Noah.

His great political power was used to turn people's minds away from God. The phrase "a mighty hunter before the LORD" (Genesis 10:8) could well have been rendered "against the LORD." It was said that he caused all the people to rebel against God.

He was also a priest in Satan's counterfeit religious system. This system, called in the Bible "Mystery, Babylon the Great" (Revelation

17:5), continued to deceive millions of people long after the actual city of Babylon was destroyed (Isaiah 13:19–22; Jeremiah 51:62).

This system not only instigated the large number of pagan religions of the world but also, amazingly, much of the world's "Christianity" (2 Corinthians 11:2–15).

Alexander Hislop's thoroughly documented work, *The Two Babylons*, goes into great detail to explain the doctrines of this system, and how it has continued to exert a profound influence upon millions in the Western world of professing Christianity to the present day.

Herodotus, the world traveler and noted historian of antiquity, studied this mystery religion at work in the various countries of the ancient world he visited. He mentioned that Babylon was the primeval source from which all systems based on idolatry flowed.[4]

The Apostle Paul expressed great concern that in his day "the mystery of iniquity" was still at work and that its adherents were attempting to gain a following amongst members of the true Church of God (2 Thessalonians 2:7).

Simon the Sorcerer

The high priest, or spiritual leader of this system at that time, has been identified by some as Simon Magus or Simon the Sorcerer (Acts 8:9–24).

Simon was a Samaritan, and the Bible points out that salvation is of the Jews—not the Samaritans (John 4:22). The book of Revelation speaks of a synagogue of Satan—the members of which claimed to be Jews, though they were not (Revelation 2:9). Just as many were prophesied to later claim to be Jews spiritually, when in fact they are condemned as being false Christians, the Samaritans, when it suited their purposes, claimed to be Jews, but in fact they were largely Babylonian by race.

The Samaritans had been settled in the area some seven centuries before the time of Christ, and had been brought from Babylon and the surrounding areas (2 Kings 17:24; Ezra 4:10). They took their Babylonian mystery religion with them into Samaria.

Although Simon was baptized by Philip, his subsequent career proves that he never really repented. He tried to buy the power to confer the Holy Spirit on his followers. There are no indications that he ever intended abandoning his former religion. Simon wanted extra spiritual power to enhance his own reputation and influence over his followers.

Peter, however, correctly perceived his motive and strongly rebuked him, pointing out that his heart was "not right in the sight of God" (Acts 8:21).

Although Simon did not repent and become a humble and convert-ed member of the true Church, he did clearly recognize the immense power of the new religion and saw in it an opportunity of extending his own spiritual influence far beyond the borders of Samaria. The new religion offered possibilities that would appeal to people everywhere—why not a universal church with himself as its leader?

Early writers often referred to Simon as "the father of the Gnostics" and Gnostic writings mention that in order to become "all things to all men" he claimed to be God the Father, in Samaria; God the Son, in Judea; and God the Holy Spirit among the Gentile peoples. Simon, it seemed, really believed in a "holy trinity."

Perhaps the most damaging and far reaching of Simon's new "Christian" doctrines was that the grace or free pardon of God gave a person the license to continue in sin.

The epistle of Jude speaks of "certain men" who "crept in un-awares" and turned "the grace of our God into lasciviousness..." (Jude 4). Simon had been dead for some time when this was written, but Jude almost certainly had in mind Simon's followers when he wrote this, who were attempting to introduce this doctrine into the true Church.

"At the head of all the sects, which disturbed the peace of the church, stand the Gnostics, who claimed ability to restore to man-kind the lost knowledge of the true and supreme God... even in the first century, in various places, men infected with the Gnostic leprosy began to erect societies distinct from the other Christians."[5]

William Cave gives further details concerning the progress of this insidious attempt to subvert the true Church: "The first ringleader of this heretical crew was Simon Magus, who not being able to attain his ends of the apostles, by getting a power to confer miraculous gifts, whereby he designed to greatly and enrich himself, resolved to be revenged of them, scattered the most poisonous tares among the good wheat they had sown, bringing in the most pernicious principles; and as the natural consequence of that patronizing the most debauched villainous practices; and this under a pretense of still being Christians.

"But besides this, Simon and his followers made the gate yet wider, maintaining a universal license to sin; that men were free to do whatever they had a mind to; that to press the observance of good works was a bondage inconsistent with the liberty of the gospel; that so men did but believe in him and his dear Helen."[6]

Helen was Simon's mistress, and it was said that his relationship with her was used by his followers as an example, which they followed in their own grossly immoral lifestyles.

Justin Martyr says of her that "A certain Helen, also, is of this class, who had before been a public prostitute in Tyre of Phoenicia, and at that time attached herself to Simon, and was called, the first idea that proceeded from him."[7]

The second-century writer Irenaeus adds that "they lived in all lust and filthiness, as indeed whoever will take the pains to peruse the account that is given of them, will find that they wallowed in the most horrible and unheard of bestialities."

These obscene orgies of Simon and his followers soon attracted the attention of the Romans, who rarely took the trouble to distinguish between the true Christians and the false. Tacitus and other writers of the period relate that Christians brought to trial were often accused by the authorities of taking part in secret orgies.

Peter seems to have had this in mind when he wrote that "many will follow their destructive ways, because of whom the way of truth will be blasphemed" (2 Peter 2:2).

Towards the end of the second century a work known as *The Clementine Homilies* was produced, which gave a long and detailed account of Simon and his activities. This bizarre record contained a confusing mixture of truth and error and has been described as " a kind of religious novel." It speaks of a visit Simon made to Egypt, at which time he embraced the doctrine of the immortal soul.

In an alleged conversation with Simon Peter the point was made that "For the soul even of the wicked is immortal, for whom it were better not to have it incorruptible. For, being punished with endless torture under unquenchable fire, and never dying, it can receive no end of its misery."[8]

112

Rome Follows Simon

This doctrine gained a following at Rome. Mosheim's history of the early church mentions a sect of Christians who met on Sundays and who sang songs in honour of the sun and moon. They taught that Christ was in both and that the souls of the dead went to these heavenly bodies to be cleansed, after which they flew out to the stars to shine for evermore.

An inscription on the tomb of a martyr found in the Roman catacombs tends to support this view. The victim had died in the Antonine persecution, which began about A.D. 160. It reads: "Alexander dead... 'is not'; but he lives above the stars, and his body rests in this tomb. He ended life under the emperor Antonine, who foreseeing that great benefit would result from his services, returned evil for good, for while on his knees and about to sacrifice to the true God, was led away to execution. Oh, sad times! in which, among sacred rites and prayers, even in caverns, we are not safe. What can be more wretched than such a life? And what than such a death? When they cannot be buried by their friends and relations. At length they sparkle in heaven. He has scarcely lived, who has lived in Christian times."[9]

Eusebius relates that after visiting Antioch, around A.D. 42, and being resisted by Peter (Galatians 2:11), Simon Magus went to Rome. Satan "seizing upon the imperial city for himself, brought thither Simon, whom we mentioned before. Coming to the aid of his insidious artifices, he attached many of the inhabitants of Rome to himself, in order to deceive them."[10]

Several New Testament passages state that two of the most prominent practices of this counterfeit system were fornication and idolatry.

A further passage from the work of Eusebius mentions that Simon's followers "prostrate themselves before pictures and images of Simon himself and of Helena, who was mentioned with him, and undertake to worship them with incense and sacrifices and libations."[11]

Justin Martyr records that Menander, a disciple of Simon, "persuaded those who followed him that they would not die." This man, in common with Satan (Genesis 3:4), deceived people into accepting the idea that a person could live a life of continual sin and yet not suffer the inevitable consequences.

Another of Simon's followers, Nicholas of Antioch, is said to have founded the sect of the Nicolaitanes (Revelation 2:15) and promoted "the doctrine of promiscuity."

The doctrine of "antichrist" was also expounded by Simon Magus: "For it is manifest, from all the accounts which we have of him, that after his defection from the Christians, he ascribed to Christ no honour at all; but set himself in opposition to Christ, and said that he was no other than the supreme power of God.

"They [Simon and his followers] could not, indeed, either call him God, or a real man. True deity was inconsistent with their notion, that he was, although begotten of God, yet every way far inferior to the Father."[12]

This evil man set himself up as "another Jesus," and gladly welcomed the actual worship of other human beings.

The religion of this movement represented a bizarre blend of Christianity and pagan, oriental philosophy. Irenaeus records that not all of Simon's followers followed him openly, but some did so in secret, appearing to the world as true Christians. It was this group who secretly infiltrated the Church of God (Jude 4).

Simon's movement had a distinct anti-Jewish bias, and rejected almost all of the Old Testament teachings. One of their methods was to allegorize teachings (such as those against idolatry and paganism). Irenaeus states that Simon taught "that the Jewish prophecies were inspired by the creator's angels; therefore those who had hope in him and Helen need not attend to them, but freely do as they would."

The law of God, which Paul described as holy, just and good (Romans 7:12) was, according to Simon's perverted reasoning, a sinister tyranny which would enslave human beings. Simon honoured the "eighth" day of the week (Sunday) rather than the Sabbath.[13]

This arch heretic died, according to Eusebius, during the reign of Claudius (A.D. 41–54), but others say during the time of Nero (A.D. 54–68).

False Teaching Corrupts the Church

Although Simon was dead his movement did not die with him. Even though the name of his sect (Simonians or Samaritans) was rarely used by his followers after the second century, the doctrines of the group gained an ever-widening following. These people now called themselves simply "Christians."

Even though the conspirators had been at work almost from the beginning of the New Testament Church, the presence and energetic activities of the apostles had, to a large extent, kept them on the outside of the Church looking in.

When Peter wrote his second epistle 65-68 A.D. (see NIV Study Bible, introduction to 2 Peter), he was able to predict—as a future event—that "there will be false teachers among you" (2 Peter 2:1).

Jude, writing a decade or two later, saw the actual fulfillment of this prophecy. Events during this period were moving very rapidly.

By June of A.D. 68 when Nero died, Peter, Paul and many other leaders and members may have already been martyred. The following year saw the flight of the headquarters church from Jerusalem to Pella, beyond the river Jordan.

Direct persecution against the Church and the upheaval caused by the Jewish wars created a leadership or power vacuum ambitious men were ready to exploit. By the closing years of the first century only John remained of the original twelve apostles, and even he was in exile for a time on the island of Patmos (Revelation 1:9).

The influence of false ministers within some local congregations had by this time become so great that even John was rejected by at least one congregation (2 John 9–10) in Asia Minor.

Clement of Rome, writing at about the same time, A.D. 95–96, expressed deep concern over a similar situation developing at Corinth. The Corinthian church, fewer than 30 years after the Apostle Paul's death, was ejecting from the ministry men who had been ordained by the apostles.

Clement, writing as a spokesman for "The Church of God which is at Rome," urges the Corinthians to "walk by the rule of God's Commandments."

He laments that "It is a shame... to hear that the most firm and ancient church of the Corinthians should, by one or two persons, be led into a sedition against its priests. But we see how you have put out some, who lived reputedly among you, from the ministry, which by their innocence they had adored. Your schism has perverted many, has discouraged many: it has caused diffidence in many, and grief in us all. And yet your sedition continues still."

He calls upon the ringleaders to repent: "Let us with all haste put an end to this sedition."[14]

It was said that the conspirators had been guilty of attempting to "violate the order of public services," primarily the Lord's Supper or Passover.

Clement's intervention may have checked the conspiracy for a while. But by the time Dionysius visited the Corinthian church, in A.D. 170, the church that in Paul's day had kept the Sabbath was now meeting for services "Sunday by Sunday."

Rome Conquers All

After the generation converted through Paul's ministry had died, inspired leadership within that local church seems to have faded quickly from the scene. With fewer converted members left with each passing year, false ministers were ultimately able to take over the entire church at Corinth.

Following Clement's death around A.D. 101 major doctrinal changes began to be introduced at Rome. The abolition of the Sabbath and annual Holy Days seems to have been the first objective of those who, at Rome, had "crept in unawares."

The introduction of Easter in place of the Passover took place according to one authority in A.D. 109; other sources put the date some ten to twelve years later, during the time of the Roman bishop Sixtus, or Xystus. Easter was observed at a different time compared to the Passover and was based on the unscriptural Good Friday-Easter Sunday tradition. Many of its features were taken directly from paganism.

Easter, according to Alexander Hislop,[15] "bears its Chaldean origin on its forehead. Easter is nothing else than Astarte, one of the titles of Beltis, the Queen of Heaven... The introduction of this festival was a gradual process and in its earliest [second century] form still retained the name of Passover."

"The festival, of which we read in church history, under the name of Easter, in the third or fourth centuries, was quite a different festival from that now observed in the Romish Church, and at that time was not known by any such name as Easter. It was called Pascha, or the Passover, and... was very clearly observed by many professing Christians."[16]

This major doctrinal change had received no approval whatsoever either from any apostle or from any who had been ordained by an apostle.

Polycarp, who had known several of the apostles, and had been ordained by John, strongly resisted the introduction of this new festival. He visited Rome in A.D. 154 to discuss the matter with Anicetus, the Roman bishop.[17]

Irenaeus described the outcome of the meeting: "For neither could Anicetus persuade Polycarp not to observe it [the Passover] because he had always observed it with John, the disciple of our Lord, and the rest of the apostles, with whom he associated; and neither did Polycarp persuade Anicetus to observe it, who said that he was bound to follow the customs of the presbyters before him."[18]

The church of Rome by this time was determined to follow its own customs and traditions, even when these were in direct conflict with the teachings and examples set by the apostles of Christ.

A series of epistles and other writings appeared during the second century, which supported the introduction of new doctrines. Many, if not most, of these works could be classed as spurious, in the sense that the individuals named as the writers of these documents were not the true authors, who had probably been dead for several decades when these works were written.

These writings do, however, reflect, with some degree of accuracy, the changes that were taking place at Rome during the second century A.D.

The observance of Sunday as a day of worship appears to have started at Rome around A.D. 120. The so-called *Epistle of Barnabas*, which was written around this time, mentions that "we observe the eighth day with gladness" (chap. 13, v. 10).

This work contains a strong anti-Jewish bias and the writer goes to great length to supposedly "prove" that the health laws of the Bible, primarily those relating to clean and unclean meats, had been written as an allegory and as such did not apply to Christians. He concludes by stating: "Wherefore it is not the command of God that they should not eat these things..." (chap. 10).

The *"Epistle of Ignatius to the Magnesians"* is another attempt to justify Sunday observance. "Wherefore if they who were brought up in these ancient laws came nevertheless to the newness of hope; no longer observing Sabbaths but keeping the Lord's Day..." (chap. 9).

By A.D. 200 the Roman church, far from calling the Sabbath "a delight, the holy of the LORD, honourable" (Isaiah 58:13) had made this a day of fasting.

God's Church Remains Faithful

"The Roman church regarded Saturday as a fast day in direct opposition to those who regarded it as a Sabbath. Sunday remained a joyful festival in which all fasting and worldly business was avoided as much as possible, but the original commandment of the decalogue respecting the Sabbath was not then applied to that day."[19]

The antagonism of the church of Rome was not confined to the weekly Sabbath but was extended to include the annual Sabbaths which pictured God's plan of salvation for mankind.

About A.D. 140 a Jew named Trypho challenged Justin Martyr, a leader in the Roman church, to explain why the Christians were not observing "festivals or Sabbaths." Justin replied that "the new law requires you to keep a perpetual Sabbath, and you, because you are idle for one day, suppose you are pious, not discerning why this has been commanded you: and if you eat unleavened bread you say the will of God has been fulfilled. The Lord our God does not take pleasure in such observances."[20]

It is also noted in the above work that "Justin never discriminated between the Sabbath of the Lord and the annual sabbaths..." Justin mentions the attitude of the Roman Christians to those of the true Church of God who continued to observe the Sabbath. They "do not venture to have any intercourse with, or to extend hospitality to, such persons; but I do not agree with them."

By the middle of the second century the few who continued to obey God, and as such constituted the true Church (Revelation 12:17) were being ejected from any fellowship with the professing Christian Church, which had substituted its own traditions in place of obedience to God.

The time predicted by Christ when "They shall put you [the true Christians] out of the synagogues" (John 16:2) had arrived.

Not only did the Roman church regard the Sabbath as a fast day but, in time, even the feast of unleavened bread began to be regarded in the same light.

The Roman congregation was instructed to "keep your nights of watching in the middle of the days of unleavened bread. And when the Jews are feasting, do you fast and wail over them, because on the day of their feast they crucified Christ... Do you therefore fast on the days of the Passover..."[21]

The changes being introduced by the Roman church did not take place without opposition. In Asia Minor, where several churches had been raised up by the apostles, Christians continued to observe the festivals which had been handed down to them by the apostles and, their immediate followers, such as Polycarp.

Church members continued these festivals even when visiting Rome, which only served to emphasize the growing differences between the church of Rome and churches from other areas.

The Roman church needed something more than the tradition of its own bishops upon which to place the seal of authority upon its changing doctrines.

A letter was circulated at Rome shortly after Polycarp's visit of A.D. 154. The letter, probably a forgery, purported to have come from the Roman bishop Pius, who had died shortly before this time, in which his brother Hermas is said to have received instructions from an angel that the Passover should be observed on a Sunday. This, it seems, gave fresh impetus to the growing Easter Sunday tradition.

About A.D. 160 Tatian, a disciple of Justin Martyr, produced the "*Diatessaron*" in which it was said [by Dionysius of Corinth] that he "selected from the gospels and patched together and constructed a gospel which is called *Diatessaron*." This work appeared to produce evidence in the form of direct quotations from the gospels to support the "Good Friday" tradition.

An honest examination of the real gospels, however, produces no such "evidence." Few in Rome, it seems, bothered to check the source of Tatian's statements.

A Shrine to Peter at Rome

At about this point in history a discovery was made at Rome which was to have tremendous significance for the local church.

Workmen, digging the foundations for a new building on Vatican Hill around A.D. 160–170, uncovered something which inspired the Roman bishop Anicetus to erect a shrine on the site of the discovery which was dedicated to the Apostle Peter.

Extensive excavations which started in 1939 and continued for several years beneath the high altar of St. Peter's have established beyond reasonable doubt that this shrine to Peter, also known as "the Andicula," was erected during the third quarter of the second century A.D.

The unknown "something" which the workmen uncovered during the second century could well have been some of the bodily remains of one, or more, of the victims of the Neronian persecution of the Christians in A.D. 64.

The site of the shrine was located only a short distance from Nero's Circus, where the Christians suffered martyrdom. A second-century will of one Gaius Popilius Horacia stipulated that he was to be buried "on the Vatican Hill near the Circus."

Bishop Lightfoot described in lurid detail the ghastly events of that time.

"The refined cruelty of the tortures—the impalements and the pitchy tunics, the living torches making night hideous with the lurid flames and piercing cries, the human victims clad in the skins of wild beasts and hunted in the arena, while the populace gloated over these revels and the emperor indulged his mad orgies—those were scenes which no lapse of time could efface. Above all... the climax of horrors... were the outrages, far worse than death itself, inflicted on weak women and innocent girls."[22]

Although there is no way of knowing for certain whether or not the workmen really did uncover the remains of Peter's body, or indeed of any body, the fact is clearly established that Peter was venerated at this shrine from about A.D. 160 onwards.

Dionysius of Corinth was the first to mention that both Peter and Paul had died at Rome (A.D. 170).

Eusebius records the statement of the Roman priest Gaius, made about A.D. 200, that: "I can show you the trophies of the Apostles. For if you go to the Vatican or to the Ostian Way, there you will find the trophies of those who founded this church."[23]

From the time of Constantine onwards Catholic churches erected on this site were built in such a manner as to incorporate the shrine within the finished building.

An interesting reference in the *"Liber Pontificalis"* would seem, on the face of it, to place the construction of the shrine some 80 years earlier than the evidence of archaeology would indicate.

It was said that Anacletus, a shadowy figure about whom almost nothing is known, "built and set in order a memorial... shrine to the blessed Peter, where the bishops might be buried." This event is dated to about A.D. 80.

So far as is known, only one shrine to Peter existed at Rome during the first few centuries of the Christian era, and intensive recent investigations have dated this to about A.D. 160. The most probable solution to this problem is that the sixth-century scribe who compiled this work, probably from earlier sources, almost certainly confused the two names of Anacletus and Anicetus (the Bishop of Rome in A.D. 160).

First Bishop of Rome: Linus, Not Peter

A bizarre twist to this story is that Anacletus did indeed dedicate a shrine to the first bishop of Rome in A.D. 80—but that man was *not* Peter. The shrine of *Memoria of Anacletus* was dedicated to the genuine first bishop of Rome. The man's name was Linus. He was ordained by the Apostle Paul (not Peter) as the first elder or bishop of the Church of God at Rome.

One of Paul's functions as an apostle was to ordain elders, or bishops in the towns and cities where churches had been established. Sometimes an assistant was delegated to handle this task (Titus 1:5). What very few have realized is that Paul also performed this task at Rome.

Several early writers mention this ordination and link the individual concerned with the Linus mentioned in 2 Timothy 4:21. Jerome gives the date of this event as A.D. 68, probably no more than a few months or weeks before Paul's martyrdom.

Of all the local bishops ordained by Paul, the bishop of Rome was not the first but the last to be ordained. This ordination could well have been his final official duty prior to his death.

Linus died, possibly martyred, in A.D. 80. His tomb has been discovered in the Roman catacombs. The amazing facts relating to this discovery are as follows: "In the Catacomb of St. Priscilla is a memorial chapel known as the *Memoria of Anacletus*. This, we are told, was built by Anacletus after the death of Linus. Dr. Spence-Jones gives an interesting account of the discovery of the Memoria and what it contained. It was evidently built in honour of Linus and as a fitting resting place for this first Bishop of Rome, who suffered martyrdom. Part of the Vatican was built over this catacomb, the oldest in Rome.

"No doubt it has been explored thoroughly in the hope of finding St. Peter's tomb, but none has been discovered with any inscription pointing to Peter. In the Memorial of Anacletus, a number of plain stone coffins were found grouped around the floor. Only one bore an inscription and it was the simple word LINUS. This was in the centre of the floor and was clearly the one for which the chapel was built."[24]

Irenaeus, who was born just 40 years after the death of Linus, confirmed his position in the early church.

"The blessed Apostles, then, having founded and built up the church, committed into the hands of Linus the office of the episcopate. Of this Linus Paul makes mention in his epistles to Timothy. To him succeeded Anacletus and after him, in third place from the Apostles, Clement was allotted the bishopric."[25]

One can only wonder why these important facts have remained hidden for so long.

The Truth About Peter
Very little is known of the movements of Peter apart from the few brief references to him given in the New Testament. These speak of him working at Jerusalem, Joppa, Caesarea, Samaria and Antioch.

His task was to preach to the Jews, not the gentile Romans (Galatians 2:7–8). Paul, not Peter, was sent to establish the church at Rome (Romans 15:16).

At the end of his epistle to the Romans, Paul lists a considerable number of his "fellow labourers in Christ," but makes no mention of Peter. No doubt he would have been the first on the list had he been the "bishop of Rome" at the time.

Some time later, probably in A.D. 59, when Paul arrived in Italy on the way to Rome he was met by some Christian brethren, but Peter was not among them (Acts 28:15).

At the time that Paul wrote his epistle to the Romans, while recognizing the existence of a Christian congregation, he speaks throughout as though this were practically a virgin soil in which he was called to sow the seed of the Gospel. The first Apostle visited Rome about A.D. 60.[26]

None of the "Prison epistles" written by Paul about this time make any mention of Peter.

William Cave mentions Peter working in Northern Asia Minor, along with his brother Andrew.

"He [Andrew] next came to Sinope, a city situated upon the same sea [Black Sea] where he met with his brother Peter with whom he stayed a considerable time."[2]

As Peter's own first epistle, written from Babylon in the early 60s (see *NIV Study Bible*, Introduction to 1 Peter), is addressed to Christians in this area, the fact that he laboured for a time along this Black Sea coast is highly probable.

The final years of Peter's life are shrouded in mystery, and scholars have rightly treated statements from early writers relating to this period with considerable caution.

Peter in Britain

Cardinal Baronius, the Vatican Librarian, quotes the tenth-century writer Simon Metaphrastes, who mentioned that "Peter spent some days in Britain, and enlightened many by the word of grace; and having established churches and elected Bishops, Presbyters and Deacons, came again to Rome in the twelfth year of Nero..." And: "This ancient account is highly probable."[28]

Although some point out that "Metaphrastes is an author of no credit" (*Fuller's Church History of Britain*, p. 9), a tradition relating to Peter's visit to Britain seems to have started at a very early date.

Gildas, in the sixth century, refers to Britain as "St. Peter's Chair." A church building, dedicated to Peter, is said to have been erected in London as early as A.D. 179 (St. Peter's of Cornhill).

Although the tradition which relates to Westminster Abbey being built on the spot where Peter once slept and had a vision seems too good to be true, and could well have been a fabrication of the Dark Ages, the fact that a church dedicated to Peter occupied the site of the Abbey from ancient times is well established.

According to Lactantius, "St. Peter came not to Rome till the reign of Nero, and not long before his martyrdom."

The twelfth year of Nero's reign is given by several early writers as the date that Peter first arrived at Rome. As this date, A.D. 66, is the year before tradition asserts that he was martyred at Rome, there is a strong possibility that the traditions are based on a measure of historical fact.

Paul, in his final epistle, the second to Timothy, reckoned to be written c. 66-67 A.D. from his Roman prison (see *NIV Study Bible*, Introduction to 2 Timothy) makes no mention of Peter and makes it clear that "only Luke is with me" (2 Timothy 4:1 1). Peter could well have been dead when this was written.

Dionysius, in the second century, mentioned that both Peter and Paul suffered martyrdom in Italy. His remarks are recorded by Eusebius.

A little later, about A.D. 200, Tertullian relates that Peter was crucified at Rome, and Origen records that he was crucified upside-down.

As the apostle to "the circumcision," Peter could well have had an interest in the Jewish community that resided in Rome at that time (Acts 28:17).

Although Peter may well have briefly visited Rome towards the end of his life, and may even have died there, this possibility in no way proves that he was the first bishop of Rome in the traditional sense of the term.

Peter was as much a "Hebrew of the Hebrews" as was Paul, and in no way would have sanctioned or authorized the doctrinal changes that the Roman church began to introduce from the second century onwards.

Christ, not Peter, was the Head of the Church (Ephesians 5:23) and He is the one who should be followed (1 Peter 2:21).

Peter, who was a married man, not a celibate priest, kept both the weekly and annual Sabbaths, and would, no doubt, had he lived, have strongly resisted any moves to change or abolish the observance of these days. Peter cannot in any way be used as an authority by those who seek to move away from "the faith once delivered to the saints."

The Lost Century

The period immediately following the deaths of Peter and Paul have, with good reason, been called "The Age of Shadows" and "The

Lost Century." For some fifty years, up to the earliest writings of the church fathers around A.D. 120, church history is almost a total blank.

Several historians have made the point that the church which we read of during the second century was in many vital respects quite different from the church which had been established by Christ and the apostles.

By the closing years of that century, Christians who faithfully continued in the teachings handed down to them by the immediate followers of Christ were rapidly finding themselves to be in a minority position.

Mosheim, in his church history, relates that: "Christian churches had scarcely been organized when men rose up, who, not being contented with the simplicity and purity of that religion which the Apostles taught, attempted innovations, and fashioned religion according to their own liking."

Paul, in his epistle to the Roman brethren, expressly warned them against boasting of their position and exalting themselves over the largely Jewish churches of the east (Romans 11:18–21).

By the closing years of the second century, however, the Roman bishop Victor attempts to "excommunicate" the churches of Asia Minor for refusing to abandon practices handed down to them from the apostles.

"A question of no small importance arose at that time. For the parishes of all Asia, as from an older tradition, held that the fourteenth day of the moon, on which day the Jews were commanded to sacrifice the lamb, should be observed as the feast of the Saviour's Passover... the bishops of Asia, led by Polycrates, decided to hold to the old custom handed down to them. He himself in a letter which he addressed to Victor and the Church of Rome, set forth in the following words the tradition which had come down to him.

"'We observe the exact day; neither adding, nor taking away. For in Asia also great lights have fallen asleep, which shall rise again on the day of the Lord's coming, when he shall come with glory from heaven, and shall seek out all the saints. Among these are Philip, one of the twelve apostles... and, moreover, John, who was both a witness and a teacher, who reclined on the bosom of the Lord... and Polycarp in Smyrna, who was a bishop and martyr... these observed the fourteenth day of the Passover according to the Gospel, deviating in no respect, but following the rule of faith.'"[29]

Victor, not content to enforce the observance of Easter, with its many pagan features, upon his own local congregation, determined to press its observance on other churches far from Rome.

Roman Hegemony

J.B. Lightfoot, the noted scholar and historian, describes the fundamental change in the office of the bishop of Rome that took place during the century that separated Clement from Victor. Although theologians of later centuries classified Clement as a Pope, Clement himself makes no mention in his writings of any such exalted position.

"The language and silence alike of Clement himself and of writers in his own and immediately succeeding ages are wholly irreconcilable with this extravagant estimate of his position.

"In Clement's letter itself—the earliest document issuing from the Roman church after the apostolic times—no mention is made of the episcopacy so called.

"There is all the difference in the world between the attitude of Rome towards other churches at the close of the first century... and its attitude at the close of the second century, when Victor the bishop excommunicates the churches of Asia Minor for clinging to a usage in regard to the celebration of Easter [i.e. Passover] which had been handed down to them from the Apostles."[30]

"Towards the latter end of the second century, most of the churches assumed a new form, the first simplicity disappeared; and insensibly, as the old disciples retired to their graves, their children, along with new converts, both Jews and Gentiles, came forward and new modeled the cause."[31]

The Roman view on Easter and Sunday observance, which was later to gain almost universal acceptance in the Christian professing world, was summed up by Justin Martyr around the middle of the second century: "But we meet together on Sunday, because it is the first day, in which God, having wrought the necessary changes in darkness and matter made the world; and on this day Jesus Christ our Saviour rose from the dead. For he was crucified on the day before that of Saturn; and on the day after that of Saturn, which is the day of the Sun, having appeared to the Apostles and Disciples, he taught the things which we now submit to your consideration."[32]

Scholars recognise that the first Christians continued to observe the "Jewish" Sabbath. By Justin Martyr's time, however, the large numbers of Gentile converts coming into the church wrongly assumed that the Sabbath was a part of the temporary ritualistic ordinances introduced by Moses at Sinai. Genesis 2, however, shows that it was instituted long before the time of Moses. [33]

Soon a new "gospel" began to be preached which extolled Christ and His virtues but denied His all-important message that He would return and set up the Kingdom of God on earth.

The "Little Flock" Branded Heretics

When the Roman or Latin form of Christianity became the state religion of the empire under Constantine, men saw less need for the return of Christ and sought to establish their own ecclesiastical empire, with Rome, not Jerusalem, as its headquarters.

Members of the "little flock" which constituted the true Church of God were now classified as "heretics" by Constantine's "Christian" empire and true to prophecy (Daniel 12:7; Revelation 12) was forced to flee into the wilderness or die as martyrs for their faith.

To those who continued to keep the Passover, in the form that it was handed down to them from the apostles and their successors, Constantine wrote the following: "Forasmuch, then, as it is no longer possible to bear with your pernicious errors, we give warning by this present statute that none of you henceforth presume to assemble yourselves together. We have directed, accordingly, that you be deprived of all the houses in which you are accustomed to hold your assemblies: and forbid the holding of your superstitious and sense-less meetings... Take the far better course of entering the Catholic Church...."[34]

Not only the Passover but the Sabbath too was to be abolished by the state, at the Council of Laodicea in A.D. 364.

Pryne records that "the seventh-day Sabbath was... solemnized by Christ, the apostles and primitive Christians till the Laodicean Council did, in a manner, quite abolish the observance of it. The Council of Laodicea... first settled the observation of the Lord's day."[35]

Those who wished to continue to keep the Commandments of God were now forced to flee for their lives into remote wilderness areas beyond the reach of their persecutors.

The new state religion, a bizarre blend of Christianity and paganism, now began to dominate Europe for over a thousand years, leaving the true Church in "a place prepared of God" (Revelation 12:6)—the remote mountains and valleys of central Europe.

Chapter Summary
When Jesus Christ established His true Church, He commanded it to preach His own gospel along with other aspects of God's Law and way of life. Why are the teachings of mainstream Christianity so different from those of the apostles? This chapter traces the introduction of "another Jesus" and "a different gospel."

Chapter Seven

A LIGHT IN THE DARK AGES

*"The despotism of Antichrist was then [A.D. 786] so far from
being universal, that it was not owned throughout Italy itself.
In some parts of that country, as well as in England and France,
the purity of Christian worship was still maintained"*
(Townsend's *Abridgment*, p. 361).

"Be faithful unto death, and I will give you the crown of life"
(Revelation 2:10).

T he period immediately following the apostolic age was
one of flagging zeal and diminishing works; a time when
the task of preaching the true gospel seems to have been
virtually abandoned. Almost no written material has survived
which relates to this "Lost Century," as it has been termed.
The "Ephesian" era of the true Church of God lost its first love
(Revelation 2:4) and like the ten virgins of Christ's parable "they all
slumbered and slept."

In Britain, the situation was much the same as it was elsewhere in
the Roman world. Gildas, writing during the sixth century, had access
to at least one very early work on the history of the British church,
which is no longer extant. He made the point that "Christ's precepts,
though they were received but lukewarmly of the inhabitants, yet
they remained entirely with some, less sincerely with others, even
until the nine years persecution under Diocletian."[1]

The apathy and indifference with which the majority of the
inhabitants greeted the gospel may well have contributed to a rapid
decline in the zeal and enthusiasm of British Christians. William
of Malmesbury in his researches into the history of the church at
Glastonbury, noted a distinct slackness among British Christians
during the early second century.

Elvanus of Avalon
Another early source on church history quoted by Stillingfleet is
Bale, who mentions one Elvanus of Avalon (known in Welsh records
as Elfan), who "was a disciple to those who were the disciples of the

Apostles." It was said that "he preached the gospel in Britain with good success."

Pitsaeus in his *Relationes Historicae de Rebus Anglicis* written in 1619, mentioned that Elvanus studied at a college or school at Glastonbury. This college, if such existed, seems to have been established for the training of ministers, perhaps during the first century, and continued during the early part of the second by the immediate disciples of the apostles.

Almost nothing is known of this institution but it seems to have been abandoned by the middle of the second century. Elvanus is the only student of whom any record has survived. William of Malmesbury records that by the closing years of that century the site had become overgrown with vegetation and a haunt of wild beasts.

In about A.D. 180 Elvanus wrote a book called *Concerning the Origin of the British Church*, an indication that even at this early date knowledge relating to the activities of the first Christians in Britain was becoming hazy, and that a source of information on that subject was by that time required.

Sadly, this work, which would have been of immense value to later historians, became lost at a very early date, probably even before the close of the Roman period; with the loss of this work and others from the early centuries of the Christian era, we are left with material which can only be described as scanty and fragmentary.

King Lucius

Bede and several later writers attribute to the second century church the shadowy and bizarre figure of King Lucius. This monarch, so the story relates, is supposed (with the assistance of Pope Eleutherius) to have made Christianity the state religion of Britain.

Most of the Lucius material, as modern scholars have correctly determined, consists of little more than fables probably concocted during the Dark Ages. The terminology used is that relating to a church much later than that of the second century.

The latest evidence from the field of archaeology indicates that the second-century British church, far from being a state religion, was, in the words of one expert, a "minority sect."

So numerous, however, are the references to Lucius in early literature (Ussher records no fewer than 23 authorities) that it seems probable that at least a few fragments of factual information lie at the root of the Dark Age legends concerning Lucius.

According to Bale, the preaching of the Gospel by Elvanus brought a strong reaction from the Druids. As Elvanus had received this "Gospel" from the immediate followers of the apostles, he was almost certainly preaching the same message of the Gospel of the Kingdom of God that had been preached by the Church of God in the previous century.

The Druids took the matter to Lucius in order to receive a settlement of the controversy. Lucius is then said to have contacted Eleutherius, the Bishop of Rome, in order to receive guidance.

Lucius (Lleuver Mawr—Lucius the Great in Welsh records) could not have been a king in the modern sense of the word, as Britain was then a province of Rome. Although a treaty was concluded in A.D. 114 which gave the Britons a measure of self government, the total freedom of religion which Lucius is supposed to have granted all British Christians is improbable in the extreme.

Lucius, if he existed at all, was probably, as Collier points out, a local British chieftain or governor, under the authority of the Roman administration, in the territory of the Regni, which probably comprised of the counties of Surrey and Sussex.

Collier also mentioned two coins which had been discovered, one of gold and the other silver, which bore the letters L.U.C. This, Collier and several other authorities of the time, took as additional proof of the existence of Lucius.[2]

The view of Dr. Mosheim on this point is worthy of consideration: "As to Lucius, I agree with all the best British writers, in supposing him to be the restorer and second father of the English churches, and not their original founder. That he was a king is not probable; because Britain was then a Roman province. He might be a nobleman, a governor, of a district. His name is Roman."[3]

According to one tradition Lucius was baptized in the Chalice Well at Glastonbury in A.D. 137 by Timotheus, the son of Rufus Pudens. In common with much of the Lucius material, however, little real evidence exists to support this tale.

Druids Turn to Christianity

There are some convincing indications that during this period, the late second century, the Druids, who had suffered persecution at the hands of the Romans, began to take an increasing interest in Christianity.

Some sources imply that Lucius gave encouragement to a blending together of the two religions.

"All the rights previously held by the Druidic hierarchy were now conferred on the Christian ministry. The Gorseddall, the various high courts of the Druids, became bishoprics, while the headquarters of the Arch-Druids at London, York and Caerleon became Archbishoprics."[4]

Describing this period, Stillingfleet adds that "it is generally agreed, that, about this time, many Pagan temples in Britain had their property altered, and the self-same were converted into Christian churches."[5]

Some Catholic writers such as Bede trace the introduction of the Catholic faith into Britain to this period. The only real evidence put forward to support this view is a letter said to have been written by Eleutherius, a second-century bishop of Rome, and sent to Lucius. Few modern scholars accept this letter as genuine, however, and many valid arguments have been put forward which indicate that it was almost certainly composed in an age much later than that of the second century.

Roman Christianity Spreads

The third and fourth centuries provide more positive evidence of the spread of Latin or Catholic Christianity in Britain.

Some sources speak of Lucius sending out bishops to establish churches in London, Gloucester, Winchester, Dover and Canterbury. He is also said to have restored the "Old Church" at Glastonbury, which by that time (A.D. 187) was in a state of disrepair.

Although much of this second-century material seems to have been somewhat distorted by legend and superstition during the Dark Ages, the clear implication must surely be that the remnants of the earlier pure apostolic faith had, by the end of the second century, all but disappeared in Britain. A new and different church was starting to emerge.

During the third century converted and zealous followers of Christ increasingly found themselves in a minority position.

The decadent condition of most professing Christians and ministers in Europe at this time is described as follows: "Each was bent on improving his patrimony: forgetting what believers had done under the apostles, and what they ought always to do, they brooded over the arts of amassing wealth. The pastors and deacons equally forgot their duty, works of mercy were neglected, and discipline was at the lowest ebb.

"Luxury and effeminacy prevailed. Meretricious arts in dress were cultivated. Fraud and deceit were practiced among brethren. Christians could unite themselves in matrimony with unbelievers, could swear, not only without reverence, but without veracity... even many bishops, who ought to be guides and patterns to the rest, neglecting the peculiar duties of their stations, gave themselves up to secular pursuits; deserting their places of residence and their flocks, they traveled through distant provinces in quest of gain, gave no assistance to the needy brethren, were insatiable in their thirst of money, possessed estates by fraud, and multiplied usury."[6]

It was during this period that foreign writers began to take note of developments in Britain.

"The extremities of Spain, the various parts of Gaul, the regions of Britain which have never been penetrated by the Roman Arms have received the religion of Christ," wrote Tertullian about A.D. 208.[7]

Some 30 years later, Origen wrote that "The divine goodness of Our Lord and Saviour is equally diffused among the Britons, the Africans, and other nations of the world."[8]

Diocletian Persecution

The church in Britain suffered its first large scale persecution during the reign of Diocletian. It was predicted to be a time of trial and distress to the "Smyrna" era of the Church of God which at this time was mainly confined to the Eastern Roman Empire. Using the "day for a year" principle (Numbers 14:34), it lasted for ten years, A.D. 303–313 (Revelation 2:10).

This persecution, which in some provinces virtually eliminated all traces of Christianity, fell with equal severity on true and false Christians alike.

Gildas records that some 10,000 died as martyrs in Britain. Bede also described some of the events of the period: "At the same time suffered Aaron and Julius, citizens of Chester [other writers give this location as Carlisle or Caerleon], and many more of both sexes in several places; who, when they had endured sundry torments, and their limbs had been torn after an unheard of manner, yielded their souls up...."[9]

Treasure at Water Newton

In 1975 an amazing discovery was made at Water Newton, near Peterborough, which illustrates the increasingly important position that Latin or Catholic Christianity was beginning to play in Britain by the early fourth century.

"Mr. A.J. Holmes found by remarkable coincidence... within the site of the Roman town of Durobrivae, a fourth-century early Christian treasure."[10]

This treasure consisted of one gold, and 27 silver vessels and plaques. There is a strong possibility that the hoard was buried, for safe keeping, during the persecution of Christians during the reign of Diocletian.

"There is evidence that the vessels were not abandoned but were put away with the intention of being recovered... but the evidence seems clear that he did destroy property, and this sort of action or even the fear of it, would have been good reason to hide the Water Newton Treasure, no matter whether the concealment was at this precise time in the fourth century or not."[11]

"In character the treasure is religious and not secular... The three major inscriptions and the use, fifteen times, of the Chi-Rho device demonstrate that the whole Water Newton Treasure is religious and Christian... The treasure seems likely, therefore, to have been in the possession of, and being used by, a practising Christian group, perhaps for refrigeria or for baptism or for Communion."[12]

Various inscriptions are found on the vessels such as the alpha and omega symbol and personal messages such as "O Lord, I, Publianus, relying on you, honour your holy sanctuary."

The increasing influence of paganism in that branch of Christianity which Constantine was soon to elevate to the position of an official state religion is also illustrated in the Water Newton hoard.

"The wording of the inscription on the Water Newton bowl is notably reminiscent of phrases in the traditional Mass, such as "sublime altare tuum" in the "Supplices," a prayer which is accompanied by the kissing of the altar. The kissing of the altar at various points in the Mass, of which the meaning was later enlarged by the idea that the altar built of stone represented Christ himself, began as a ceremony borrowed from ancient culture. The custom of greeting holy places with a kiss was continued in Christendom, with only a change of object."[13]

"The Water Newton silver is not later than the fourth century A.D. The group includes religious plaques which are pagan in type and vessels which are ordinary secular types used for Christian religious purposes. The objects throw light on areas of the history of Christianity of which we know almost nothing. The Water Newton treasure is the earliest known group of Christian silver from the whole Roman Empire.[14]

Christian Art

During the fourth century the Chi-Rho monogram, which the pagans used as a numerical symbol, appeared in large numbers in various examples of "Christian Art."

"Archaeologists have been amazed to discover, in recent years, a large number of Chi-Rho monograms in Romano-British buildings. This symbol, consisting of the first two letters of the name of Christ in Greek, is quite distinctive and unmistakable. The most striking example was found in a beautifully preserved mosaic floor, at Hinton St. Mary, in Dorset.

"At the centre of the design is a head with the Chi-Rho behind it. It could well be a portrait of the owner of the house with the symbol which would show him to be a Christian. In Canterbury Museum is a silver spoon with the Chi-Rho engraved on it, dated by the experts as the second century.

"A number of lead tanks have been found, leading to the conclusion that they may have been used for adult baptism. The missionaries regarded a baptistery as essential, that converts might be baptized immediately."[15]

Inscriptions of a Christian nature in the Greek and Latin languages have been discovered on drinking vessels and other objects. They include such statements as "May you live in God... Hail, sister! may you live in God! " And: "In God is hope."

As the Roman period drew to its close in Britain the influence of paganism within Christian art increased. A "Christian" mosaic discovered at Frampton includes the ocean god Neptune and also a cupid—well known in pagan art as a symbol of souls in paradise.

The male bust in the Hinton St. Mary mosaic is thought by some authorities to represent Christ, having a Chi-Rho monogram behind the head. The panel also contains a picture from pagan antiquity—Bellerophen on Pegasus slaying the Chimaera.

The first Christians, in common with the Jews, had a horror of anything which came even close to breaking the second commandment which expressly forbids the use of images of any kind in the worship of the true God (Exodus 20:4–5).

Religious pictures, including those used in pagan cultures, were definitely included in this ban. The Israelites, at the time of their invasion of Canaanite territory, were ordered to "destroy all their pictures, and destroy all their molten images, and quite pluck down all their high places" (Numbers 33:52).

As late as the time of Constantine we find Eusebius outraged with a request from the sister of Constantine that he send her a portrait of Christ. He pointed out that such pictures were not to be found in churches and were forbidden among Christians.

By about A.D. 400 the influx of pagan influence led to a trend towards the increased use of pictures for worship. In A.D. 691 the Catholic Council of Constantinople officially sanctioned the use of images and pictures in churches.

The professing Christian church which received the official sanction and approval of the Roman state during the time of Constantine, began persecuting and driving from the empire those who refused to conform to the new laws which promoted Sunday observance and prohibited the keeping of the seventh-day Sabbath.

God's Church Goes Into the Wilderness

The "little flock" which constituted the true Church of God was driven, as prophesied, into the wilderness. For nearly two centuries after the Roman legions left Britain in A.D. 410, the country was almost entirely free from both the political and ecclesiastical domination of Rome. It proved a suitable haven for many of God's people.

The church historian, Jones, gives an interesting account of the scattering of God's Church: "Multitudes, however, fled like innocent and defenseless sheep from these devouring wolves. They crossed the Alps, and traveled in every direction, as Providence and the prospect of safety conducted them, into Germany, England, France, Italy, and other countries. There they trimmed their lamps, and shone with new luster. Their worth everywhere drew attention, and their doctrine formed increasing circles around them. The storm which threatened their destruction only scattered them as the precious seeds of the glorious reformation of the Christian Church."[16]

The factors which led to the promotion of Sunday observance at Rome were present long before the time of Constantine.

In the apocryphal *Gospel of Peter*, dating to the late second century, the first reference is found to the "Lord's day." Regular Sunday

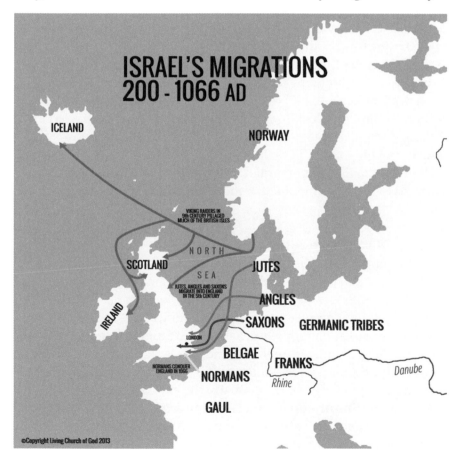

ISRAEL'S MIGRATIONS
200 - 1066 AD

ICELAND

NORWAY

VIKING RAIDERS IN
9th CENTURY PILLAGED
MUCH OF THE BRITISH ISLES

NORTH

SCOTLAND

SEA

JUTES

JUTES, ANGLES AND SAXONS
MIGRATE INTO ENGLAND
IN THE 5th CENTURY

ANGLES

IRELAND

SAXONS   GERMANIC TRIBES

LONDON

BELGAE   FRANKS

NORMANS CONQUER
ENGLAND IN 1066   NORMANS   Rhine   Danube

GAUL

©Copyright Living Church of God 2013

meetings for church services are mentioned in the apology of Justin Martyr, written around the middle of that century.

Several writers have noted the early abandonment of the Sabbath at Rome. Clement in his epistle to the Corinthians (A.D. 95–96) not only fails to even hint at Sunday services but speaks of the "sacrifices and services" which were "offered at the appointed times" in the temple at Jerusalem as "things the Master has commanded us to perform."

"On the other hand, a few decades later we find in Ignatius, Barnabas and Justin not only the opposite attitude toward Jewish institutions, but also the first timid references to the resurrection, which is presented as an added or secondary reason for Sunday worship."[17]

The Jewish War of A.D. 66–70 provoked an outburst of anti-Semitism among the Roman population, which was to last until well into the second century. This led to a contempt for all things associated with the Jews—including the Sabbath.

"The introduction of Sunday worship in place of 'Jewish' Sabbath-keeping—the latter being particularly derided by several Roman writers of the time—could well represent a measure taken by the leaders of the Church of Rome to evidence their severance from Judaism and thereby also avoid the payment of a discriminatory tax."[18]

"... anti-Judaism has emerged as a primary factor which contributed to the introduction of Sunday observance in place of the Sabbath."[19]

Sunday Observance

A second important reason for Sunday observance was the great popularity of sun worship among pagan Romans.

"The two different designations ("the day of the sun" and the "eighth day") could well epitomize two significant factors which contributed to the change of the Sabbath to Sunday, namely, anti-Judaism and paganism. We might say that while the prevailing aversion towards Judaism in general and towards the Sabbath in particular caused the repudiation of the Sabbath, the existing veneration for the day of the Sun oriented Christians towards such a day both to evidence their sharp distinction from the Jews and to facilitate the acceptance of the Christian faith by the pagans."[20]

New Testament Christians observed the *death* but *not* the resurrection of Christ (1 Corinthians 11: 26). The resurrection was not observed on a Sunday, or indeed on any other day of the week.

It is unlikely that Sunday observance in any form was practised by the Jewish Christians of Palestine prior to the Barkokeba revolt of A.D. 135. Many Christians in Asia Minor and other eastern regions followed the example of the Jewish church members.

The Church of God people who arrived in England after fleeing as refugees from the persecution in Continental Europe could hardly have experienced a quiet or easy life in their new country.

Although the papacy had obtained political power and great authority in Europe, by this time a reverse situation prevailed in England. No longer protected by the Roman legions, after their withdrawal in A.D. 410, the land became a prey to merciless invaders: Angles (who gave their name to England), Saxons and Jutes.

They swept through the island like a forest fire, burning churches (mainly Catholic by this period), cities and towns. Altars were smashed and the shattered bodies of the worshippers left to become food for birds and wild animals.

Bede records the depressing events that had occurred by about A.D. 450: "Public as well as private structures were overturned; the priests were everywhere slain before the altars; the prelates and the people, without any respect of persons, were destroyed by fire and sword; nor was there any to bury those who had been thus cruelly slaughtered. Some of the miserable remainder, being taken in the mountains, were butchered in heaps."[21]

In the following century civil war among the Britons increased the misery of the population. According to Gildas even the legendary King Arthur was considered by many of his own countrymen to be a rebel and tyrant.

Celtic Christianity Survives

The western extremities of Britain, along with Wales, Ireland and Scotland enjoyed a greater measure of stability and peace however, and in these regions the pre-Catholic Christianity that had survived from Roman times continued to flourish.

The Celtic church of this period often termed itself "the Church of God." How many of its members were really converted Christians, however, is difficult to determine. In some respects this group was similar to "the church in the wilderness" described by Stephen in Acts 7:38. As we have seen in an earlier chapter the Celtic peoples were the descendants of those Israelites in the wilderness, having migrated westwards after their Assyrian captivity and then settled in Britain and other parts of Europe.

In areas of Britain where the Celtic church was able to exert political influence, the laws and statutes contained in the first five books of the Bible—the "book of the law"—formed the basis of civil law as had been the case in ancient Israel. Even as late as the time of King Alfred, English law was heavily influenced by a wide range of legal precepts taken directly from the Old Testament. No other system of law so completely adopted the principles of the Mosaic Law.

The Bible formed the basis of doctrine and lifestyle for the Celtic Christian. Great stress was placed on obedience to the Law of God.

"The Scriptures were supreme. Literally interpreted, rigidly obeyed, biblical regulations lay at the foundation of Celtic Christian belief and life."[22]

"But while the Celtic theologian was keenly interested in the whole of the scriptures, his preoccupation with the Ten Commandments was even deeper."[23]

The seventh-day Sabbath was observed by Celtic Christians. They began their Sabbath at sunset each Friday. "The Sabbath was held to be a day of blessing in Wales as well as in Ireland and other Celtic lands."[24]

Sin was defined as the transgression of God's Law. "Adamnan invariably employed the original biblical name, Sabbath, for the seventh day of the week, and spoke of it in a manner betokening a respect which is not detected in writers two centuries later."[25]

The Passover was observed on the 14th day of the first month (Nisan). Bede records that some Christians in Scotland continued this practice until the seventh century A.D.[26]

The foot-washing ceremony instituted by Christ (John 13:4–12), was also carried out. Some sources indicate that the Celtic Christians observed Pentecost and perhaps some of the other Hebrew feast days.

Repentant adults were baptized by immersion for the remission of their sins and any practice or belief found to be at variance with the Scriptures was rejected.

The Celts believed in a literal interpretation of the Genesis account of the creation of man and the universe. Free moral agency was stressed, salvation could not be forced on anyone. Obedience of the Ten Commandments was a vital requirement for one wishing to obtain salvation, but even so, the Celtic Christian did not believe in salvation by works. Salvation was granted by the grace of God through faith.

Prayer and Bible study were considered to be of great importance. Sincere prayer was advocated as vain repetition was not acceptable.

There was no invocation of saints, angels or martyrs in the early Celtic Church. It was believed that Satan along with one third of the angels had rebelled against God and had been cast down to the earth; following this event Satan's main objective was to influence human minds.

Several of the most well-known ministers of this period were Sabbath-keepers.

"There is strong incidental evidence that Columba, the leading minister of his time among the Culdees, was an observer of the ancient Sabbath of the Bible." His dying words as preserved by Gilfillan are as follows: "Today is Saturday, the day which the Holy Scriptures call the Sabbath, or rest. And it will be truly my day of rest, for it shall be the last of my laborious life."[27]

Even Patrick, "the apostle of Ireland," is believed by several authorities to have kept the Sabbath.

"In the *Senchus Mor*, ancient Irish laws believed to have been framed with the help of Patrick... These Christianized Brehon laws required that 'every seventh day of the year' should be devoted to the service of God. This code also mentions the payment of tithes and offerings."[28]

"The early life of Patrick by Muirchu has two stories indicating Patrick's attitude towards the seventh day. These traditions had persisted for more than two centuries after the saint's death."[29]

Muirchu records that Patrick met with another minister on every seventh day of the week for worship and spiritual contact.

"Almost five centuries later, when the movement to Sabbatize Sunday was underway, in accounts of Patrick's activities several comminatory anecdotes for Sunday observance are fathered on the saint. Patrick's journeys were occasionally terminated in the records by the phrase 'and he rested there on Sunday.' Then stories were introduced into his activities as propaganda for stricter Sunday observance."[30]

A few decades after Patrick's death we find that the Sabbath and Sunday were both being observed in Wales. This is mentioned in *The Book of David*, dating to A.D. 500–525.

Beliefs of Patrick

Patrick's understanding of the role of the Holy Spirit in a Christian's life is interesting. Its task was to "inspire belief, in man, which in turn would lead to salvation.... inducing men to obey the divine laws, and enabling them to become sons of God and joint heirs with Christ."[31]

The concept of the Holy Spirit as a "third person" of a trinity seems to have been quite foreign to the real Patrick of authentic history. His own writings and biographies written about him shortly after his death, reveal a clear understanding of the nature of Christ and of man's ultimate destiny.

Christ, it was said, had always existed with the Father. He returned to His former glory when He ascended to heaven. His death brought about the atonement between God and man. Christ was the *only* mediator between God and man; Patrick makes no mention of angels, saints or priests having this role. The Holy Spirit, Patrick noted, was the agency through which God revealed truth to man; it also brought about a change (conversion) in the human mind.

Patrick believed that man's ultimate destiny was to join the family of God and inherit eternal life. He did not believe in an immortal soul but that the converted Christian would be resurrected at the second coming of Christ, and would reign with Christ on the earth.

Columba, Patrick, and others of their generation believed themselves to be living in the final decades before Christ's coming and that their duty was to preach the Gospel as a witness (Matthew 24:14). As Patrick died only four years before the fall of Rome in A.D. 476, which to many represented the "end of the world," his error on this point is understandable.

A number of spurious documents, attributed to Patrick, were circulated during the centuries that followed his death. These writings abound in superstition and the miraculous. The *Epistle* and *Confessions*, however, are of an entirely different nature and probably represent the only authentic writings of Patrick still extant. He states in his *Confessions* that his mission was "from God." There is no mention of any commission from the Pope, nor any reference to church councils or tradition. His only source of doctrine is Scripture.

The early life of Patrick was traumatic. Living in a now unlocated Roman coastal town, perhaps situated somewhere along the Bristol Channel coast, he was captured by pirates at about the age of 16 years. Taken by them to Ireland, he spent six years in a state of slavery.

During this time he claims to have found "the living God." In a dream he saw the Irish calling to him, which he took as a sign that God wanted him to preach in Ireland.

The Catholic Church in Britain seems to have opposed his career at all stages. The early Irish church was independent from Rome. This is a clear historical fact. It was not until about A.D. 700, more than 200 years after Patrick's death, that Ireland became reconciled to Rome.

"O'Halleron's *History of Ireland*, p. 172, reports that the Irish church 'adhered more closely to the Jewish customs than did the Roman Catholics. St. Patrick never was connected with Rome, and was a Sabbath-keeper, according to Seventh Day Baptists. And St. Columba's establishment of a Sabbath-keeping community on the island of Iona was the result of St. Patrick's teaching'... some Irish Sabbath-keepers remained until the nineteenth century."[32]

Celtic Colleges

References to "monasteries" within the context of the early Celtic church are regrettable; these communities bore very little resemblance to the great celibate institutions that dominated Europe during the Middle Ages.

The earliest Celtic monasteries could perhaps have been more accurately called colleges. They were modeled on the Old Testament cities of refuge, and were communities where Christian men, women and children, living in family groups along with single people, were able to avoid overly close social contact with their pagan neighbours, and enjoy Christian fellowship.

The Bible was studied, copied out by hand (this was prior to the invention of printing), and perhaps in some cases even translated into other languages. In time these institutions became centres of education and culture; they provided an environment in which musical, and other skills, could be developed.

"Monasticism in the Celtic Churches was mainly for the purpose of copying and disseminating the Sacred Scriptures, and was singularly free from the vain acts of physical mortification typical of Latin Christianity."[33]

In process of time, however, Latin or Catholic views began to influence and eventually dominate these institutions. The celibate lifestyle was accepted and a gradual segregation of the sexes developed.

Women had a restricted role as "spiritual wives," which meant that they were employed in cleaning, cooking and other domestic functions; the monks were clearly informed however, that they "are not for any other purpose."[34]

Records that have survived from this period tend to imply that the relationship between monks and "spiritual wives" (which meant that they were employed in cleaning, cooking and other domestic functions), was often of a sexual rather than spiritual nature. Increasingly severe rules were introduced by the authorities to limit the contact between men and women, and to keep this to a minimum.

Moral standards had declined so much by the sixth century that one rule had to be introduced that "If anyone from drunkenness cannot sing though being unable to speak, he is to lose his supper."[35]

When Augustine arrived in A.D. 596 to convert the English to the Catholic faith, he found that many were still observing the Sabbath.

"Augustine reports in his biography that he found the people of Britain in 'grievous and intolerable heresies,' because they were 'being given to Judaizing, but ignorant of the holy sacraments and festivals of the church."[36]

Scottish Christians, too, continued to keep the Sabbath, until well into the Middle Ages.

"Scottish Queen Margaret (Saint Margaret) in her attempt to harmonize the Scottish church with the rest of Europe, had to contend with those who 'did not reverence the Lord's day, but... held Saturday to be the Sabbath.' Not until 1203 did Scotland submit to Rome and its Sunday."[37]

"Welsh Sabbath-keepers were prevalent until 1115, when the first Roman Bishop was seated at St. David's."[38]

In England, Catholic doctrine and authority spread rapidly. At the Council of Whitby (A.D. 664) the English churches agreed, with some reluctance, to abandon their earlier doctrines, including the observance of the Passover on the 14th day of Nisan, and to adopt the rites and practices of the church of Rome.

Rome Takes Over the British Churches

Theodore of Tarsus was a successful advocate of the Roman church in Britain. During his day increasing prominence was given to Sunday observance, to the exclusion of the Sabbath. He drew up seven Canons dealing with Sunday observance. Considerable debate continued for some time between advocates of the Sabbath and those who supported Sunday. Some wished to keep both days.

In one sermon of the period it was even suggested that the word "Sabbath" in Exodus 20:8–11 should be changed to read "Lord's day."

The first English Sunday Legislation was introduced in A.D. 692: "Ina, king of the West Saxons, by the advice of Cenred his father, and Heddes and Erkenwald his bishops, with all his aldermen and sages, in a great assembly of the servants of God, for the health of their souls, and the common preservation of the kingdom, made several constitutions, of which this was the third: 'If a servant do any work on Sunday by his master's order, he shall be free, and the master pay thirty shillings; but if he went to work on his own head, he shall be either beaten with stripes, or ransom himself with a price. A freeman, if he works on this day, shall lose his freedom or pay thirty shillings; if he be a priest, double.'"[39]

The Romanizing of the Celtic church continued rapidly during the period A.D. 700–900. In A.D. 886 a spurious *Epistle of Christ* was brought to Ireland from Rome which stated that "Whoever shall not keep Sunday... his soul shall not enter heaven." The "Cain Domnaig," which was Ireland's first Sunday law, was introduced at about the same time.

Even during this period of the Dark Ages, however, the light of God's true Church was not entirely extinguished. "The despotism of Antichrist was then [A.D. 786] so far from being universal, that it was not owned throughout Italy itself. In some parts of that country, as well as in England and France, the purity of Christian worship was still maintained."[40]

Little is known of the activities of the Church of God in Britain during this period; indeed, the numbers could well have dwindled to the point where the "light" of God's people was about to flicker out.

Chapter Summary

The Dark Ages, which lasted some 500 years from the end of the Roman empire, was a difficult time for the people of God. Catholic domination of Europe during this period made it all but impossible to preach the true gospel. Only a small number had the courage and determination to hold fast to the truth of God at this time.

Chapter Eight

THE CHURCH IN THE WILDERNESS

"The Waldenses... abandoned their beautiful country; and fled, like the woman mentioned in the Apocalypse, to these wild mountains, where they have, to this day, handed down the Gospel, from father to son, in the same purity and simplicity as it was preached by St. Paul"
(D.H. Macmillan, *"The True Ecclesia,"* p. 23).

"Then the woman fled into the wilderness, where she has a place prepared by God..."
(Revelation 12:6).

During the long dark night of the Middle Ages, God's true Church, as prophesied, "fled into the wilderness, where she hath a place prepared of God..." (Revelation 12:6). For 1,260 years the Church of God was driven by the persecuting power of the "Holy Roman Empire" into the remote mountains and valleys of Europe, there to preserve the purity of the true faith.

A variety of names were applied to God's people during this period; "Paulicians," "Publicans," "Puritans," "Waldenses," "Vaudois" (meaning "Valley Dwellers"), "Henricians," "Bogomils" ("Friends of God") and several others. Names such as these, however, were generally used by those outside of the Church. In their own writings church members normally employed the title "Church of God."

Church historians have been able to demonstrate that regardless of the differing names used, "These branches, however, sprang from one common stock, and were animated by the same religious and moral principles."[1]

"Indeed, from the borders of Spain, throughout the greatest part of the south of France, among and below the Alps, along the Rhine, and even to Bohemia, thousands of the disciples of Christ, as will hereafter be shown, were found, even in the very worst of times, preserving the faith in its purity, adhering to the simplicity of Christian worship, patiently bearing the cross after Christ, men distinguished by their fear of God and obedience to His will, and persecuted only for righteousness' sake."[2]

Seventh-Century Leaders and Beliefs

As the earlier "Smyrna" (Revelation 2:8–11) era of the true Church had been classified by the world as "Ebionites," so the members of the "Pergamos" (Revelation 2:12–17) era came to be known as "Paulicians" ("the followers of the Apostle Paul").

This group of Christians became very numerous during the seventh century and were distinguished by their zeal, knowledge and the simplicity of their lives.

About A.D. 650 a well-educated man named Constantine of Mananali began to study portions of the Bible that he had received as a gift. Amazed by the truth which he found revealed he began preaching in the regions of Cappadocia and Armenia. Several evangelists were trained to assist him in the ministry and soon tens of thousands were being converted to the truth.

This Constantine plainly taught that the Pope was not the representative of God, and perhaps because of this and other reasons, he was martyred in A.D. 684.

Simeon, an officer sent by the Emperor at Constantinople to destroy Constantine and other church leaders, was so impressed by the faith and courage displayed by Constantine and several of the other martyrs, that he became convinced that these were truly God's people. Three years later, his service to the Emperor completed, he returned to the area and was placed by Christ into the office of an apostle, vacated by the death of Constantine. Following a three-year ministry Simeon was burned at the stake.

A third great leader, Sergius, was later raised up by God to lead the church.

Paulician doctrines, along with those of other groups, are described in a work entitled *The Key of Truth*, which was translated into English by Fred C. Conybeare. They preached the gospel of the Kingdom of God, baptized believers by immersion, practised the laying on of hands for the reception of the Holy Spirit, and observed the Sabbath, the Passover on the 14th day of Nisan and the Festival of Unleavened Bread.

This era of the Church was not without its problems. A trend towards spiritual and moral decline set in early; many who associated with the Church were not really converted but simply cleaved to the true Christians with flatteries (Daniel 11:34).

148

Others held to the "doctrine of Balaam" (Revelation 2:14), that one could commit spiritual "fornication" and coexist with sin and false doctrine. When these people were permitted to fellowship with local church congregations, the corruption only spread to many more members.

In an attempt to correct His people, Christ allowed severe persecution to afflict them—multitudes perished but few repented.

"During a period of one hundred and fifty years, these Christian churches seem to have been almost incessantly subjected to persecution, which they supported with Christian meekness and patience; and if the acts of their martyrdom, their preaching, and their lives were distinctly recorded, I see no reason to doubt that we should find in them the genuine successors of the Christians of the first two centuries. And in this, as well as former instances the blood of the martyrs was the seed of the church.

"A succession of teachers and churches arose: and a person named Sergius, who had labored among them in the ministry of the gospel thirty-seven years, is acknowledged, even by their vilest calumniators, to have been a most exemplary Christian. The persecution had, however, some intermissions, until at length Theodora , the Greek Empress, exerted herself against them beyond all her predecessors. She sent inquisitors throughout all Asia Minor in search of these sectaries, and is computed to have killed by the gibbet, by fire, and by the sword, a hundred thousand persons."[3]

Paulician leaders including Sergius and Sambat taught that the same Holy Spirit was in them, and other true Christians, that was in Jesus Christ. Their persecutors, seemingly unable to grasp this point, charged that these Paulician teachers called themselves "Christs," as if this were a matter of blasphemy.

The Paulicians claimed that they were the "holy universal and apostolic church" and as such represented a direct continuation of the first-century church established by Jesus Christ. They urged that all Christians, ministers and laymen, should study the Scriptures and that priests who prevented the people from studying were in error and were in fact hiding the truth of God.

Biblical church offices (Ephesians 4:11) were held by Paulician ministers and leaders. Those of highest rank were termed "apostles" and "prophets," others who held office were called "evangelists," pastors" or "teachers." They exercised the power of "binding and loosing" (Matthew 18:17–18). "Elders... rulers" and "readers" are also mentioned. "Teachers" were responsible for hand-copying the Holy Scriptures.

Ministers were expected to be married men, not celibate priests. Ordinations were conducted by the laying on of hands. Apostles were inducted into office by the direct inspiration and selection of Jesus Christ.

The Paulician faith eventually came to dominate large areas of Armenia and Albania but with many this was nothing more than an outward "form" of religion; truly converted members were never numerous. Many reached a state of compromise with the dominant Catholic state religion. They conformed externally but followed Paulician teachings in secret.

In time the alternatives narrowed to apostasy or martyrdom. By the ninth century most had drifted so far from the true doctrines that they were drawn to seek political or military solutions to their persecution problems. Anatolia, one of the earliest Paulician homelands, became a desolation and wilderness ravaged by decades of warfare; thus the "Pergamos" era of the true Church came to its inglorious conclusion.

The Waldenses

The next era of the Church of God—"Thyatira" (Revelation 2:18–29)—began to conduct a work of some significance around A.D. 1000. Although having its headquarters and centre of operations located in the mountains and valleys of northern Italy and southern France, the work rapidly spread through large areas of Europe and even into Britain. The names most commonly applied to these people were "Vaudois," "Waldenses" or "Waldensians."

The Waldenses, says Popliner, "spread not only through France, but also through nearly all the European coasts, and appeared in Gaul, Spain, England, Scotland, Italy, Germany, Bohemia, Saxony, Poland and Lithuania."

Crosby records that: "For in the time of William the Conqueror [A.D. 1070] and his son William Rufus, it appears that the Waldenses and their disciples out of France, Germany and Holland, had their frequent recourse, and did abound in England. The Berlingarian, or

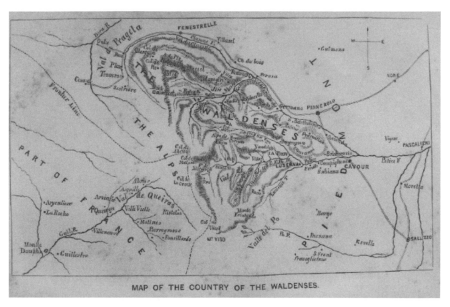

MAP OF THE COUNTRY OF THE WALDENSES.

Map of Waldenses Region

The Waldenses lived in an area of the Alps bordered by northern Italy and southern France. They suffered great persecution from the Inquisition and specifically from the Duke of Savoy.

Waldensian heresy, as the chronologer calls it, had, about A.D. 1080, generally corrupted all France, Italy, and England."[4]

A wide variation of opinion exists concerning the precise origin of the Waldenses. Some have traced their roots back to apostolic times.

"From among many testimonies I quote that of Henry Arnold, who superintended the 'glorious return' of the Waldenses to their valleys in 1689. He says: 'The Vaudois are, in fact, descended from those refugees from Italy: who, after St. Paul had there preached the Gospel, abandoned their beautiful country; and fled, like the woman mentioned in the Apocalypse, to these wild mountains, where they have, to this day, handed down the Gospel, from father to son, in the same purity and simplicity as it was preached by St. Paul.'"[5]

Several authorities, including Reimer, trace them back to the fourth century, but Reinerius Saccho, an inquisitor and implacable enemy, admits that they flourished about A.D. 600.

There seems to be general agreement amongst almost all

non-Catholic writers that the Waldenses represented a continuation of the true Church of God.

Even Oliver Cromwell, the Lord Protector of England, recognised the true status of this group. He employed the diplomatic channels available to him in an attempt to bring an end to the persecution of the Waldenses.

In a letter sent to the Lords of the United Provinces in 1655, Cromwell points out: "But if, on the other hand, he shall continue firmly resolved utterly to destroy and to drive to a state of distraction those men, among whom our religion was either planted by the first preachers of the gospel, and so maintained in its purity from age to age, or else reformed and restored to its primitive purity more early than among many other nations, we hereby declare ourselves ready to advise, in common with you, and the rest of our brethren and allies of the reformed religion, by what means we may most conveniently provide for the preservation and comfort of these distressed people."[6]

The Waldenses possessed a version of the Bible in their own language and stressed obedience to the commandments, including the observance of the seventh-day Sabbath. They also baptized by immersion repentant believers, and kept the Passover or Lord's Supper once a year in the first month.

The lifestyle of these people tended to be simple but industrious. They raised cattle and sheep and had considerable success in the cultivation of olives, figs and grapes. Visitors to their pleasant and well kept villages and hamlets noted the happiness of the people and merry voices of the children at play.

Waldensian doctrines were based on "the doctrine contained in the Old and New Testaments and comprehended in the Apostles' Creed, and admitted the sacraments instituted by Christ, and the Ten Commandments... They said they had received this doctrine from their ancestors, and that if they were in any error they were ready to receive instruction from the Word of God."[7]

High moral standards were a part of the Waldenses' way of life and like a bright light shining in a dark place these people set a fine example to all who came into contact with them.

"Claudius Seisselius, archbishop of Turin, is pleased to say, that 'their heresy excepted, they generally live a purer life than other

Christians. They never swear but by compulsion, they fulfill their promises with punctuality; and living for the most part in poverty, they profess to live the apostolic life and doctrine.

"'They also profess it to be their desire to overcome only by the simplicity of faith, by purity of conscience, and integrity of life; not by philosophical niceties and theological subtleties.' And he very candidly admits that 'in their lives and morals they were perfect, irreprehensible, and without reproach among men, addicting themselves with all their might to observe the commands of God.'"[8]

Peter of Bruys and Henry

The Paulician and Bogomil evangelization of the Alpine region led to a fruitful harvest of conversions; so much so, in fact, that the Pope in 1096 described the Valley Louise in Dauphiny, France, as being infested with "heresy."

It was in this region, at Embrun, that Peter of Bruys, about 1104, began to preach a message of repentance from sin. This work spread throughout Languedoc and Provence. Peter rejected infant baptism; only persons old and mature enough to understand the importance of the step that they were taking were baptized, and that only after real repentance.

The Catholic teaching that the priest in the Mass was able to produce the literal flesh of Christ was also rejected, along with purgatory, prayers for the dead, reverence for crosses, and several other Catholic precepts.

Peter's preaching, which lasted for "nearly twenty years," was highly successful. Many during this period were led by the Holy Spirit to conversion. The true Gospel of the Kingdom was spread in the south of France.

After Peter was seized and burned at the stake, his disciple, Henry, took over his position as an apostle, and continued the work. They were calumnied by the Catholic church for remaining faithful to the whole law of God, including the observance of the Sabbath.

The historian, Mosheim, adds that they abstained from eating meats which were prohibited under the Mosaic economy, and refused to accept the "Trinity" doctrine. They seemed to have understood that God is a family, which converted Christians may join at the return of Christ.

Peter was martyred by burning at a town called St. Giles in 1126. Henry was burned at Toulouse in 1147; some; sources, however, state that he died in prison in 1149.[9]

"So zealous were the Inquisitors in destroying the writings of Bruis [Peter of Bruys] and Henry, that we scarcely know anything of their tenets save what we can learn from... an Abbot of Clugny."[10]

The "heretical" teachings of Peter and Henry were summarized by the Abbot as follows:

"(1) They rejected infant baptism and held that it was the faith of the individual candidate, which along with baptism saved him. One cannot be saved by the faith of another. (2) Church buildings are not necessary, worship can take place anywhere by those who are close to God. (3) Crucifixes should not be employed as a part of worship. (4) The bread and wine of the Passover or Communion service are only symbolic—they do not change into the literal body and blood of Christ. (5) They denied that any prayers, alms or other sacrifices by the living could assist the dead."[11]

The followers of Peter were said by the Abbot to have gathered up as many crucifixes as they could find on a certain Good Friday and made a large fire of them upon which they roasted some meat and had a good meal. This story seems highly improbable and could have been mere propaganda.

Peter is said to have made the remark that "churches are vainly built, since the Church of God consists, not in a mass of coherent stones, but in the unity of the congregated faithful."[12]

Henry, Peter's disciple, spoke out against chanting and other forms of repetitious prayer.

During the ministry of Peter of Bruys the people of God were nicknamed "Petrobrusians." They later became known as "Henricians" after Henry. The people themselves, however, used the name "Church of God."

Regarding the work carried out by Henry, Monastier records that "his preaching made a powerful impression on his hearers. The people were fascinated."[13]

Two views which were promulgated by Peter and Henry, which almost certainly contributed to the persecution which they suffered, were: "That the priests and monks ought to marry, rather than be the prey of lust, or give themselves to impurity" and "That God is mocked by the chants which the priests and monks repeat in the temples; that God cannot be appeased by monkish melodies."[14]

These ministers could clearly see the need for sincere prayer which was from the heart.

Persecution of the Vaudois "Heresy"

Several of the Vaudois concepts were committed to writing during this period. Examples of their works include *The Noble Lesson* written in 1100, *Treatise on Antichrist* (1120), and *Treatise on Purgatory* (1126).

Shortly after the death of Henry the work spread from France into England.

"From Provence they passed into Languedoc and Gascogne, whence their so-called heresy penetrated into Spain and England."[15]

William of Newbury mentions that about the year 1160, "In the same days, certain vagabonds came into England, of the race (it is believed) of those whom they commonly denominate Publicans." Other sources classify these people as Waldenses or "Thirteen Valdensian families."

"These formerly emigrated from Gascony" and "they seemed to be multiplied beyond the sand of the sea." They were accused of "seducing the simple under a pretended display of piety."

"At that time [during the reign of Henry II], however, somewhat more than thirty individuals, as well men as women, dissembling their error, entered here, as it were peacefully, for the sake of propagating their pestilence; a certain Gerard being their leader."[16]

They seemed to have spread their doctrine in England for only a short time before being arrested, and put into prison. The king directed that they be tried by a council of bishops at Oxford. At their trial they claimed to be Christians, following the doctrines of the apostles and rejected several points of Catholic belief.

The group was sentenced to be branded on the foreheads, whipped and driven from the city. After receiving this punishment they were "ejected from the city, through the intolerance of the cold (for the season was winter) no one showing to them even the slightest degree of mercy, they miserably perished."[17]

Another authority on this era (*Authentic Details of the Valdenses*, written in 1827) mentions that others were burned at the stake, also at Oxford.

Bale in his *Old Chronicle of London* records "one burnt to death tainted with the faith of the Valdenses" in the year 1210. Some, fleeing from persecution in various parts of Europe, reached England to face what must have been an uncertain future.

A treatise dating to about 1160 speaks of "many well disposed persons devoting themselves to the preaching of the Gospel, notwithstanding the persecution which had been set on foot against the members of Christ."[18]

Peter Waldo's Ministry

This period marks the beginning of one of the most important phases of God's work during this era. The later works of this "Thyatira" Church were "to be more than the first" (Revelation 2:19).

It was at about this point in history that Peter Waldo, perhaps the most important leader in this Church era, began to preach. A successful and wealthy merchant of Lyons, France, Waldo was shocked by the sudden death of one of his friends. This traumatic experience prompted the question, "If I had died what would have become of my soul?"

Being a Catholic, Waldo asked a theologian, "What is the perfect way?" The reply, quoted from Scripture, was, "If thou wilt be perfect, go, sell that thou hast and give to the poor, and thou shalt have treasure in heaven; and come take up thy cross and follow me."

Waldo gave his wealth to the poor, but also used a part of it to produce a translation of the Scriptures. In his personal study, he was struck by Christ's command to the apostles to preach the gospel of the Kingdom of God. Bringing an intelligent and orderly mind to the study of God's word, Waldo's understanding of the truth increased rapidly.

After a time Waldo began to preach and share his newly discovered truths with others. A group of helpers or "co-workers" began to assist in this work as the "Poor Men of Lyons." The education and business expertise that Peter Waldo brought to the work of God was soon to lead to significant and steady growth.

The bold and determined stand that Waldo took, based on teachings which he found revealed in Scripture, was to lead to major personal problems within his own family. His Catholic wife and two daughters supposed that he had lost his mind, and as a result of this

Petrus Waldus. Vom Lutherdenkmal in Worms.

Peter Waldo (died 1218)

Waldo was a wealthy merchant who gave all of his possessions away in 1170. He became acquainted with the Waldenses who kept the seventh-day Sabbath. Waldo translated the Bible into the language of the Waldenses.

they separated themselves from him; one of his daughters entered a convent. There are some indications, however, that his wife later became reconciled to him and provided financial assistance from the money which he had given to her.

Little is known of the early stages of Waldo's ministry, but he is known to have gone, along with a group of his followers to Picardy, in northern France. After suffering persecution in that area they moved into Flanders and the Netherlands. By 1182 many converts from those regions had joined their cause. Everywhere they went, the Waldenses took their translation of the Bible with them.

In about 1176 the archbishop of Lyons forbade Waldo and his followers to preach. "We must obey God rather than man" was the reply which they gave, and when they persisted in spreading their message they were ordered to appear before Pope Alexander III.

Peter Waldo went boldly to Rome in 1178 where he urged that the Provencal translation of the Bible, which could be understood by the people of southern France, and by those in parts of Spain and Italy, be made available to the people. A decision on the matter was left to the Lateran Council, which in 1179 stated that Waldo and his followers could only preach at the invitation of local priests.

The response to this decision was that Christ had sent them to preach and that this was what they would continue to do. Several years of persecution were to follow, during which period they were eventually driven from Lyons. A group of Waldenses became established in Italy.

The courage displayed by Waldo in defending the true doctrine is further described by Townsend.

"About 1160, the doctrine of transubstantiation was required by the court of Rome to be acknowledged by all men. This led to idolatry. Men fell down before the consecrated host and worshiped it as God. The impiety of this abomination shocked the minds of all men who were not dead to a sense of true religion. The mind of Peter Waldo was aroused to oppose the abomination, and to strive for a reformation. A fear of God, in union with an alarming sense of the wickedness of the times, led him to conduct with courage in opposing the dangerous corruption's of the hierarchy.

"As Waldo grew more acquainted with the Scriptures, he saw that the general practice of nominal Christians was totally abhorrent from the doctrines of the New Testament: and in particular, that a number of customs, which all the world regarded with reverence, had not only no foundation in the divine oracles, but were even condemned by them. Influenced with equal zeal and charity, he boldly condemned the reigning vices, and the arrogance of the Pope. He did more: as he advanced in the knowledge of the true faith and love of Christ, he taught his neighbours the principles of practical godliness, and encouraged them to seek salvation by Jesus Christ.

"John de Bekos Mayons, archbishop of Lyons, a distinguished member of the corrupt system, forbade the new reformer to teach anymore, on pain of excommunication, and of being proceeded against as an heretic."

Although Waldo continued to preach, God it seems took steps to protect His courageous servant.

"All things operated so strongly in his favor, that he lived concealed at Lyons three years.

"Waldo fled from Lyons, and his disciples followed him. By this dispersion, the doctrine of Waldo was widely disseminated throughout Europe .... Persecuted from place to place, he retired into Picardy. Success attended his labors; and the doctrines which he preached appear to have so harmonized with those of the Vaudois, that they and his people were henceforth considered as the same."

Phillip Augustus, a prince of France, attacked the Waldenses and destroyed much of their property. He drove many of them into Flanders.

"Not content with this, he pursued them thither, and caused many of them to be burned. It appears that, at this time, Waldo fled into Germany, and at last settled in Bohemia, where he ended his-days about the year 1179. He appears to have been one of whom the world was not worthy, and to have turned many unto righteousness. The word of God then grew and multiplied."[19]

The Waldensian Work

A school or college was established for the training of qualified ministers and other labourers in the expanding work of God. It consisted of three small stone buildings and was located in the Angrogna Valley of the Cottian Alps. The college and town of La Torre became the new headquarters of the Church of God. Articles and small booklets were written and copied by hand and provided free of charge to those who were interested in them.

Tithes and offerings from many countries were used to finance the operating costs of the college and, as the work spread, translations of the Bible were produced in various languages.

Entrance to La Torre

An etching copied from Israel of the Alps (1852) showing the entrance to La Torre, a Waldensian town in the Alps of northern Italy. It was here that these faithful followers of Christ built a college for training their ministry. They were sent out "two by two" with the younger man learning from the experienced.

"Their pastors were named barba, the Vaudois term for uncle. It was in the almost inaccessible solitude of the Pra-del-Tor, a deep gorge... that their school was situated."

"There they learned by heart the gospels of St. Matthew and St. John, the catholic epistles, and a portion of those of St. Paul. They were instructed, further, in Latin, Romane [old French] and Italian. After this they passed several years in retirement, and they were then consecrated ministers by the administration of the sacrament and imposition of hands."[20]

Ministers were mature and well qualified men. Because of long evangelistic journeys and the extreme personal danger that such trips sometimes produced, few of these men married; this was based on practical rather than religious grounds. They condemned priestly celibacy for scriptural reasons (1 Timothy 4:1–3).

Biblical offices were restored for the ministry. Evangelists, pastors, elders and deacons were ordained. Peter Waldo, according to his fruits, was an apostle but called himself "chief elder."

"They were supported by the voluntary contributions of the people, distributed among them annually in a general synod. A third of these contributions was given to the ministers, a third to the poor, and a third was reserved for the missionaries of the church."

"These missionaries traveled in pairs, a young man and an old man. They traversed all Italy, where they had fixed stations at different points, and in almost all the towns adherents.

"The younger men thus became initiated in the delicate duties of evangelization, each being under the experienced conduct of an elder whom discipline established as his superior, and whom he obeyed in all things, alike from duty and from deference. The old man, on his part, thus prepared himself for his repose, by forming for the church successors worthy of it and himself."[21]

They visited the sick and sang hymns and believed in "free salvation by Jesus Christ—and above all, faith working by charity."

"They recommended fasting, whereby men humble themselves; but fasting without charity is as a lamp without oil: it smokes, but shines not. Prayer is, with them, inherent in love; patience is the support; gentleness, resignation, charity, the seal of a Christian."

"They deny that the Christian should ever take an oath."[22]

Ministers were encouraged to learn a trade in order to be able, if necessary, to earn their own living. Many received special training in the laws of physical health and dietary matters.

A system of elementary schools was established for children. Even young children learned to memorize and recite entire chapters of Scripture.

Waldenses observed not only the weekly Sabbath and Passover, but also assembled once a year in September or October for a conference or synod. Some believe that this was in fact the biblical "Feast of Tabernacles."

Special ministerial conferences were also held from time to time. On one occasion 143 pastors met together—they came from several different countries.

"They also had extraordinary meetings by deputies from all parts of Europe, where Vaudois churches existed."[23]

The first Waldenses prohibited participation in wars and even avoided taking military action in self-defense, they also refused to take oaths of any kind. Later generations of Waldenses, however, began to reject these views.

They "instructed their children in the articles of the Christian faith and the commandments of God."[24]

"In like manner, also, their women are modest, avoiding backbiting, foolish jesting, and levity of speech, especially abstaining from lies or swearing, not so much as making use of the common asseveration, 'in truth,' 'for certain,' or the like, because they regard these as oaths, contenting themselves with simply answering 'yes' or 'no.'"[25]

Some 80,000 Waldenses were said to have lived in the Austrian Empire during the fourteenth century.

The Lollards

In 1315 Walter the Lollard, a leading Waldensian minister, along with his brother, Raymond, carried the true Gospel into England. His work seemed to have been highly successful as it was said that he spread the Waldensian doctrine all over England.

This zealous leader in God's work also preached in other parts of Europe. "It is known that the celebrated Lollard who laboured with such zeal to diffuse the Vaudois doctrines in England, was not only a native of our valleys [Alpine valleys of northern Italy], but preached in them for a length of time with great success."[26]

The name "Lollard" came from the Flemish word "Lollen" or "Lullen," meaning to mumble or speak softly. Waldenses were thought to mumble to themselves, or at least this was the impression gained by outsiders as a result of the habit which they practised of memorizing and repeating to themselves, or others, passages from the Scriptures.

Walter Lollard was seized and burned at Cologne, Germany, in 1322. His death, according to one authority, was "highly detrimental" to the cause of his followers, but in England the movement seems to have prospered.

Later, during the second half of the fourteenth century, the name "Lollard" was also applied to the followers of John Wycliffe, the eminent Oxford theologian and Bible translator. Because of this confusion, the later history of the original Lollards becomes somewhat obscure.

A large number of sympathizers joined themselves to the Lollard cause, but it would appear that the objective of most of these people was to introduce reforms into the Catholic church, rather than to come to personal repentance and to assist in the preaching of the true Gospel.

In 1401 a law was introduced which forbade the teaching of "new doctrines" by the Lollards. Faced with fines, imprisonment or the ultimate penalty of being burned to death, many recanted and made their peace with the Catholic church. The true Lollards remained faithful to the Church of God, however, and several were hunted down and martyred.

As late as 1494 a group of 30 people known as "the Lollards of Kyle" were tried for "heresy" in Scotland; happily, they escaped execution.

The "Thyatira" era of the Church had major internal problems relating to compromise with false doctrine (Revelation 2:20). In the Waldenses' ancient *Book of Antichrist* we read that the "Jezebel" of Bible prophecy was equated with the Roman papacy.

The Roman church during the Middle Ages used various means, including the threat of persecution, to induce the Waldenses to participate in Sunday services and the Catholic mass. Many allowed themselves to compromise and commit spiritual "fornication," some even allowed Catholic priests to "baptize" their infant children.

Apostasy and Persecution

Generations of coexistence with sin led the Thyatira Church to gradually depart from its doctrines. By 1380 many members no longer had the faith to rely on God for protection and began to use military force to resist their persecutors. This was in spite of the fact that God, on several occasions, had caused a wall of dense fog to separate the Waldenses from their enemies.

The probable justification for using military action against their enemies, rather than to follow Christ's instructions to flee from persecution, was that the ancient Israelites had used military might, along with God's assistance to defeat their enemies, and as the Waldenses looked upon themselves as "Israel of the Alps," why should not they do likewise?

Most, by the fifteenth century, had forgotten that the Church of God is a holy and spiritual nation, using spiritual rather than carnal weapons (1 Peter 2:9). Although the first Waldenses had obeyed the command of Christ to "swear not at all" (Matthew 5:34–37), by the time of the Synod of Angrogna in 1532 they had departed so far from their earlier true doctrines that they now held "that a Christian may swear by the name of God."

The Sabbath seems to have been rejected by the Waldenses at about this date, or perhaps even earlier. One of the 17 articles of their faith written in 1532 states "that on Sundays we ought to cease from our earthly labours."[27]

At the Synod of Angrogna the Waldenses declared their solidarity with the Swiss Calvinists and the Protestant Reformation. From this time they copied more and more of the ways of the Protestant churches.

The later history of the Waldensian movement is dominated by persecution. This period must be ranked as one of the blackest episodes in the entire history of man's inhumanity to his fellow human beings. God appears to have permitted the mass slaughter of multitudes of these people, perhaps in order to induce them, by means of these severe trials, to repent and return to their former true doctrines and godly way of life.

As the centuries of persecution progressed to a grisly climax, entire villages and communities of these unfortunate people were butchered until it was said that the valleys ran red with the blood of men, women and children.

"Children, cruelly torn from their mother's breast, were seized by the feet, and dashed and crushed against the rocks or walls... their bodies were cast away on common heaps.

"The valleys resounded with such mournful echoes of the lamentable cries of the wretched victims, and the shrieks wrung from them in their agonies, that you might have imagined the rocks were moved with compassion, while the barbarous perpetrators of these atrocious cruelties remained absolutely insensible."[28]

On one occasion fires were lit at the mouth of a cavern where a group of Vaudois were hiding.

"When the cavern was afterwards examined there were found in it four hundred infants suffocated in their cradles, or in the arms of their dead mothers. Altogether there perished in this cavern more than 3,000 Vaudois...."[29]

One young man was tied to an olive tree and used as target practice by the soldiers, until the fifth bullet terminated his sufferings.

"Daniel Revelli had his mouth filled with gunpowder, which, being lighted, blew his head to pieces.

"Another martyr, Mazzone, was stripped naked, his body shredded with iron whips, and the mangled frame then beaten to death with lighted brands."[30]

Many villages were burned to the ground. In one such incident, "Some women having been surprised in the church, they were stripped naked, subjected to indescribable outrages, and then compelled to hold each other by the hand, as in a dance, were urged, at the pike's point, up the castlerock, whence, already severely wounded and suffering, they were precipitated, one after the other into the abyss beneath."[31]

Men were sometimes sold to ship owners as galley slaves and women and girls who survived the horrors of those days often were sold to the highest bidder.

"I speak not of the young women and girls who were seized and taken into these dens of iniquity; the atrocious outrages to which they were subjected may not be described."[32]

Some women, unable to contemplate an obscene and violent death, or survival under such unthinkable conditions, took their own lives.

Houses were burnt and goods plundered, thousands were forced to flee into the mountains where many perished of cold and hunger.

"So monstrous were the cruelties with which the extermination was accompanied, that several even of the officers who had been appointed to "execute it were struck with horror, and resigned their commands, rather than fulfill their orders."[33]

When the persecutions ended in 1686, a French officer observed that "All the valleys are wasted, all the inhabitants killed, hanged or massacred."[34]

As we read of this very sobering aspect of church history, it is good to remember that history does indeed repeat itself. A time, yet future is predicted, when the final era of God's Church, the Laodicean era, will also be exposed to the wrath of Satan, and those human instruments that he can influence. Is it not far better to learn the lesson that the Waldenses failed to heed, and to stay close enough to God that we are counted worthy to receive His protection (Revelation 3:7–13)?

Chapter Summary

During the long dark night of the Middle Ages, God's true church, as prophesied, fled into the Wilderness. The alternative was to face arrest and martyrdom. Only a few individuals such as Peter of Bruys and Peter Waldo, had the courage and qualities of leadership to do the Work of God in an age of great spiritual darkness.

Chapter Nine

THE MAN WHO WROTE TO A KING

*"James Ockford was another early advocate in England of the claims of
the seventh day as the Sabbath. He appears to have been well acquainted
with the discussions in which Trask and Brabourne had been engaged"*
(Andrews, *History of the Sabbath*).

"You will be brought before kings and rulers for My name's sake"
(Luke 21:12).

M any of us use the *King James Version* of the Bible, first
published in 1611, for our personal study of God's word.
Have you ever wondered how God's Work was conducted
during this interesting period of history?

In Tudor England, the recently discovered process of printing was
being put to good use. The English translations of the Bible, by men
such as John Wycliffe and William Tyndale, were pouring from the
presses.

For centuries, the Bible had been beyond the reach of all in Britain apart from theologians and scholars. The limited number of
hand-written copies in existence were all in the Latin language. Even
those who wished to study were generally discouraged from doing so,
for fear that they would begin to embrace some form of "heresy."

Stunned by the savage persecution of Protestants by "Bloody
Mary" Tudor (1553–58), the nation under Elizabeth I experienced a
new spirit of toleration. For a time, men could study the newly published Bibles without fear of arrest should they begin to discuss with
others the new points of doctrine that were coming to light.

Sabbath Observance

God began opening the minds of a few to His truth, including the
Sabbath. Thomas Bampfield, a Church of God minister who lived
during the seventeenth century, claimed that there were some who
observed the seventh-day Sabbath during the reign of Edward VI
(1547–53), although some of his critics denied this.

There is little real evidence of any activity by the Church of God in

Tudor England. Only brief references are found, many writers who used the word "Sabbath" could well have been talking of Sunday.

John Stockwood, writing in 1584, mentioned that: "A great diversity of opinion among vulgar people and simple sort, concerning the Sabbath day, and the right use of the same."

Gilfillan pointed out that: "Some maintaining the unchanged and unchangeable obligation of the seventh-day Sabbath."

"At what time the seventh-day Baptists began to form churches in this kingdom does not appear; but probably it was at an early period; and although their churches have never been numerous, yet there have been among them almost for two hundred years past, some very eminent men."[1]

Several Sabbatarian writers of the seventeenth century, including Francis Bampfield and Vavasor Powell, use the term "Church of God" in their writings as the official, and scriptural, name of the true Church. The word "Sabbatarian" was also used from time to time, mainly by outside writers.

During the eighteenth and nineteenth centuries, the term "Seventh Day Baptist" was employed by the great majority of Sabbath-keepers in Britain; the term "Church of God" seems to have been almost entirely abandoned. The Seventh Day Baptists ultimately became a separate denomination, whose doctrines, with the exception of the Sabbath and baptism by immersion, were almost identical to those of other Protestant churches.

Theophilus Brabourne

Theophilus Brabourne, a former Puritan minister from Norfolk, published books in 1628 and 1632 advocating the true Sabbath. He sent a copy of the latter work to King Charles I. Original documents still held by the British Museum Library reveal the amazing facts.

Brabourne made the point to the King that the nation's problems, at least in part, were occasioned by neglect of the fourth commandment. He strongly urged that the King should use his royal powers to change the national day of worship from Sunday to Saturday.

The King, grappling with his own problems of state which were soon to lead to the Civil War, was neither impressed nor amused by Brabourne's arguments. The matter was passed to Francis White, Bishop of Ely, one of the nation's leading scholars and theologians.

John Wycliffe (1320–1384)
John Wycliffe translated the Bible from the Vulgate into vernacular English in
1382. He was incensed by the excesses of the papacy and the corruption of many
priests of the Roman church. His translations led to the King James Bible of 1611.

In 1635 Bishop White published his *A Treatise of the Sabbath Day*
in which he refuted Brabourne's thesis. Under pressure from the
authorities Brabourne later agreed to conform to the teachings of the
established church, stating that his former views had been "a rash
and presumptuous error."

The ironic thing is that Francis White's treatise against the Sabbath probably did more good to God's Church than harm. In this thorough and well written work he traced the history of Sabbath-keeping groups from the earliest times to his own day. Several later writers have used this book in their own works on church history.

White's treatise reveals a little of the concern felt by the authorities of the time over the impact that God's Church was beginning to have on the nation.

"Now because his [Brabourne's] treatise of the Sabbath was dedicated to His Royal Majesty, and the principles on which he grounded all his arguments (being commonly preached, printed and believed, throughout the kingdom) might have poisoned and infected many people, either with Sabbatarian error or some other like quality: it was the King our gracious master, his will and pleasure, that a treatise should be set forth, to prevent further mischief, and to settle his good subjects (who have long time been distracted about Sabbatarian questions) in the old and good way of the ancient and orthodox catholic church."[2]

This incident throws an interesting light on the problems faced by writers during the early days of printing.

Sabbath Preaching

R. Cox in his *Literature of the Sabbath Question* gives the following information about Brabourne: "Brabourne is a much abler writer than Trask, and may be regarded as the founder in England of the sect at first known as Sabbatarians, but now calling themselves Seventh Day Baptists.

"The book is very ill printed, for which he apologises by informing the Christian reader that 'by reason of some troubles raised up against both myself and this my book, I was enforced to absent myself, and there to dispose my work where I could not be present at the press, to peruse, correct, and amend the faults therein.' From the oddities of its spelling, it looks as if printed either by a foreigner unacquainted with English, or at a private press where the stock of some of the vowels was inadequate...."

The book was entitled *A Defence of that most Ancient and Sacred Ordinance of God's, the Sabbath Day*. It was said that "he submitted for the time to the authority of the Church of England, but sometime afterward wrote other books in behalf of the seventh day."[3]

Although the major activity of God's Church seems to have taken part in the London area, others were busy preaching the true doctrines in different parts of the nation.

"About this time Philip Tandy began to promulgate in the northern part of England the same doctrine [as Brabourne] concerning the Sabbath. He was educated in the established church, of which he became a minister. Having changed his views respecting the mode of baptism and the day of the Sabbath, he abandoned that church and 'became a mark for many shots.' He held several public disputes about his peculiar sentiments.

"James Ockford was another early advocate in England of the claims of the seventh day as the Sabbath. He appears to have been well acquainted with the discussions in which Trask and Brabourne had been engaged.

"Being dissatisfied with the pretended conviction of Brabourne, he wrote a book in defense of Sabbatarian views, entitled, *The Doctrine of the Fourth Commandment*. The book, published about the year 1642, was burnt by order of the authorities in the established church."[4]

Chapter Summary

By the seventeenth century, the Protestant Reformation had produced a limited measure of freedom of religion. Theophilus Brabourne, a Sabbath keeper, wrote to King Charles I urging him to use his royal powers to change the national day of worship from Sunday to Saturday. As might have been expected, his request was turned down.

Chapter Ten

THE PERSECUTED CHURCH

*"Mrs Trask lay fifteen or sixteen years a prisoner for her
opinion about the Saturday Sabbath... Her diet for the most part during
her imprisonment... was bread and water, roots and herbs..."*
(Andrews, *History of the Sabbath*).

"Yes, and all who desire to live godly in Christ Jesus will suffer persecution"
(2 Timothy 3:12).

The measure of religious freedom that existed under Queen Elizabeth I was not to last for long. During most of the seventeenth century, up to 1687, freedom of religion was available only to those who followed the precepts of mainstream Protestant theology in the form of the established Church of England.

In that year, James the Second suspended all penal laws against dissent and released those in prison, granting freedom of worship to all. Shortly afterwards, William and Mary passed "The Toleration Act," a measure described as 'An Act exempting their Majesties' Protestant subjects dissenting from the Church of England from the penalties of certain laws.'

Before these freedoms were granted, the Church of God in England had experienced a time of severe trials. It was not without good reason that these people often called themselves the "Poor" Churches of God. Fines for failure to attend the Sunday services of the established church of 20 pounds a month might seem modest in today's society, but such a sum three centuries ago represented the income of the average employee for two years. Failure to pay such fines often led to a prison sentence. In many such instances this was almost as bad as a sentence of death.

Conditions in the prisons of the day were appalling. Food was described as "rubbish," hygiene precautions almost non-existent, and disease rampant.

It was recorded that at the Bridewell Prison in Bristol in 1664, 55 women (probably mainly Quakers) shared five beds. When two of the women died, the cause of death was given simply as "the stench."

The Incredible History of God's True Church

The severity of persecution varied greatly from area to area. Among the Sabbath-keeping churches the indications are that the ministers and leaders were the main targets.

Much depended upon the attitude of local officials and magistrates. If the lay members lived quiet, industrious lives and were respected within their communities, local magistrates often turned a "blind eye" and no action was taken against them.

The Preaching of John Trask

Religion dominated the thoughts of many of the nation's scholars during this period; the literature published at this time is full of religious debate and controversy. The Sabbath in particular was the subject of almost endless discussion. Some understood the academic reasons for keeping the seventh day, but only a few were really willing to obey God in the face of strong opposition.

John Trask, one of the most powerful speakers of his day, began to preach. He understood not only the truth of God's Sabbath but also the facts regarding clean and unclean meats. Four evangelists were ordained around 1616 and many were being brought to real conversion.

The authorities were swift to take action against Trask; public debate over God's law was one thing, but actual obedience was an entirely different matter.

"John Trask began to speak and write in favour of the seventh day as the Sabbath of the Lord, about the time that King James I, and the Archbishop of Canterbury, published the famous *Book of Sports for Sunday*, in 1618. His field of labour was London, and being a very zealous man, he was soon called to account by the persecuting power of the Church of England... He was censured in the Star Chamber to be set upon the pillory at Westminster, and from thence to be whipt to the Fleet [Prison], there to remain a prisoner. This cruel sentence was carried into execution, and finally broke his spirit. After enduring the misery of his prison for one year, he recanted his doctrine."[1]

Trask is said to have founded the Mill Yard Church in London shortly after his arrival in the capital from Salisbury. At least one writer, however, has traced the establishment of this church back to 1580—long before the time of Trask. As the records of this church up to 1673 were destroyed in the fire of 1790, it is impossible to know the facts with any degree of certainty.

There are some indications in the writings of the period that Trask later returned to Sabbath observance, but there is no record of him playing any major part in the church after his release from prison.

Trask's wife was also imprisoned for her faith and spent the remainder of her life behind bars.

Obedience to God during this somewhat grim period of history often cost more than loss of a job and personal liberty, it could also have devastating effects upon family relationships.

Conditions often became so difficult that some were required to sacrifice all hope of a normal marriage and family relationship. Many in this era lacked faith and dedication and were described by Christ as being spiritually dead (Revelation 3:1). He did, however, commend the few who were willing to go all the way in obedience.

"Thou hast a few names even in Sardis which have not defiled their garments; and they shall walk with me in white: for they are worthy" (Revelation 3:4).

"Mrs. Trask lay fifteen or sixteen years a prisoner for her opinion about the Saturday Sabbath; in all which time she would receive no relief from anybody, notwithstanding she wanted much. Her diet for the most part during her imprisonment, that is, till a little before her death, was bread and water, roots and herbs; no flesh, nor wine, nor brewed drink. All her means was an annuity of forty shillings a year; what she lacked more to live upon she had of such prisoners as did employ her sometimes to do business for them."[2]

The Fate of John James

Although most of these persecutions involved fines or imprisonment, at least two of the leaders of God's people at this time suffered direct martyrdom. One of those who gave his life in this manner was John James.

"It was about this time [A.D. 1661], that a congregation of Baptists holding the seventh day as a Sabbath, being assembled at their meeting-house in Bull-Stake Alley, (London) the doors being open, about three o'clock P.M. (Oct. 19), whilst Mr. John James was preaching, one Justice Chard, with Mr. Wood, an headborough, came into the meeting place. Wood commanded him in the King's name to be silent and come down, having spoken treason against the King. But Mr. James, taking little or no notice thereof, proceeded in his work.

"The headborough came nearer to him in the middle of the meeting place and commanded him again in the King's name to come down or else he would pull him down; whereupon the disturbance grew so great that he could not proceed."[3]

John James was arrested and brought to trial, found guilty under the new law against non-conformity. He was sentenced to the barbaric fate of being hung, drawn and quartered.

It was said that "This awful fate did not dismay him in the least. He calmly said 'Blessed be God, whom man condemneth, God justifieth'"!

James was held in high esteem by many and whilst in prison under sentence of death several people of rank and distinction visited him and offered to use their influence to secure his pardon. His wife sent two petitions to the King, but all these moves failed to save him.

In his final words to the court he simply asked them to read the following scriptures: Jeremiah 26:14–15 and Psalm 116:15. In keeping with the gruesome custom of the time, after his execution his heart was taken out and burned, the four quarters of his body fixed to the gates of the city and his head set up on a pole in Whitechapel opposite to the alley in which his meeting-house stood. Such was the horrible price that some were prepared to pay for obedience to the higher laws of God in seventeenth-century England.

Little is known of the organizational structure of the Church during this period. No information has come down to us regarding the numbers attending services. During the time that Sabbath-keeping was illegal it is highly unlikely that any form of written records were kept; a high degree of secrecy must have existed, but even so many members were arrested by the authorities.

Chapter Summary

In time, freedom of religion in Britain was narrowed to only apply to those who followed the teachings of the Church of England. Those who held and preached other doctrines were subjected to large fines, imprisonment and even, in a few cases, execution.

Chapter Eleven

THE AMAZING LIFE OF SHEM ACHER

*"One of them in the name of the rest, in prayer to the LORD, did
by stretching out his hands, as others also of them did, commend
him to the Lord in a special message to the sabbath churches in
Wiltshire, Hampshire, Dorsetshire, Gloucestershire and Berkshire ..."*
(*Autobiography* of Francis Bampfield).

*"You have a few names even in Sardis who have not defiled their
garments; and they shall walk with Me in white, for they are worthy"*
(Revelation 3:4).

Although there were several talented writers among God's
people during the seventeenth century, few of their works
have remained extant. The bulk of such writings were seized
and destroyed by the authorities.

One remarkable document did escape destruction, however. A
single copy of Francis Bampfield's autobiography *The Life of Shem
Acher* has been preserved by the British Museum Library.

In his book, Bampfield draws a parallel between his own calling
and ministry and that of the Apostle Paul. Like Paul, he too was not
called by men into the ministry but by God. He was also an educated
man and talented scholar of Hebrew.

Born in Devonshire in 1614 it was said that he was "designed for
the ministry from his birth." He entered Wadham College, Oxford,
in 1631 and left in 1638 with a degree in the Arts. Shortly after this he
was ordained a deacon in the Church of England by Bishop Hall.

He was later given a position, within that church, in Dorset with a
salary of 100 pounds per year. A zealous and hardworking minister,
he purchased books and Bibles for his congregation out of his own
pocket.

His personal study of the Bible brought him to an understanding
of the truth of God. For a time he was permitted to preach these newly discovered truths to his Dorset congregation; in 1662, however, he
was forced to make a decision—would he obey God or the State?

"But being utterly unsatisfied in his conscience with the 'conditions of conformity (as laid down by the new law),' he took his leave
of his sorrowful and weeping congregation in 1662, and was quickly

after imprisoned for worshipping God in his own family. So soon was his unshaken loyalty to the King forgotten… that he was more frequently imprisoned and exposed to greater hardships for his non-conformity than most other dissenters."

Such was the zeal of this man that during his nine years of imprisonment at Dorchester he raised up a church congregation within the prison and regularly preached to the other prisoners.

He was arrested yet again in 1682 and given a life sentence in Newgate—he died in prison on February 16, 1684. Such was his reputation among God's people that a great company of mourners attended his funeral.

"All that knew him will acknowledge that he was a man of great piety. And he would in all probability have preserved the same character, with respect to his learning and judgment, had it not been for his opinion in two points, viz., that infants ought not to be baptized, and that the Jewish Sabbath ought still to be kept."[1]

Bampfield Anoints The Sick

Bampfield raised up the Pinners Hall Sabbatarian Church in London, probably only one of many—the details of his ministry are far from complete. He mentions the "Church of God" and sometimes the "Churches of Elohim" in his books.

Jesus Christ used this very able minister to reveal to His Church of that day what was to them "new truth." In reality it was old truth about a vital doctrine which, over a period of many years, the Church had neglected and lost sight of.

The practice of anointing the sick (James 5:14) was unknown by the time of Bampfield, and had probably been neglected in Britain for several centuries. One of the major problems of this church era was that being in a spiritually dead or dying condition, several vital points of true doctrine became neglected and over a period of time forgotten, only to come to light years or centuries later as "new truth."

Very much aware of this tendency, Jesus gave the church of this period (Sardis) the clear warning that it should "be watchful, and strengthen the things [important points of doctrinal truth] which remain, that are ready to die" (Revelation 3:2).

It was of vital importance that this era, even if not performing many "works" itself, should preserve certain main points of true doctrine that it had received from the previous (Thyatira) era. There was a need to pass on these truths to the later dynamic Philadelphia church (Revelation 3:7).

As a result of personal study, Bampfield became aware of the truth of this doctrine. He took up the point with other ministers only to find them either apathetic or openly in opposition to his views. He began to waver in his own conviction on the point. Jesus Christ, who was keenly aware of what was taking place within His Church, decided to intervene.

Using the same "still small voice" that He had used when speaking to Elijah (1 Kings 19:12–13), He told Francis Bampfield, who was sick at the time, to go ahead and anoint himself.

Bampfield, in his book, described what happened: "This was brought upon his heart, that the Ordinance of Anointing the sick had not been used: he was convinced of the need and use of this Ordinance, of the standing preceptive and the promising part of it; but, knew not whither to his satisfaction to go, or send for a right Administrator, the Ministers in those parts at that time, either not having Light or Faith therein, and some of them openly opposing it.

"Hereupon a secret voice whispers, that, as a messenger from Christ, he should administer it upon himself, the case being so circumstanced; which accordingly he did, and felt the healing strengthening effect of it quickly."[2]

After this incident he continued to use the method and the knowledge spread to others in Britain and later to the church in America.

Bampfield's Ministry

In this book the author refers to himself and his wife by the names "Shem Acher" and "Gnezri-jah." During this time of persecution the precaution was clearly necessary to obscure personal identities from the authorities.

During his ministry Francis Bampfield, in common with the Apostle Paul, suffered trials and persecutions both from "within and without." So-called "brethren" who probably should have been disfellowshipped years before, continually resisted his work.

Although he believed in the principle of tithing, he often refused to accept the tithes of members in an attempt to counteract false accusations that he "was only in it for the money."

After beginning his ministry in the west of England, he later spent much time in London. In 1674 he observed the Lord's Supper at Bethnal Green and mentions the fact that he conducted a number of baptisms in the Thames near Battersea.

A very lengthy treatise was written on the Sabbath, and after coming to this knowledge he relates that: "Since that, Shem never met with any objection, that could shake or stagger him, but all wrought for his fuller Confirmation and Establishment."

The widespread impact of Bampfield's ministry is indicated in the following passage from his book: "One of them in the name of the rest, in prayer to the LORD, did by stretching out his hands, as others also of them did, commend him unto the Lord in a special message to the Sabbath churches in Wiltshire, Hampshire, Dorsetshire, Gloucestershire and Berkshire, which was undertaken by him, and prospered with desired success, the report whereof at his return, caused joy to all the brethren and sisters in fellowship."

"Eccentric" Servants of God

Francis Bampfield's courtship and marriage must surely be one of the saddest romances on record. His wife came from a prosperous and respected Dorchester family. She began visiting Bampfield and a few others during one of his terms of imprisonment. After his release she began joining him in his preaching tours.

After a time rumours began to circulate that "something was going on" between them and at this point he decided to ask the lady to marry him.

Bampfield describes his wife in the following glowing terms: "Excelling almost all her sex in the whole town of Dorchester for humility, patience, diligence, faithfulness, zeal... having undergone many hardships and difficulties for him, Shem Acher married her."

This unusual situation and the initial reluctance to marry might seem odd to us, but it was very similar to that mentioned in 1 Corinthians 7:26; it was simply not a good time to marry and raise a family.

It is difficult to imagine the kind of married life this couple experienced. Francis Bampfield spent most of his life from 1662 onwards either in prison or "on the run" from the authorities. There was no mention made of any children born to the couple, which was probably just as well.

There can have been few leaders in God's Church with more zeal than Francis Bampfield. Even when detained at Dorchester Prison, his leadership and speaking ability resulted in large crowds of people from the town flocking to the prison to hear him preach. As he was unable to go out and do God's Work, God, it seems, brought "the work" to him.

The prison authorities, embarrassed by this situation, eventually took steps to prevent the local people from coming to the prison.

Damaris Bampfield, who had married Francis at the Mill Yard Church in 1673, survived her husband by less than ten years—she died in 1693.[3]

The world looked upon the Bampfields, not as dedicated servants of God, but as mere eccentrics: "The Bampfields were typical English eccentrics such as this country only can produce."[4]

"Bampfield's Seventh-Day church flickered out in 1863, watched only by a zealous antiquarian."[5]

Chapter Summary

The life and experiences of Francis Bampfield. This zealous and talented minister wrote his autobiography, under the name of Shem Acher, in order to hide his identity from the authorities. He preached the truth of God, including the Sabbath doctrine, for several years but was arrested and ended his life in prison.

(My grateful thanks are extended to the Baptist Union of Great Britain and Ireland for making available the above works on Baptist history.)

Chapter Twelve

SARDIS IN DECLINE

"I have considerations of the great sufferings of the Church of God of old, and the ground of their comfort which is Christ. From Revelation 12, I was much refreshed to consider that the church when she went into the wilderness was by the wings that God gave her"
(Vavasor Powell, *Confessions of Faith*, 1662).

"I know your works, that you have a name that you are alive, but you are dead"
(Revelation 3:1).

Among the people that God was calling during the seventeenth century were several whose lives were filled with great personal accomplishments. Dr. Peter Chamberlen was one such individual. Born in 1601, he was baptized in 1648 and started keeping the Sabbath about three years later. He died in 1683, and was buried at Malden, Essex.

During his long and interesting life he became "'Physician in Ordinary to three Kings and Queens of England... As for his religion he was a Christian keeping the commandments of God and faith of Jesus, being baptized about the year 1648 and keeping the seventh day for the Sabbath above 32 years."[1]

Becoming a Fellow of the College of Physicians in 1628, he was a man of progressive ideas, especially in the field of medical science. Chamberlen advocated reforms in midwifery and other areas of public health and hygiene. In 1818 a secret room was discovered in his house—it contained some of his midwifery forceps.

He suggested that a professional body be set up to care for the needs of London's midwives. The eradication of disease was also a subject which interested him; to this end he urged that a system of public baths be established. Chamberlen also had an inventive mind, he patented a method of writing and printing phonetically. He also traveled extensively in Europe and spoke several European languages.

A Non-Conformist church at Lothbury is believed, under his leadership, to have begun Sabbath observance. In 1653 he became pastor of the "Mill Yard" church.

An educated man and Cambridge graduate, Peter Chamberlen wrote on a variety of subjects, but primarily on religious topics such as the Sabbath and baptism, along with scientific and medical works.

"What shall we say," he wrote, "of those who take away of those ten words [Ten Commandments] or those that make them void and teach men so? Nay, they dare give the lie to, and make Jesus Christ not only a breaker of the law, but the very author of sin in others, also causing them to break them! Hath not the little horn played his part lustily in this, and worn out the saints of the Most High, so that they become little horns also!"[2]

Vavasor Powell

During the period when the English Civil war was raging another faithful servant of God was doing a powerful work in Wales. Vavasor Powell traveled thousands of miles over mountains and through valleys preaching the Word of God by day and night, ultimately dying in prison for his faith.

He wrote a book, during his confinement, relating to his experiences. It bore the curious title *The Chirping of a Bird in a Cage*. This book was addressed to "the Churches of God, and Scattered Saints throughout Wales."

In another of his books, *Confessions of Faith*, published in 1662, he reflects on the sufferings of God's people at that time.

"I have considerations of the great sufferings of the Church of God of old, and the ground of their comfort which is Christ. From Revelation 12, I was much refreshed to consider that the church when she went into the wilderness was by the wings that God gave her."[3]

Ten years later, shortly after Mr. Powell's death, one of his followers wrote of some of his experiences. This work was published in 1672 but the name of the author is not given.

"About the year 1647, the island of Anglesey in North Wales being unreduced, the Parliament forces went to reduce it, and their chief officers sent for me to preach to that brigade of soldiers, and as I marched with them into the place, either the night immediately before or the night before that, it was revealed unto me in my sleep that I should be wounded, and two of my fingers cut (and the very fingers pointed out), which accordingly came to pass; yet when I was in extreme danger between several enemies who fell upon me, receiving that and some other wounds, there being no likelihood of escape, I heard a voice, as I apprehended, speaking audibly to me, 'O Lord, then bring me off'; and immediately God guided my horse (though he was very wild and not well commanded) to go backward out of the barricade that I had entered at, and so I was indeed miraculously preserved.

"One time, coming from preaching, I lost my way, and being out till it was far in the night in a wood or forest, among lakes, briars and thorns, I went up and down until I was quite weary. But by looking up to the Lord, I was presently directed into my way.

"The like experience I had another time, when another preacher and myself had lost our way in a very dark night, and had tired ourselves in searching to and fro to no purpose. At last calling to mind how God had formerly heard in that case where I sought unto Him, we called upon the Lord, who immediately pointed out our way, and it seemed as clear to us as if it had been daylight."

Joseph Davis

Joseph Davis was a wealthy linen merchant and Sabbath-keeper. He suffered greatly for his beliefs. A member of the Mill Yard church, he left this congregation a yearly allowance. His experiences were described in the following manner: "About the time the king entered London, I was illegally seized by the county-troops, and carried a prisoner seven miles from my habitation and calling, to Burford, and there detained two days, being oftentimes tempted to drink the king's health.

"My second imprisonment was after Venner's unlawful insurrection; when the militia of the county Horse and Foot, came on the seventh day in the evening to our town and Mr. Hoard, one of the captains of the county troops came to my shop, asking my name and demanding arms, rudely made me Prisoner for nothing... my house was rifled by his soldiers, who took away my goods feloniously...

"He was held in Oxford Castle until his trial, following which he was imprisoned for ten years."[4]

Davis wrote to members of the Newport, Rhode Island Church in 1670, whilst he was a prisoner at Oxford. He was released on September 13, 1672.

When describing his beliefs he twice used the term "Church of Christ." He believed in God the Father, Jesus Christ, and that the Holy Spirit was not part of a "Trinity" but rather the power of God. He knew that men are justified by the faith of Jesus Christ, not the works of the law, but that God required of men obedience and good works.

He stated that: "I believe there is but one true visible Church. The members of the Gospel visible Church, in the latter times, that Anti-Christ prevailed, are noted by the Spirit in Revelation 14:12 to be such as keep the Commandments of God, and the Faith of Jesus, and such are, and shall be Blessed, Revelation 22:14... They are the Lord Christ's Church..."[5]

The Stennett Family

Through the ages God has often carried on His work not only through individuals, but also families. The talented Stennett family was an example of this in action. Four generations of this family faithfully served the Church of God in England.

The Stennetts, in common with other ministers of their time, were prolific writers. In 1658 Edward Stennett wrote the book *The Royal Law Contended For*, and in 1664 he published a work on a very common theme entitled *The Seventh Day is the Sabbath of the Lord*.

"He was an able and devoted minister, but dissenting from the established church, he was deprived of the means of support.

"He suffered much of the persecution which the Dissenters were exposed to at that time, and more especially for his faithful adherence to the cause of the Sabbath. For this truth he experienced tribulation, not only from those in power, by whom he was kept a long time in prison, but also much distress from unfriendly dissenting brethren, who strove to destroy his influence, and ruin his cause."[6]

Edward Stennett was one of the few, at that time, who could clearly see the very real danger of allowing apostates," as he called them, to continue in fellowship with the church. These false "brethren," when permitted to remain within the local congregations, often did as much damage to the work of the true servants of God as "outside" persecutors.

Stennett spoke out strongly on this point, but being little more

than one voice in the wilderness had little effect on the general trend
within the church.

The absence of a strong central authority at this time led to a lack
of unity within the church. A wide variation of opinion existed on
even the most basic points of doctrine.

Regarding the Sabbath doctrine, Edward Stennett was stating the
"official" position when he wrote that "its observance ought to be
commenced, after the manner of the Jews, at sunset on Friday." A
great deal of controversy existed as to exactly when "sunset" should
begin.

One ex-member described some of the extreme views that were
held by at least a number who considered themselves as a part of the
Church of God.

"Now that which about this time (1671) shewed forth itself, was
of a Sabbath-keeper in the town where I lived (and she hath more
fellows abroad), a Sabbath-keeper so strict in her Sabbath-keeping,
that few others of them (if any at all) do match her for her zeal
therein... Who is so far in her owning of the Sabbath, and the Law
whence the rule of it is taken, that she shames not openly to disown
the Gospel, and the Lord Jesus Christ, the author and revealer
thereof having cast out of her Bible the whole New Testament of our
Lord and Saviour Jesus Christ... disowning all those writings from
the beginning of Matthew to the and of Revelation."[7]

"As a rector of the Established Church, Edward Stennett did not
hold to the Sabbath in 1631, when Brabourne wrote against him. A
Parliament supporter, Stennett lost his ministerial position in 1660
with the Restoration of the crown. He turned to the medical profession to support his family, and gave his children a liberal education.

"Stennett began keeping the Sabbath, holding secret meetings in
his Wallingford Castle, which was immune from search warrants."[8]

In the work entitled, *Work of Joseph Stennett*, published in 1732,
we find that an interesting sequel has been added by another writer
relating to Joseph's father, Dr. Edward Stennett. It tells of how God
was protecting some of His leading ministers at that time.

"He dwelt in the castle of Wallingford, a place where no warrant
could make forcible entrance, but that of a chief justice; and the
house was so situated that assemblies could meet, and every part
of religious worship be exercised in it, without any danger of a legal

conviction, unless informers were admitted, which care was taken to prevent: so that for a long time he kept a constant and undisturbed meeting in his hall."

A local clergyman became so incensed that these meetings of God's people were, because of a technical point of law, being held legally, that he hired a number of false witnesses to wrongly claim that they had attended the meetings and by doing so had obtained "evidence" of illegal worship.

"The assizes were held at Newbury; and when the time drew near, there was a great triumph in the success the gentlemen proposed to themselves, when of a sudden the scene was changed.

"News came to the justice that his son, whom he had lately placed at Oxford, was gone off with a player; the concern whereof, and the riding in search of him, prevented his attendance in the court.

"The clergyman, a few days before the assizes, boasted much of the service which would be done to the church and the neighborhood by his prosecution, and of his own determination to be at Newbury to help carry it on; but to the surprise of many his design was frustrated by sudden death."

One by one all of those involved in the case either died, became sick, had accidents or decided not to give evidence. The result was that "when Mr. Stennett came to Newbury, neither prosecutor nor witness appearing against him, he was discharged."

In 1686 Edward Stennett moved from Wallingford to London where he apparently gathered together the members of Francis Bampfield's Pinner's Hall Sabbatarian Church. This church had been dispersed a few years earlier at the time of Bampfield's imprisonment and death.[9]

Dr. Edward Stennett died in 1689.

"His son Joseph Stennett succeeded him as pastor of the Pinner's Hall Church, and four generations of Stennetts continued to be Sabbatarian leaders in England. On his parents' tombstone, Joseph engraved an epitaph that they were heirs of immortality."

"Joseph Stennett, son of Edward, pastored the Pinner's Hall Church, 1690–1713." Very well-educated, "he preached on Sunday to other Baptist churches, but remained the faithful pastor of the Pinner's Hall Seventh-day Baptist church until his death. He wrote several Sabbath hymns."[10]

One of his hymns includes the words:

> *"Another six days' work is done,*
> *Another Sabbath is begun;*
> *Return, my soul, enjoy thy rest,*
> *Improve the day that God has blessed."*

A rather touching picture is given of the death of Joseph Stennett. "In the beginning of the year 1713, Mr. Stennett's health began apparently to decline. Many heavy afflictions at that time crowded upon him.

"When he drew near his dissolution, he called his children around him, and in a peculiar manner gave his dying advice to his eldest son, with respect to the management of his studies and the conduct of his future life."

He informed those present, "That if they were found walking in the ways of true religion, his God would be their God, to whose providence he could in faith commit them."[11]

He was buried in the churchyard of Hitchenden, Bucks.

"His son, Joseph Stennett II, became a minister at the age of 22. He declined to become pastor of the Mill Yard Church." Later, as "it was quite customary in those days for a seventh-day minister to serve a first-day," he at the age of 45 became pastor of a First Day Baptist Church in London, although he remained a 'faithful' Sabbath-keeper for the rest of his life. One of the most eloquent preachers of the day, and a dissenter, he was known personally to King George II."[12]

Sabbath-Keeping Declines

A great many Church of God ministers of the seventeenth century were former ministers of the Church of England. The reason why God called these men was probably that few others in that age had the necessary education and leadership qualities. Even the ability to read was by no means as universal a skill as it is today. A few such men even held high political office prior to their conversion.

"Thomas Bampfield had been Recorder of Exeter, member of the Commonwealth Parliament, Speaker of Richard Cromwell's Parliament. He lived at Dunkerton, near Bath, and about 1663 blossomed out in extraordinary costume considering himself commissioned to found a new sect. Francis won him to Seventh Day Baptist principles, and he subsided into a quieter life.

"In 1692 and 1693 Thomas Bampfield was publishing on the Sabbath question, eliciting three or four rejoinders: in the latter year he died."[13]

In 1646 seven congregations are said to have met in London, but by the time that Francis Bampfield wrote in 1677, persecution had reduced this number to three. The locations of those three congregations were Mill Yard, Bell Lane, and Cripplegate.

One of the earlier congregations, of which John James was pastor, for a time met at "Bull Stake Alley," Whitechapel. It is probable that many, if not most, of the meeting halls of the first Sabbatarian groups were destroyed in the "Great Fire of London," which, in 1666, burnt down most of the city.

There is considerable variation among sources regarding the number of congregations outside London. One source states that "in the seventeenth century eleven churches of Sabbatarians flourished in England, while many scattered Sabbath-keepers were to be found in various parts of that kingdom."[14]

The cities and towns where congregations are known to have met are as follows: Sherborne, Dorchester, Salisbury, Chertsey, Wallingford, Norweston, Tewkesbury, Braintree, Colchester, Woodbridge, Norwich, Leominster, Derby, Manchester, and Hexham.

In Wales at least one Sabbath meeting was held regularly at Swansea, there were also a number of scattered members in this area.

Sabbath-keepers also met in Ireland, although there are no indications that they had any contact with the English groups.

"A small remnant of Sabbath-keepers has persisted in Ireland unto this time; a church or society being found there as late as 1840."[15]

John Bunyan, the well-known author of *Pilgrim's Progress*, wrote a book against the Sabbath in 1685, but it was never published.

"Another very early church is that of Natton, or Tewkesbury, on the River Severn. There is evidence here of Sabbath-keepers as early as 1620, and a church by 1640. Complete organization was not achieved until 1650. Prior to 1680, Natton was a mixed congregation of both first and seventh day observers."[16]

John Purses was said to have been the first pastor at Natton (1660–1720). He was followed by Edmund Townsend (1720–1727), Philip Jones (1727–1770), and Thomas Hiller (1770–1790).

"He [Thomas Hiller] died a few years ago [written in 1848] since which time the church, now dwindled to a mere handful, has been destitute of a pastor, but has enjoyed the assistance of a worthy Baptist preacher from Tewkesbury."[17]

The Pinner's Hall Church followed a similar pattern of decline. This group—which met together on Broad St., London (and also from time to time at Cripplegate and Devonshire Square), had been gathered together by Francis Bampfield and later pastored by Edward and Joseph Stennett.

"The church continued to meet at Pinner's Hall till 1727, when they moved to Curriers Hall, where they assembled for divine worship till the expiration of the lease in 1799, when they removed to Redcross Street.

"In former days this church appears to have been pretty numerous, but it has declined latterly, and at present (1808) consists of only a very few members."[18]

The historic Mill Yard Church probably dates back to 1607, but one authority (Daland) traces its establishment to 1580. One of its earliest pastors was John Trask (1617–1619). Later ministers included Dr. Peter Chamberlen, John James, William Sellers and Henry Soursby.

Until 1654 the group met for worship "near Whitechapel." The next meeting place was "Bull Stake Alley." In 1680 they were at East Smithfield. Between 1691 and 1885 they worshipped in Mill Yard Goodman's Fields in Middlesex.

By 1900 the congregation was meeting in two private houses, one the home of Lt. Col. Richardson and the other the house of the church secretary.

At the time of writing, a "Mill Yard" Seventh Day Baptist Church still meets. The latest official membership figures supplied by the Seventh Day Baptist headquarters indicate that 15 members and 29 children (members of a Sabbath school) meet together for worship.

By the eighteenth century the prophecy of Jesus Christ relating to this "Sardis" era of the Church had become a sobering reality: "know your works, that you have a name that you are alive, but you are dead" (Revelation 3:1).

On The Brink of Extinction

From this period onwards most British Sabbath-keepers abandoned even the name "Church of God" (John 17:11). This scriptural name is given twelve times in the New Testament. The warning of Christ to "strengthen the things which remain, that are ready to die" (Revelation 3:2) went largely unheeded. As a result, a period of decline which was to lead to almost total extinction set in.

"The middle of the eighteenth century marks the virtual disappearance of the Seventh Day Baptist churches. Their numbers had never been considerable but they had several churches in London and the Provinces. By 1754, there was no Seventh-Day minister left, though ordinary Baptist ministers were willing to do double duty."[19]

Books were written advocating Sabbath observance in the years 1801, 1825 and 1851.

Writing in 1848, Benedict records that "only three Sabbatarian churches now remain in England out of the eleven which existed there one hundred and fifty years ago.

"There can be little doubt, that the observance of the Sabbath upon a different day from the one commonly observed, is connected with great inconvenience."[20]

As zeal diminished still further no attempts were made to preach the gospel. In time only the doctrines of the Sabbath and baptism by immersion remained.

"An April 13, 1901, article in the *Birmingham Weekly Post* stated that the Natton Church was the only Seventh Day Baptist Church left in the provinces. The minister there, as usual, also ministered to a First Day Baptist Church at Tewkesbury. The writer of the article remarks, 'There is nothing in the type of service to differentiate it from that of an ordinary nonconformist service.' And he was amazed that this sect, which few know about, had continued to exist for two and one-half centuries, because 'there appears to be little attempt to propagate the faith, and without such effort the number of adherents is not likely to increase.' The writer concluded that the interested person had better hurry up and find out about the group 'before it passes out of existence altogether.'

"The official Seventh Day Baptist history gives three reasons for the decline of British Sabbath-keeping churches: (1) lack of organized fellowship among the churches (improper government); (2) dependence on charitable bequests for finances (tithing not enforced); and (3) employment of first-day pastors (failure to keep the Sabbath properly)."[21]

In a recent letter to the author, a leader of the Seventh Day Baptist church, writing from its headquarters in Plainfield, New Jersey, mentions that "Our most recent statistics show 50 members in Britain, 5,150 members in the United States, and a worldwide total of 52,700."

A limited evangelistic work is being conducted by this group and a magazine *The Sabbath Recorder* is published on a monthly basis. This church has made available much valuable material on church history, for which I thank them.

Chapter Summary
The later years of the "Sardis" era of the Church of God. Interest in the truth of God diminishes. The introduction of false teachings. Many problems were experienced during the eighteenth and nineteenth centuries.

Chapter Thirteen

THE NEW WORLD

*"The great majority of the 'Free inhabitants of the Towne of
Westerly' on a list dated May 18, 1669, at the time were or were
later to become members of this church. Also, outstanding
Rhode Island leaders of the pre-revolutionary era during the struggle
for independence from England... were members of this church"*
(*Seventh Day Baptists in New England*, Karl G. Stillman).

*"The blessings of your father have excelled the blessings
of my ancestors, up to the utmost bounds of the everlasting hills.
They shall be on the head of Joseph "*
(Genesis 49:26).

D uring the period when the Church of God in England was
suffering some of its most severe persecution, Jesus Christ
caused His Church to be established in America. It was
here, in the area which was later to become the United States of
America, that the new congregations, free from much of the persecution and other restrictions suffered in England, would have a new
base from which to flourish and grow.

Stephen Mumford Leads the Way
"Who was the first Sabbath-keeper in America? It is not known, but
the first recorded Sabbatarian was Stephen Mumford, who came to
America in 1664. There may have been others prior to Mumford, for
as early as 1646, Sabbath discussion embroiled New England. Some
of the earliest books published in America supported the keeping of
the seventh-day Sabbath.

The Baptist historian Griffiths reports that the earliest Sabbath-
keepers were at Newport, Rhode Island, in 1644. 'It is said that in
the province of Rhode Island, there were adherents of that faith
[Sabbath-keepers] at its early settlement contemporary with the
founding of the first Baptist Church.'"[1]

"Stephen Mumford came over from London in 1664, and brought
the opinion with him that the whole of the Ten Commandments, as
they were delivered from Mount Sinai, were moral and immutable;
and that it was the Antichristian power which thought to change
times and laws, that changed the Sabbath from the seventh to the

first day of the week. Several members of the first day church in Newport embraced this sentiment, and yet continued with the church for some years, until two men and their wives who had done so, turned back to the keeping of the first day again."[2]

Mumford, who originally came from Tewkesbury, was sent to Newport, Rhode Island, by the Bell Lane Sabbatarian Church of London. He was not a minister.

Religious Freedom in America

"There is no doubt that Stephen Mumford decided to migrate across the Atlantic Ocean because of the difficult circumstances in which not only the Seventh Day Baptists but other Baptists and Dissenters found themselves in England at the time. They hoped to find greater freedom over the seas."[3]

When King Charles II came to the throne in 1660 the measure of religious freedom that had been permitted during the time of Oliver Cromwell was not to continue.

Several Acts of Parliament were passed designed to enforce uniformity of religion in Britain, which in effect meant conformity to the teachings of the Church of England.

"The third Act was the Conventicle Act of 1664 which forbade the assembly of more than five people in addition to the family of the house for religious services except according to the Prayer Book, under penalty of fines and transportation. For the third offense they could be banished to the American plantations, excepting New England and Virginia. If they should return or escape, death was the penalty. Many were sent to the West Indies where they endured great hardship. Vast numbers suffered in all parts of England and Wales. It is said that 8,000 perished in prison during the days of Charles II. It may have been this Act which led Stephen Mumford to decide to migrate to Rhode Island, to banish himself by so doing rather than wait for the Government to do it."[4]

Rhode Island Sabbath-Keepers

Further information on Mumford's arrival in Rhode Island is given by Richard Nickels: "Mumford may have been induced to come by Dr. John Clarke, pastor of the Newport First-Day Baptist church, who was agent of the colony to the court of King Charles II. The King's charter held by Clarke granted 'unlimited toleration in religion to all people of Rhode Island.' Mumford could thus be escaping religious persecution by coming to the New World.

"Mumford did not succumb to Sunday-keeping, nor did he keep his Sabbath beliefs to himself. Apparently on October 6, 1665 he wrote to several Sabbatarian churches in England for advice.

"The first of his 'converts,' called 'the first person upon the continent to begin the observance of the Bible Sabbath'... was a woman, Tacy Hubbard, wife of Samuel Hubbard, who commenced its observance a little later...

"The Hubbards joined Mumford in Sabbath observance in 1665. The group increased with Ruth Burdick, wife of Robert in 1665, and Rachel Langworthy, wife of Andrew (daughter of the Hubbards), and Bethiah and Joseph Clark in 1667, living in Misquamicut, Rhode Island. Apparently they continued to go to church on Sunday and also met in private homes on Saturday. Others who embraced the Sabbath were William Hiscox, Roger Baster, Nicholas Wild and wife, and John Solomon and wife."[5]

Opposition to Sabbath-Keeping

Problems and persecution for the little group were not long in coming. John Clarke and several other local ministers began to preach against them, charging them with being heretics and schismatics. Clarke taught that all of the Ten Commandments were done away.

Early in 1669 four of the Sabbath-keepers (the Wilds and Solomons) renounced their faith and returned to Sunday worship. This action deeply disturbed the other Sabbath-keepers who were perplexed by the question. Should we continue to fellowship with a church which includes apostates?

They wrote to the church in London for advice and guidance. Dr. Edward Stennett wrote to them from London as follows: "If the church will hold communion with these apostates from the truth, you ought then to desire to be fairly dismissed from the church; which if the church refuse, you ought to withdraw yourselves, and not be partakers of other men's sins..." The letter was dated March 6, 1670.[6]

Dr. Stennett's letter was one of several which were written from England to encourage the infant Sabbath-keeping church in America.

"Before this the Bell Lane Church in London, which seems to have been gathered by John Belcher the bricklayer in 1662, kept in touch with Stephen Mumford at Newport. Their letter was dated 26 March 1668, four years after he had migrated, and signed by eleven members of Bell Lane. Among those signatures appear the names of Belcher and William Gibson who later came to Newport and was the second pastor of the Seventh Day Baptist Church there. A month before this, on 2 February 1668, Edward Stennett wrote to Newport from his place in Abingdon, Berkshire.

"Another Sabbath-keeper in England wrote to those in Newport two years later. This was Joseph Davis, Sr., who had accepted the Sabbath in 1668 and was in prison at Oxford Castle in 1670 as a result of a fresh wave of persecution for attending conventicles. It would seem that those in Newport had heard of him because they wrote to him on 4 July 1669, and to this letter he replied that Baptists and Independents were preaching against the Sabbath. He exhorted the Sabbath-keepers on Rhode Island not to be discouraged by opposition."[7]

In June, 1671 the trials of the Newport group reached a climax when Elder Holmes preached a blistering sermon against the Sabbath-keepers, claiming that the Ten Commandments were given to the Jews but were not binding on Gentiles. Several meetings were held to discuss the points of difference between the two factions.

William Hiscox pointed out that "The ground of our difference is, that you and others deny God's law." It took the Sabbath-keepers over six years to learn the lesson that it is not possible to keep the Sabbath and, at the same time, remain in a church which kept a different day and preached against God's law. They withdrew from further fellowship with the Sunday congregation and formed a new Sabbath-keeping church in December 1671.

The Newport Church Starts

"In 1671... Stephen Mumford, William Hiscox, Samuel Hubbard, Roger Baster, and three sisters, entered into church covenant together, thus forming the first seventh-day Baptist Church in America."[8]

"For more than thirty years after its organisation, the Newport church included nearly all persons observing the seventh day in the states of Rhode Island and Connecticut..."[9]

Although Baptist historians almost always define these early American Sabbatarian congregations as "Seventh Day Baptist," it becomes very clear when reading the actual records left by these people that they considered themselves to be "the Church of God" at Piscataway, New Jersey, or "the Church of God dwelling at Shrewsbury" (New Jersey).[10]

It was good that the close relationship which the Sabbath-keepers had with other churches ceased at an early date. Had this not been so, they would quickly have lost many of the distinctive features of their faith.

Had the first-day people been of the same mind, the light of the Sabbath would have been extinguished within a few years, as the history of English Sabbath-keepers clearly proves.

But, in the providence of God, the danger was averted by the opposition which these commandment-keepers had to encounter.

"When the London Seventh-day Baptists, in 1664, sent Stephen Mumford to America, and in 1675 sent Eld. William Gibson, they did as much, in proportion to their ability, as had been done by any society for propagating the gospel in foreign parts."[11]

For a time growth in church membership was slow. The entire population of the Rhode Island colony was less than 3,000; the inhabitants found themselves in conflict with the Indians and also in dispute with Massachusetts and Connecticut over boundaries. Four other people soon joined the original seven.

"Owing to the fact that the roll of the Church for many years is not extant, if one was kept at all, it is difficult to tell in some cases who did belong to the church."[12]

Records of the Newport Church begin in 1692. Samuel Hubbard reported that in 1678 there were 37 Sabbatarians in America; 20 in Newport, seven at Westerly (also known as Hopkinton) and 10 at New London, Connecticut.[13]

Three years later the number of members reached 51; of this group two were Indians.

"William Hiscox, the first minister, served from 1671 to his death in 1704. When, if ever, he was ordained, is unknown.

"In 1675, Mumford went to London, and on October 16, 1675, he returned with a new assistant elder, William Gibson of the Bell Lane church. Gibson was probably already ordained when he arrived, for he preached at New London, and eventually settled at Westerly. Gibson worked effectively against the Rogerine sect, and upon Hiscox's death, he became full pastor."[14]

Sabbath Keeping Expands to the Mainland

As time went on, many of the Newport members moved on to the western wilderness of Westerly and Waterford and as early as 1680 a branch of the Newport Church was established on the banks of the Pawcatuck River at Meetinghouse Bridge in Westerly which was known for nearly half a century as the Sabbatarian Church of Westerly. These early settlers went back and forth to Newport when Indian raids were threatened particularly at the time of King Philip's war in 1675, traveling by boat.

"Many of the members of the Newport Church were outstanding citizens of the times and some were intimates of Roger Williams. The Redwood Library, the first library to be established in the Colonies, was erected on a site given by Henry Collins, a Seventh Day Baptist and a well known goldsmith, benefactor of the arts, and contributor to many projects which would make better business men and better citizens."[15]

Members were received into these early New England churches by profession of faith, baptism and the laying on of hands.

"The great majority of the 'Free Inhabitants of the Towne of Westerly' on a list dated May 18, 1669, at the time were or later were to become members of this church. Also, outstanding Rhode Island leaders of the pre-Revolutionary era during the struggle for independence from England, notably Samuel Ward, Joshua Babcock and others, were members of this church.

"At Boom Bridge, a large tree was felled, mounted on a post in a horizontal position, weighed at the short end and so adjusted that it could support an individual at the long end and swung around to reach the far bank. The bolder Sabbatarians took this shorter route to church risking an occasional dunking while others chose the 'Saturday Path,' safer but longer. Boom Bridge derives its name from this novel apparatus."[16]

By 1683 the American churches had realized the need of closer personal contact between the members. With one church at Newport, on an island, and various scattered members on the mainland, they found great difficulty in meeting together as a group.

On October 31 of that year Hubbard wrote to Elder William Gibson, who at the time was living in New London, "O that we could have a general meeting! But winter is coming upon us."

General Meetings Begin

The first general meeting was held in late May 1684, shortly after Pentecost. All the brethren in New London, Westerly, Narraganset, Providence, Plymouth Colony and Martha's Vineyard were invited.

"The object of this meeting was to bring the members, so widely scattered together at a communion season."[17] This was the first recorded general meeting of Sabbath-keepers in America. According to Hubbard 26 or 27 people were in attendance. Prayers were given and discussion took place on several doctrinal issues.

"By this time, more members lived on the mainland than at Newport. Sabbath-keepers had lived at Westerly since 1666, converts of Mumford. At a yearly meeting of the Church, at Westerly, on September 28, 1708 (New Style), the decision was made to separate into two churches. There were 72 at Westerly and 41 at Newport [The Feast of Tabernacles for that year started Saturday, September 29]. Previously it was common to hold the yearly meeting at Westerly. Its first elder, John Maxson, was ordained October 1, 'by fasting and prayer and laying on of hands.'"[18]

There are strong indications that many of these annual meetings took place either during the fall Holy Day season or near Pentecost. Although these people probably had only a limited knowledge of God's Plan of Salvation, pictured by these days, they were at least attempting to follow the Holy Day pattern that God had ordained.

Four Sabbatarian churches were established around Philadelphia towards the end of the seventeenth century and early years of the eighteenth. Little historical record has survived concerning these churches and they seem to have died out by the early 1800s.

An important local congregation of "the Church of God" was established at Piscataway, New Jersey, in 1705. Edmund Dunham was its first pastor.

Articles of Faith

The Articles of Faith of this church are given in *Seventh-Day Baptist Memorial*:

I.   "We believe that unto us there is but one God, the Father, and one Lord Jesus Christ, who is the mediator between God and mankind, and that the Holy Ghost is the Spirit of God.

II.   "We believe that all the Scriptures of the Old and New Testaments, given by inspiration, are the Word of God—and are the rule of faith and practice.

III.   "We believe that the ten commandments, which were written on two tables of stone by the finger of God, continue to be the rule of righteousness unto all men.

IV.   "We believe the six principles recorded in Hebrews 6:1, 2 to be the rule of faith and practice.

V.   "We believe that the Lord's Supper ought to be administered and received in all Christian churches.

VI.   "We believe that all Christian churches ought to have church officers in them, as elders, and deacons.

VII.   "We believe that all persons thus believing ought to be baptized in water by dipping or plunging, after confession is made by them of their faith in the above said things.

VIII. "We believe that a company of sincere persons, being formed in the faith and practices of the above said things, may truly be said to be the Church of Christ.

IX.   "We give up ourselves unto the Lord and one another, to be guided and governed by one another, according to the Word of God."[19]

Extensive scriptural evidence was given to support these Articles of Faith.

Mixed Fruit of Expansion

Only "a few names" in the Sardis era of the Church were truly converted and dedicated Christians (Revelation 3:4). During the eighteenth century numerous Sabbath-keeping congregations were being formed in various parts of America, but as time went on an increasingly small proportion of the people in those congregations were really drawing close to God through prayer and Bible study. Many joined local churches after having accepted the doctrinal "argument" of the Sabbath. The fruits indicate that only a small number had deeply repented of their former ways. Some even continued to take part in wars and politics.

As a result of being in this weakened spiritual state several members were influenced by false teachers who came into the church with a view to obtaining a following for their own style of belief.

One such "evangelist" was William Davis. Born in Wales in 1663, Davis studied at Oxford in order to become a minister in the Church of England. He changed his mind about this and became a Quaker instead. After migrating to Pennsylvania, he found himself in disagreement with other Quakers which resulted in him joining the Baptists.

Because Davis's view of Christ differed from that held by the Baptists—he did not believe that Christ was divine—he was excommunicated from that church; but some time later was introduced to the Sabbath by Abel Noble, who, according to some sources, was also a former Quaker.

Mr. Davis applied for membership of the Newport Church in 1706 but was turned down on doctrinal grounds. Four years later he tried again, and even though some still objected, he was finally accepted. In 1713 he was given authority by this congregation to preach and baptize.

For the rest of his life Davis was continually "in" and "out" of fellowship due to his belief in the Trinity, immortal soul, and the idea of going to heaven after death. His views were accepted by an increasing number of people and eventually became a part of Seventh-Day Baptist doctrine.

In one of his letters William Davis strongly defends his doctrinal views against those who rightly rejected them as being unscriptural.

"Now all this enmity against me among Seventh-day men arose against me originally from a noted seventh-day man and soul sleeper (one who rejected the immortal soul belief) in this country, who above twenty years ago opposed me about my principles of immortality of human souls, and afterward proceeded to differ with me about my faith in Christ and the Trinity, who having poisoned several other seventh-day men with the mortal and atheistical notion, and set them against me, he secretly conveyed this drench [accusation] against me over to Westerly to the persons beforenamed [various elders in the Rhode Island Church of God], who, complying with him in their judgments in the Socinian and Anti-Trinitarian error, drank it greedily down before I came among them..."[20]

This man had many descendants in New Jersey, New York, Pennsylvania and West Virginia who perpetuated his views long after his death.

In the early 1700s several debates were held on the question of the Sabbath. Episcopalians, led by Evan Evans and George Keith were able, by their arguments, to cause some leading Sabbatarians in Upper Providence to give up the Sabbath.

Public debates, conducted by leading ministers on both sides, were held in 1702 at Philadelphia. At Pennepek the Sabbatarians lost their place of worship when its owner returned to the Church of England.

Exemplary Lifestyle
The lifestyle of the members of the Sabbatarian "Philadelphia Movement" churches has been compared to that of the Quakers. They spoke directly and simply, dressed plainly and refused to engage in war or to take oaths.

A London minister, Elhanan Winchester, described them in 1788: "Such Christians I have never seen as they are, who take the Scriptures as their only guide, in matters both of faith and practise... they are so afraid of doing anything contrary to the commands of Christ, that no temptations would prevail upon them even to sue any person at law. They are industrious, sober, temperate, kind, charitable people. They read much, they sing and pray much... they walk in the commandments and ordinances of the Lord blameless; both in public and private, they bring up their children in the nurture and admonition of the Lord... and whatsoever they believe their Saviour commands, they practise without inquiring what others do."[21]

"Another church began through Piscataway as the mother church, at Oyster Pond, Long Island, with Elder Elisha Gillette. He joined the Piscataway church in 1769, but continued to live on Long Island. Upon request of the Piscataway church during its yearly meeting of 1786, Gillette was ordained by Elder William Bliss of Newport, Elder John Burdick of Hopkinton, and Elder Nathen Rogers [who in 1787 became pastor of Piscataway].

"Gillette soon organised a Sabbath church in Long Island, which in 1791 was recognized as a sister church of Piscataway. The church was short-lived, for it made the fatal mistake of admitting into membership Sunday keepers, and soon dissolved."[22]

Another important reason for the spiritual decline of the eighteenth-century Sabbatarian churches was involvement in politics. Richard Ward, a member of the Newport Church, even held office as governor of Rhode Island from 1741 to 1742.

Prominent Members

"One of the outstanding leaders of the Colonial and Pre-Revolutionary War periods in American History was Samuel Ward, a founder of Rhode Island College (Brown University), Colonial Governor of Rhode Island and a Seventh Day Baptist. He was a participant in the deliberations of the Continental Congress in Philadelphia and would have been a signer of the Declaration of Independence had he not been stricken by small pox from which he died before that document was in final form. He was a descendant of Roger Williams.

"His home was located at the corner of the Shore Road and the road to Weekapaug in Westerly not far from the Atlantic Ocean, the present location of the home of Clifford A. Langworthy. Here came Benjamin Franklin and other leaders for conferences and planning discussions as to policies and procedures to be followed by the Colonies in their struggle for independence.

"Samuel Ward's wife was Anna Ray from Block Island and Benjamin Franklin struck up a friendship and corresponded regularly with a sister of Mrs. Ward who came over to the mainland at times when Franklin was in the area. It is recorded that he accompanied her to Weekapaug Breachway from where she took off for Block Island in a small boat bidding her goodbye as she began her dangerous trip over the rough waters of Block Island Sound.

"A bronze tablet marks the spot where the Ward home was located, erected and dedicated by the Children of the American

Revolution in 1904. Governor Ward's granddaughter, Julia Ward
Howe, author of the Battle Hymn of the Republic, was present and
participated in the dedication ceremonies. Tea was served by the
ladies of the Pawcatuck Seventh Day Baptist Church and other
members of Phebe Greene Ward Chapter of the D.A.R. [Daughters of
the American Revolution] to the assembled guests."[23]

"Among the prominent Seventh Day Baptists of the Eighteenth
Century residing in Westerly was Dr. Joshua Babcock born there
in 1707, graduated from Yale College and who studied 'physic and
surgery' in Boston, later completing his education in England. He
then settled in his native town where he built up a very large practice.
Later he established a retail store which carried as wide a variety
of merchandise and handled as large a volume of business as any
between New York and Boston.

"The Babcock house is located on Franklin Street named in
honour of Benjamin Franklin and is greatly admired for its rugged
strength and beauty. Its interior features, Dutch tiles around its
fireplace, many elaborate cupboards and ceilings, a carved elegant
staircase, secret closets and other architectural features provide us
today with an authentic example of a fine Colonial home."[24]

Dr. Babcock died in 1783 and his memory is kept alive in the
Babcock Junior High School of Westerly.

Although American Sabbatarians enjoyed a far greater measure
of religious freedom than had their European counterparts of earlier
generations, subtle pressures were exerted at times to induce them
to conform to the beliefs of their Protestant neighbours. The mea-
sures taken to combat such pressures were often controversial and,
at times, even comical.

"Fourteen of the early New London Sabbath-keepers petitioned
the church in Hopkinton June 28, 1784 asking 'that they be incorporated a church in covenant relations with the mother church.' The
request was granted and they became a separate church November
11, 1784. Early meetings were held in private homes and eventually
the church had three different places of worship."

"We are disturbed today by the numerous mass demonstrations
against this or that unpopular cause and are inclined to think of them
as being unique and a present-day phenomenon. However, history
records the fact that early Seventh Day Baptists in the New London

area were so determined to have freedom to worship on the Sabbath and not be compelled to conform to Congregational pressures that some of the womenfolk took their knitting with them to a church service on Sunday while the men noisily pushed loaded wheelbarrows up and down the church steps."[25]

Yearly Meetings

Interesting and significant records have been preserved which reveal that for several generations the early American Sabbath-keeping congregations did keep, within the limitations of their understanding, the Feast of Tabernacles. This term does not seem to have been in general use, however, and the festival was normally termed the "Yearly Meeting," or the "General Meeting," or the "Sabbatarian Great Meeting."

"The journeys to attend them were often performed by ox teams, a distance of one hundred miles... great multitudes thronged to them for the spiritual profit to be gained, and great multitudes more attended for curiosity or pleasure. No event, during the year, caused more excitement. The old members of the church, who attended them in their earlier times, love to live over again and again those pleasant and profitable meetings. Their social intercourse was of a holy and sanctified character, the influence of which still lingers in the hearts of those who enjoyed them.

"The meeting was regarded somewhat in the light of the yearly feasts of the Jews when all the tribes went up to Jerusalem to worship. It was a time when the members of the Church, generally, were expected to come together for a spiritual re-union... The Lord's Supper was commonly observed at these General Meetings.... At a Church meeting of the 15th of September 1722, was celebrated the ordinance of Bread and Wine."[26]

Records of these early festivals indicate that, in common with the Biblical observance of such feasts, the moderate use of alcohol was permitted to those attending. Crowds of local people would sometimes gather around the places where alcohol was on sale and create trouble for those attending the festival. At times, problems of this nature would become so serious that state laws in Rhode Island and New Jersey were introduced which prohibited the sale of intoxicating drinks within a mile of the place of the meeting.

Passover Considerations

The observance of the Lord's Supper or Communion during the autumn or fall festival described by James Bailey, was clearly a departure from "the faith once delivered to the saints."

"The 1926 Seventh Day Baptist Manual notes that the 'Mill Yard Church, of London, the original Seventh Day Baptist Church, celebrates it once a year, at the time of the Passover, from the Jewish Church.' But besides the South Fork of the Hughes River Church in West Virginia, no record has been found of any other Seventh Day Baptist church observing communion on the time of the Passover.

"A.H. Lewis, Seventh Day Baptist counterpart of the Seventh Day Adventist, and Sabbath historian, John N. Andrews, said that the crucifixion was on Wednesday, and the resurrection on Saturday. Further, he admitted, 'The earliest Christians, i.e. those of the New Testament period, continued to observe the Passover; and since Christ died at that time, they associated his death with that festival. In this way the Passover became the festival of Christ's death.' The scriptural time, Lewis knew, was the 14th of Nisan, without reference to Sunday or any day of the week.

"If the Mill Yard church observed communion at the time of the Passover throughout its history, it appears that the American churches deviated from English practices from the start. The very purpose of holding yearly meetings (the first recorded one was May 14, 1684, Old Style) was to bring scattered members together 'at a communion season.' From its earliest records, communion at Newport has been reported to have been held in April, May, September, and other times of the year. On December 1, 1754, Newport communion time was set on the last Sabbath of every month. It was still observed on the last Saturday of the month in 1771.

"On July 12, 1746, the Shrewsbury church voted communion once in two months in conformity with the practice of the Westerly church. On March 3, 1775, the church voted communion to be held quarterly, on the last Sabbath in November, February, May and August.

"In 1811, the Piscataway church was also observing communion quarterly, with the Friday before communion Sabbath, a day of fasting and prayer.

"Formerly, fermented wine and unleavened bread both, only, were used. But contents of the 'cup' changed to grape juice; and today [among Seventh Day Baptists], even regular, leavened bread, is often used.

"According to the 1833 'Confession of Faith' it is the duty of members to take the Lord's Supper as often as the church shall deem it expedient and the circumstances admit.

"If the Mill Yard 'mother church' of London, England, always observed communion once a year on the date of the Jewish Passover, why didn't American Sabbatarians do the same? The exact reason is unclear. But the fact that the Americans had forgotten how they had received their doctrines and beliefs (Revelation 3:3) cannot be denied."[27]

The practice of foot-washing as a part of the celebration of the Lord's Supper seems to have been carried out by several Sabbatarian congregations during the eighteenth century.

A letter written by the Shrewsbury Church of Christ during this period gives some interesting instructions on the subject: "And now, dear Brethren, we shall use the freedom to acquaint you with one thing, and do heartily desire to recommend it to your serious and Christian consideration, and that is about the duty of washing one another's feet.

"This is a duty and work which some of us have been long thoughtful and in part persuaded of... and have concluded to put it in practice some time since, in the following manner; viz, at the... Lord's Supper... the Elder, in imitation of the Lord, takes a towel and girds himself, then he pours water in a basin and begins to wash the disciples' (viz., the brethren's) feet, and from him they take it, and the brethren to the brethren, and the sisters to the sisters, they wash one another's feet through the present assembly.

"The practice of feet-washing was continued by this church after its removal to Virginia but was probably abandoned at some time during the first half of the nineteenth century."[28]

Wartime Upheavals
In 1775 Jacob Davis was ordained a minister of the Shrewsbury Church. During the ordination ceremony he was asked the question, "Have you entire freedom to administer the ordinances of God to them as to a Church of God; to pray with them and for them and

endeavour to build them up in the faith?" The new minister was given a solemn charge. "Brother Davis, I charge thee before God and the Lord Jesus Christ, that thou take charge of the church of Christ dwelling at Shrewsbury."[29]

At Piscataway major internal problems were aroused due to members' attitudes towards the Revolutionary War. They "differed among themselves in relation to the justness of the war." The church broke up for several years and some members joined the Patriot army; others fled to the north and a number suffered the destruction of their farms during the war.

The Shrewsbury Church was also split by the war. Jacob Davis became a chaplain in the Continental Army and several members joined their pastor in taking a part in the conflict.

At least one member, however, took an entirely different position. Simeon Maxson, was temporarily disfellowshipped in 1776 for violently disagreeing with the others and calling them "children of the devil" for supporting carnal warfare.[30]

"Impoverished and decimated by the Revolutionary War, the Shrewsbury church sold the church building and on September 6, 1789 as a body moved to Woodbridgetown, Pennsylvania, and soon thereafter to New Salem, Virginia, on land donated by William Fitz Randolph. It is probable that the Shrewsbury emigrants were joined by recruits from Piscataway, New Jersey.

"It is reported that some Sabbatarians had removed from Shrewsbury to southwestern Pennsylvania and Western Virginia as early as 1774. After the war, small colonies went even further west, into Ohio, Illinois, Iowa and Nebraska."[31]

Near the close of the war, other members of the Rhode Island churches were migrating to Berlin, New York. By 1797 there was a church established at Brookfield, New York. Sabbath-keepers were soon to spread into western New York, and elsewhere. From the Newport and Piscataway movements sprang churches of Sabbath-keepers in North, Central, and Western New York, northern Pennsylvania, Illinois, Wisconsin, Minnesota, Kansas and western Nebraska.

In 1794 a Sunday "blue law" was passed in Pennsylvania which caused great hardship to the Sabbatarians. Richard Bond, of the Nottingham church, refused to serve on a jury during the Sabbath.

Church Expansion... and Weakness

"In America the number of churches gradually increased as the gospel was spread from state to state. But so nearly dead were these congregations that in 1802 many began to organize themselves together into a General Conference... At this serious juncture, most of the local churches joined themselves together to form the Seventh-day Baptist General Conference... Soon they began teaching the pagan Trinity doctrine and the immortality of human souls!

"Several faithful congregations did not become members of the Conference because they would not submit to the new Protestant doctrines being introduced... For another half century the congregations maintained the little truth they possessed, although most of them did not go all the way in obedience to God. John aptly described this period: 'Be watchful, and establish the things remaining, which are about to die, for I have not found thy works perfect before my God' (Revelation 3:21)."[32]

A circular letter was sent out by the 1802 General Conference: "Beloved brethren, we having received the kind letters from various churches in our fellowship, are bound by the love of God and the law of gratitude, to give thanks to God for the common salvation he has provided for us all, and for civil and religious liberty, and for the day and means of grace and hopes of glory through our Lord Jesus Christ.

"To effect so good an end and to keep order in the house or church of God, let every member have a home, or be under the watch and care of faithful brethren, and not scattered in the wide world where no church can see them walk or discipline them. Let them be careful to keep God's holy Sabbath, and join in social worship, statedly; likewise in private duties.

"It is expected that all the churches in our Communion will send letters or messengers, or both, to our next Yearly Meeting... with a statement of their liberality toward defraying the charges of the missionaries. As purity of heart and morality of life constitute our chief happiness, and we all are but stewards of the manifold grace of God, let us give unto all their due. The grace of the Lord Jesus Christ be with you all. Amen."[33]

One source gives the number of members of the Seventh Day Baptist church, at the time of this Conference, as 1,130, with nine ordained ministers.

The minutes of the Seventh-Day Baptist General Conference for 1846 reveal that by 1807, numbers had risen to 1,648, and by 1846 they had increased to 6,092.

In 1818 the name "Seventh-Day Baptist" was officially adopted by the majority of Sabbatarian congregations.

By about 1917 this church had 73 church congregations and 6,000 members."[34]

At the time of writing, membership of this church, the figures provided by Seventh-Day Baptist headquarters in Plainfield, New Jersey, are "5,150 members in the United States, and a worldwide total of 52,700."

Conference records during the nineteenth century reveal a gradual change in attitude and doctrine. By 1803 decisions affecting Seventh-Day Baptists were reached by the process of voting. Each church had from one to four votes depending on its size. The Conference could only advise local churches; it assumed no powers over the churches beyond this. All contributions to the Conference were to be voluntary.

In 1804 a Circular Letter indicated that internal dissention was prevalent: "...do nothing to wound the weak and feeble lambs of Christ, who cannot endure much; and be not offended with those who cannot see as far and walk as fast as you... establish nothing new, although it might be for the better, until the whole be generally agreed thereon, that peace and harmony may be established among ourselves...."

A "have love" philosophy was advocated towards those of differing beliefs, including the preachers and people of other denominations at the 1820 Conference.

Two years later members were advised "not to sacrifice the Sabbath in marriage." In 1833 members voted unanimously to abstain from alcohol except for medicinal purposes.

A condition of "coldness and apathy" was said to have prevailed in 1836. By 1864 Seventh Day Baptists were "greatly absorbed in national affairs," meaning the Civil War. A policy of cooperation with Seventh Day Adventists was agreed in 1870.[35]

Seventh Day Baptists
Not all American Sabbath-keepers were in agreement with the "General Conference." One such church was established on the

212

South Fork of the Hughes River in West Virginia. The congregation was raised up following revival meetings held by an evangelist, Alexander Campbell, in 1833. A public debate on the Sabbath was also conducted with a local Methodist minister, which resulted in several of the listeners accepting the Sabbath. Church services began in 1834. The people called themselves "the Seventh Day Baptist church" and also the "Church of Christ."

Some of the practices of this group were described as "Mosaic." Biblical laws of "clean" and "unclean" meats were observed. The communion service was held "once in twelve months on the four-teenth day of the first Jewish month." The foot-washing ceremony was also observed by this group.

They believed that a Christian should not hold public office, that tithing is commanded, and that a Christian should not marry a non-Christian. This church was governed from the top down with the ministers firmly in control.

Rules were imposed relating to courtship, dating and child rearing. A standard of dress was enforced, the violation of which even resulted in some being excommunicated.

Randolph records that more than 130 people belonged to the South Fork congregation during its half-century of existence.

Because of its rigid and literal application of the Bible, this group experienced severe persecution from "Christian" sources which viewed their beliefs as "half crazy ideas."

A group of five disaffected members established their own oppo-sition church in order to challenge the "heretics" of South Fork; for several years a fierce struggle continued between the two factions. The dissidents eventually gained control of the "mother church." In 1885 they ordained a woman as a minister.[36]

The West Virginia churches were closely associated with Sabbath-keepers in Ohio. A church was raised up in 1824 at Pike, Clarke County, Ohio. A division took place over the question of alcohol and a "Temperance Reform" movement began which led to the separation of "wet" and "dry" churches in the area.

The nineteenth century saw a growing acceptance of Catholic and Protestant doctrines by Seventh-Day Baptists. Their 1833 General Conference produced an "Expose of Sentiments" which included a statement on the Trinity.

"We believe that there is a union existing between the Father, the Son, and the Holy Spirit; and that they are equally divine and equally entitled to our adoration.

"Members were received only upon the vote of a Sabbatarian Baptist church at a business meeting. In the Westerly church (Hopkinton), a written confession of faith was required of candidates for membership, so that the initiate knew the step he was taking.

"After baptism, laying on of hands was generally performed. The Newport church practiced this from the start, in accord with the English Sabbatarian churches, and the 1833 *Expose of Faith* upholds it.

"Much internal dissension occurred within the churches. Personal and business differences among members were taken before a church council composed of the elders, deacons and several leading members. Recalcitrant members were sometimes excommunicated, with a formal 'Awful Sentence of Excommunication.' A frequent reason was for continual breach of Sabbath or other offense."[37]

Lukewarm and Apathetic

The general trend amongst Sabbath-keeping churches of the nineteenth century seems to have been that they desired to be more and more like the churches around them. They overlooked the fact that they were to be "a special people" (1 Peter 2:9) set apart by God for a particular purpose. This trend is evident in the observation of religious festivals.

"No fact is more fully established than that Sunday and its associate festivals came into Christianity through pagan influence." This included Easter, Christmas, Whitsunday, and others. This was the general Seventh-Day Baptist view until the late 1800s, when Christmas influence began to show itself in the holding of 'Founder's Day' on December 23, in order to hold the interest of the children during the holiday season. It was really only a pretense; a Christmas observation two days early. Now Christmas and Easter are commonly observed among Seventh-Day Baptists.[38]

This period is marked by declining membership and spiritual power. True conversion was sadly lacking in the majority of Sabbatarians.

"Conference reports are rife with admissions of the cold and lethargic state of the Sabbatarian churches at the turn of the nineteenth century. In 1836, there was said to be 'general coldness and apathy' in the whole church. In 1840, despite the 'revivals' in the church, there remained 'widespread, apathy and backsliding.' By 1846, little interest was shown in denominational matters.

"Periodical after periodical published by Seventh Day Baptists folded due to lack of support. In fact, the history of nineteenth-century Seventh Day Baptists is the record of one paper's demise after another.

"A 'tent campaign' began in 1878, with several evangelist preachers in the effort. But the program was soon abandoned, because church members would not support it. A feeble revival of the program was attempted in 1895, with few visible results."[39]

Rise of the Adventists

Sabbatarian history in the mid-nineteenth century is dominated by the Adventist movement.

During this time the Advent movement among Sunday observing churches was begun by William Miller. "In 1843 several followers of Miller in Washington, New Hampshire, became acquainted with the truth of the Sabbath. It was not until after the miserable disappointment of 1844, however, that the general body of Adventists had the Sabbath question called to their attention. A small number accepted the Sabbath and soon united with the few remaining Church of God brethren who refused to be affiliated with the Seventh-Day Baptist Conference.

"They called themselves the 'Church of God' and began publishing 'The Advent Review and Sabbath Herald.' Their first songbook was dedicated to 'The Church of God scattered abroad.'"[40]

"The 'transition period' of Church of God history, from the 1840s to early 1860s, is difficult to record. History seems to focus almost entirely on those Sabbath-keepers who adhered to the 'visions' of Mrs. White, or on those who had lost the proper church name, or history focuses on Adventists who held to the name, 'Church of God,' but did not observe the Sabbath.

"Independent Sabbath-keepers existed throughout the period of 1840–1860 in New York, West Virginia, Ohio, Michigan, and elsewhere. Of these, remnants of Sabbatarian Baptists in West Virginia in the late 1850s combined Sabbath-keeping, Passover observance, and keeping of Biblical food laws with other beliefs strikingly similar to the modern Church of God (Seventh Day)."[41]

"With each passing year, new and different doctrines were being introduced by Ellen G. White to explain away the Adventist failure of October 22, 1844," the predicted date for the second coming of Christ. "The original Church of God brethren generally did not go along with the 'inspired testimony' of Ellen G. White. Finally, a meeting was held by some of the members in Battle Creek, Michigan, September 28 through October 1, 1860."[42]

Seventeen delegates attended the Conference, the purpose of which was to discuss "loyal organization." Most of the speakers held the view that organization when applied to a church was of the devil, that "organization is Babylon." There seemed to be no clear understanding as to how the true Church should be organized and governed.

The Conference did agree, however, that it should legally organize a publishing association. It also recommended that local Sabbath churches be organized.

Another subject considered by the delegates was that of a church name. Some pressed for "Church of God" and others "Seventh Day Adventist," objecting to the former name because it failed to emphasize the Sabbath and the belief in the Second Coming of Christ.

The name "Seventh Day Adventist" was finally chosen. Only one man, from Gilboa, Ohio, voted against this decision, holding out for "Church of God." Many delegates did not consider that a church name had any major significance whatsoever.

In 1863 the first Seventh Day Adventist General Conference was held at Battle Creek. The membership of this church in that year totaled 3,500.

Not all Sabbath-keepers agreed to the new name. Those of Ohio determined to retain the name "Church of God."

"For another seventy years conditions remained almost unchanged. The remaining brethren retained the name 'Church of God,' with headquarters finally at Stanberry, Missouri. Among local congregations only a few individuals repented and strengthened the truth that was ready to perish in their midst. But most of the ministers resorted to organising pitifully weak evangelistic work on the pattern of state conferences rather than yielding themselves to

God's government and direction in the carrying of the gospel with power.

"In fact, instead of the true gospel, most ministers taught a 'third angel's message,' which they had accepted from the Adventist people. They also published a small paper called the *Bible Advocate*."[43]

During this period an evangelistic work took place at Marion, Iowa. Early in 1860 a man named M.E. Cornell arrived in the town and began to preach on the Second Coming of Christ, Sabbath observance and the unconscious state of the dead. His preaching created something of a stir and the ministers of various local churches began to oppose him.

One such minister challenged Cornell to a debate on the Sabbath and state of the dead questions. The debate caused even more local interest as the ministers were unable to counter Cornell's arguments. As a result of this, a new congregation was established at Marion, consisting of about fifty people drawn from several churches in the area.

Separation From Adventists

The new group agreed together to keep the commandments of God and faith of Jesus and to use the Bible alone as their rule of faith and practice. A crisis quickly developed for the new church when a move was made to change the name from "Church of Jesus Christ" to "Seventh Day Adventist." The members were also required to accept the visions of Ellen G. White as having equal authority with the Bible.

"Fully half of the members refused to enter the new organization with its new conditions, but remained firm to the original organization, and to those that remained were added quite a few persons who had been holding back, now came forward and united with them, which made them much stronger than the party that reorganized. Other churches in Iowa were organized, who shortly were also disrupted, and then more or less associated themselves with the Church of Christ in Marion, later known as the Church of God.

"As soon as it was discovered that some of the members of these neighboring churches clung to their original faith, a circular letter was written calling for a conference of the scattered believers which was responded to by meeting of such a conference at Marion, Nov. 5, 1862, when the above circular letter was ordered printed for the call of a conference of a more general nature. The Church at Marion was without a pastor at that time, so one of their members, V. M. Gray, who took charge of the meetings, was voted in as elder of the church."[44]

Another powerful preacher that rose to prominence around the middle of the nineteenth century was a former Seventh Day Adventist, Elder Cranmer. He left that church because he would not accept Mrs. White's visions and the "Shut Door" policy of the Adventists.

"Henceforth Elder Cranmer preached as the Spirit directed, and got quite a following, including several ministers." Persecution had to be endured. "While meetings were in progress at Hartford or near there... they were served with a shower of eggs of no recent date, but the Elder came out of it unharmed, while others were not so fortunate. His wife had on a very nice dress which was nearly spoiled. The perfume of the eggs broke up the meeting that night...

"One more effort was made by the enemy; this time a large bucket of water was placed over the speaker's stand with a string attached. When Elder Cranmer was in the midst of his sermon the string was pulled and down came the water, but the trick did not work as the promoters had expected, for the Elder was unharmed, but a little child lying asleep nearby was nearly drowned.

"Organization was now discussed and was finally effected in the year 1860." Other ministers united until there was a total of twelve. Gilbert Cranmer was the founder of the Church of God in Michigan, and was the first president of the Conference. One writer stated: "To have known Elder Gilbert Cranmer at any time during his life, and especially in his earlier Christian ministry, is to have known one of the most powerful and eloquent ministers of his day."[45]

The Hope of Israel

On August 10, 1863, a new magazine was published with the title *The Hope of Israel*. It was printed at Hartford, Van Buren Co., Michigan, with a subscription price of 75 cents a year. The Resident Editor was Enos Easton; Gilbert Cranmer and John Reed were Corresponding Editors.

The editorial policy was based on ten principles:

1) That the Bible alone contains the whole moral law and that its precepts are sufficient to govern God's people in every age without the addition of humanly devised creeds.

2) That the penalty of sin is death, and that the dead are really dead and "know not anything."

3) That sin is "the transgression of the law," which in effect means breaking the Ten Commandments.

4) Man, having sinned, is under the sentence of death. His only hope of eternal life is by means of a resurrection from the dead, the penalty for sin having been paid by the sacrifice of Christ.

5) This hope in eternal life was a major motivation in Israel and the primitive church.

6) The setting up of the Kingdom of God on earth and return of Jesus Christ is imminent.

7) The reward of the righteous and punishment of the wicked will take place on the earth.

8) The earth will provide the final abode of the faithful saints.

9) That paradise will be restored to the earth and that God will dwell in the New Jerusalem.

10) Man will finally have access to the tree of life and will experience life without pain, death and sorrow.

The effect of this new magazine was to draw together a host of scattered believers and to provide a vehicle through which views on many different religious topics could be shared with others.

One of the first issues carried an article by Elder Cranmer in which he related his experiences in the ministry. His labours had resulted in the ordination of eight ministers and the conversion of several hundred members in the state of Michigan.

He wrote of divine healings, numbering about 100, which included the restoration of sight to the blind and hearing to the deaf.

The *Hope of Israel* attracted interest, it seems, from many parts of the United States, and even beyond. A letter was included in the second issue from a Mr. Tanton Ham of Bristol, England, in which he described the pagan origins of the immortal soul doctrine.

Bible prophecy and its relationship to world news was a common theme and the progress of the Civil War received good coverage in the early issues.

In some areas the preaching activities of ministers was disrupted by the influence of spiritualists, but the magazine reported that the "devils were cast out."

The pages of the *Hope* were available for the expression of widely differing opinions on a variety of subjects. Various opinions were expressed; for example on the subject of whether or not fermented wine should be drunk by church members.

Hope of the End

Booklets were advertised and readers could even send for a book containing "105 choice hymns" for 45 cents. Many contributors to the magazine were convinced that they were living in "the last days" and some even set the date for the end of the world and the return of Christ. One such "prophet" predicted that this event would occur in 1873, basing his prediction on the book of Daniel and added the ominous warning, "Reader, this just leaves ten years to the end of the world..."

This general belief that the end was near seems to have stimulated a measure of zeal and enthusiasm among members. The *Hope* carried several reports of evangelistic campaigns.

The Civil War created many problems for God's people. Most were firmly opposed to participation in warfare and several were sentenced to periods of imprisonment for their refusal to join the army when drafted. One member, John L. Staunton, was disfellowshipped in 1865 for enlisting in the U.S. Army.

Articles covered such subjects as "The Plan of Salvation," "The Mark of the Beast" and "When Does the Sabbath Begin?"

The *Hope* also carried news of conferences and meetings: "At one meeting a Sister Carter of Otsego, who for a long time had been deprived of her power of speech, had a moving experience: her speech was perfectly restored again. Glory to God!"

From time to time readers were urged to increase their contributions in order that the size and quality of the magazine could be enhanced. It was suggested that members might give up the use of tobacco, described as "the poisonous weed" and donate the money saved to "our little paper."

In 1864 the magazine subscription was increased to $1.00 per year, that was for 26 issues. This period seems to have been marked by a measure of growth within the Church of God. Procedures were laid down for the ordination of ministers. Such men had to be full of faith and the Holy Spirit and also to meet the qualifications listed in I Timothy, chapter 3. They were set apart by prayer and the laying on of hands.

Although ministers were ordained partly that order and discipline should exist within congregations, each local church was an independent unit and not under the authority or jurisdiction of any higher church authority. Regular communications did exist between churches, however, in order that their common cause should be promoted.

The need for unity was stressed and so far as the church name was concerned the members used either "The Church of God" or "The Church of Christ." Division was to be avoided and all were to strive for "one faith" and "one baptism."

Several articles and letters appeared which discussed the precise time of the crucifixion and resurrection of Christ. Although most writers took the "three days and three nights" to mean exactly that—72 hours—a measure of confusion existed over the actual time that these events took place.

Hope Declines

The *Hope of Israel* was often plagued by financial problems. H.S. Dille, the office editor, was paid $4 per week, which even in 1865 was considered a low wage. At one point the church owed him between $60 and $70. Even the most dedicated of workers could hardly be expected to continue indefinitely under such conditions; his health began to decline and several issues of the *Hope* did not appear.

Members were constantly urged to do their part and support the magazine financially; some had even neglected to pay their own subscription.

The October 1865 issue was the last one to be published at Waverly, Michigan. No further issues were produced until May 1866, and by this time the paper had been moved to Marion, Iowa. It now had a new editor, W.H. Brinkerhoff, and was published on a semi-monthly basis. The subscription price by this time had increased to $1.50 per year and each issue contained 16 pages.

One of the most energetic ministers of this period was Elder J.H. Nichols. He began preaching for the Church of God in 1861 and continued until his death in 1916. It has been said that he was the first person to take the Sabbath truth west of the Rocky Mountains when he preached on the site of Santa Rosa, California in 1862.

Articles and letters on a wide variety of subjects appeared in the *Hope*. One such article examined "that dreadful disease known as Trichinosis." The writer produced evidence to show that the only certain way to avoid contracting the disease was to avoid eating pork products.

"Clean" and "unclean" meats appeared to have been the theme of several articles.

The magazine contained reports from church conferences and of various evangelistic work conducted by the ministers. In June 1866, H.S. Dille was disfellowshipped for joining the Mormons.

For several years a running battle was fought in the pages of the *Hope and Review* and *Herald* between the Church of God people and the Seventh Day Adventists. The two main points of issue were the validity or otherwise of Mrs. Ellen G. White's visions and the interpretation of the prophecies of the book of Revelation.

By about 1870 a decline in the zeal and enthusiasm of many of the members may be detected. One reason for this could well be the lack of real leadership in the church and the fact that the *Hope*, which was the only real contact that many members had with others of like faith, seemed to lack a clear, decisive and united policy on many vital points of doctrine.

An example of this is the controversy that surrounded the question of whether or not the "wicked dead" would be resurrected. Articles in favour of this and against appeared in the magazine, including the obvious answer that in order to have a "second death" there would have to be a resurrection from the first death.

As a wide variety of often-conflicting opinions were given equal space in the magazine it seems probable that many readers became confused and began to lose interest.

Hope Becomes *The Advocate*

The *Hope* seems to have ceased publication for a period of about two years (1869–71). When it resumed in June 1871, it published "Mr.

Miller's Apology and Defense" being William Miller's reasons why Christ had not returned in 1843–44 as he had predicted.

In 1872 the name of the magazine was changed from *The Hope of Israel* to *The Advent and Sabbath Advocate and Hope of Israel*. This rather cumbersome new title was favoured because the former title did not draw the attention of the reader to the key doctrines of the Church—the Second Coming of Christ and the seventh-day Sabbath. Publication of the paper was suspended between October 1873 and March 1874, due to differences of opinion between the editor and the managers of the Publishing Association.

It was about this time that A.F. Dugger appears on the scene. As a first-day preacher, he had been asked by his denomination to write a book against the seventh-day Sabbath. The material uncovered by his research convinced him, however, that the seventh day and not the first was the true Christian Sabbath.

A letter to the *Advocate* in 1881 suggested that the practice of tithing be introduced. This seems to have been a new doctrine to the Church of God of this period.

The centre of activity for the church appears to have been in Missouri at this time. A series of "camp meetings" were held, which drew crowds of from 1,200 to 1,500 people. These meetings were occasions for both preaching services and social gatherings. They seem to have been quite successful.

The *Advocate* ceased publication for some two years between 1882 and 1884; when it resumed publication, information was given relating to the establishment of a branch of the Church of God at Stanberry, Missouri.

In 1884 Elder A.F. Dugger, who was working from Fairfield, Nebraska, announced the creation of a system of Sabbath school work for young people.

Views were expressed in the *Advocate* that seem strange to a modern reader. During the period 1885–86 several articles appeared which deplored "the evils of the skating rinks."

Magazine Name Changes
The General Conference of the Church of God for 1886 was held at Marion, Iowa. Some interesting statistics were produced at the time, showing how small and lacking in any real impact on the world the

Church of God really was during these final years of the "Sardis" era. Reports revealed a membership of 75 in four churches in Kansas, 440 in 13 churches in Missouri and 365 in the eight churches of Michigan. Total membership of the Church of God in 1887 stood at about 1,000. There were 122 conversions in that year and 30 ministers.

About 1890 the name of the magazine was changed yet again. This time to *Sabbath Advocate and Herald of the Advent*. By 1892 a branch of the Church of God had been established in South Dakota. The following year a songbook of hymns and music was produced that was said to be slanted towards truth so that members could freely sing them; it was advertised in the *Sabbath Advocate*.

So "liberal" was the editorial policy of the magazine that in 1894 several articles were submitted which were against the Sabbath. They were rejected by the editor.

The closing years of the nineteenth century saw a work being done by the church in Oregon, Pennsylvania, North Dakota and several other areas. In 1900 a sanitarium was opened at White Cloud, Michigan. The name of the magazine was changed once again in that same year—this time to *The Bible Advocate and Herald of the Coming Kingdom*.

At the General Conference of 1902 it was suggested that an academy or college for the Church of God should be established.

In 1905 A.F. Dugger became the editor and manager of the *Bible Advocate*. The Conference of that year passed a resolution to reaffirm belief in the doctrine that tithes and offerings were the means by which the Work should be supported.

By 1907 Elder Dugger's health was failing and he retired as editor of the *Bible Advocate*. The vacancy was reluctantly filled by Brother Brinkerhoff. On December 20 of that year a fire destroyed a large part of the *Advocate* building, although most of the printing type was rescued. Some of the machinery and many of the tracts were destroyed by fire and water. The $700 insurance on the building and printing materials covered only a part of the loss, but contributions from members from many parts of the country made up the balance of the loss.

Dugger and The *Bible Advocate*

In 1910 Elder A.F. Dugger died, but by this date we find his son Andrew N. Dugger active in the ministry. The November 1912 issue of the *Bible Advocate* carried news of a series of meetings held by Andrew Dugger in schoolhouses at Empire Prairie, some eight miles from Stanberry. The meetings were moderately successful and it was said that several of those attending had minds receptive for the truth.

Mr. Dugger became quite well known in later years as one of the authors (along with C.O. Dodd) of *A History of the True Religion*. He died in the mid 1970s after one of the longest ministries in Church of God history.

A good deal of space in the magazine was devoted to prophecy and its relationship to world news. The "Eastern Question" concerning the Balkan war and the decline of the Turkish Empire was a favourite theme during 1913. These events were often linked with the Biblical "Times of the Gentiles."

Several articles appeared during 1914–18 on the prophetic significance of World War I. Many writers considered these events as a fulfillment of some of the prophecies of Daniel. During this period A.N. Dugger became editor of the *Bible Advocate*.

A number of public debates were held in 1916 between Church of God ministers and those of other persuasions. Several conversions were reported as a result of these activities. In April of the following year when the United States entered World War I, A.N. Dugger, together with a Congressman from Missouri, had a personal meeting with President Woodrow Wilson, which resulted in the young men of the Church being exempted from combatant service.

The capture of Jerusalem by the British General Allenby towards the end of 1917 led to a series of articles in the *Bible Advocate* entitled "Condensed History of Jerusalem and the Jews."

Church records for 1919 reveal that more than 60 new members were added in the states of Oklahoma, Texas and Missouri. The subject of growth within the church seems to have been on the minds of some at this time as a proposal was submitted that the Church of God establish a college for the training of ministers.

By March 1920, pledges and special offerings for this purpose had been received that totaled $59,083.25 This sum also included several wills. Not all within the church were in favour of the project. Some held the view that God did not need a college for His Work, that the inspiration of the Holy Spirit was sufficient and that colleges and schools were of the Devil.

The Incredible History of God's True Church

The *Bible Home Instructor*

A *Bible Home Instructor* was produced in 1920 and it was offered to book agents who reported good sales. During this period a tent campaign was conducted at Sabatha, Kansas and Maryville, Missouri. Forty-three new members were added to the church.

Numerous campaigns and debates were held in various parts of the United States during 1922 but results were hardly encouraging. By this time field ministers numbered about 40, and their goal was to bring 1,000 new members into the church during 1922. This was probably an optimistic objective.

During that year a new church was established in Mexico City and interest in the Work was reported in China, India, New Zealand and Jerusalem.

Milton Grotz of Bethlehem, Pennsylvania visited Stanberry in 1923. He appears to have had quite a reputation for his healing ministry. People came to his services not only from the local area but also from many miles away.

There were several reports of healing miracles. Grotz, accompanied by Elder Dugger, also conducted evangelistic campaigns at Bassett, Nebraska. It was said that people with all manner of diseases, including cripples, were healed. A local church of more than 80 members was established shortly after the end of the campaigns.

By 1923 the number of ministers had increased to 126 and church membership estimated at 1,000 to 1,500. During the late 1920s the main thrust of the Work seems to have been concentrated in a very aggressive program to sell *Bible Home Instructors*. The salesmen or "Colporteurs" appear to have been pioneers in several new areas. Ministers followed along later and raised up churches after a sufficient level of interest had been aroused.

A very limited foreign work was also being conducted at this time. Some of the church literature was translated into the Swedish and German languages. Some, at this time, began to see the potential of radio as a means of reaching mass audiences, and efforts were made to raise money for a radio work.

The need for unity in preaching and writing was recognized and by 1929 ministers were being urged to speak and write the same thing. It soon became clear, however, that differences of opinion still existed on a variety of doctrinal subjects.

226

It was during this time that a very special ministry was about to begin in the state of Oregon, which was to have a profound impact on the next era of the Church of God.

Chapter Summary
The truth of God established in what was to become the United States of America. In 1664 Stephen Mumford leaves England to establish a Sabbath keeping congregation in Newport, Rhode Island. The later history of the Church of God in the United States of America.

Chapter Fourteen

GO YOU INTO ALL THE WORLD

*"It was like a miracle! And indeed, it WAS a miracle! The very
Holy Spirit of God had come into and renewed my mind"*
(*Autobiography of Herbert W. Armstrong*, Vol. 1, p. 321).

*"And this gospel of the kingdom will be preached
in all the world as a witness to all nations ..."*
(Matthew 24:14).

W e now come to the modern era of the Church of God, a
phase of God's Work, which in several important respects
was quite unlike the earlier eras that had preceded it.
Prior to the twentieth century the Church had experienced only a
limited impact upon the world. During Roman times it was confined
to the Roman Empire and a few areas beyond its borders. For more
than a thousand years during the Dark and Middle Ages, the true
Church was driven underground and subjected to almost continual
persecution. Any public preaching of the true Gospel was on a small
scale and of limited duration.

Even when the fires of persecution began to die down and flicker
out some three centuries ago, the church had become so worn out
by the privations that it had suffered that it could do little more than
hang on to the true doctrines that had been handed down to it from
ancient times. Little by little much of this truth had slipped away and
become lost by the beginning of the twentieth century.

Christ, however, had predicted that a time would come when the
Gospel of the Kingdom of God would be preached *"in all the world"* as
a witness and warning of His imminent return to the earth to set up
the Kingdom and Government of God. The witness would go *"unto
all the nations"* (Matthew 24:14). Although the church itself was still
to be small in number, still a "little flock," it would have set before it
"an open door" through which to reach "all nations" (Revelation 3:8).

The context of these verses and the reference to a worldwide
crisis, shortly before the return of Christ, proves that this passage
was largely prophetic relating to our modern age. The "open door"

through which a small group having "a little strength" could reach the whole world must surely be such present day means of mass communication as radio, television and publishing.

Christ also stated that at the end of the age there would come an Elijah-like figure prior to His return, to perform a similar role. "And Jesus answered and said unto them, Elias truly shall first come, and restore all things" (Matthew 17:11). It is important to realize that John the Baptist, who was a type of Elijah (see vv. 12–13), was already dead and his work completed when this statement was made (Matthew 14:1–12).

This end time "Elijah" would "restore all things," including the knowledge of how to have happy family relationships (Malachi 4:5–6), and to proclaim the gospel on a worldwide scale (Matthew 24:14).

A Worldwide Work Bursts Forth

An "Elijah-type" work, carried out on such a large scale, involving the expenditure of vast sums of money, could not be handled by one man alone. It had, of necessity, to be supported by a group, an entire era of the Church of God (Revelation 3:7–13). Christ said that one should evaluate the fruits—the results—of His ministry. In this chapter we will examine the life and work of Mr. Herbert W. Armstrong and the Worldwide Church of God, which truly did an unprecedented "Elijah-type work" in the twentieth century.

This story "is the incredible story of something never done before—never done this way—a seemingly impossible achievement utterly unique in the world!

"By all the criteria of organizational and institutional experience, it simply could never have happened.

"Every phase of this globe-girdling Work has been something altogether unique—a first—the blazing of a new trail.

"Ambassador College is astonishingly unique among institutions of higher learning.

"*The Plain Truth* magazine is utterly unique in the publishing field.

"The *World Tomorrow* program, viewed and heard by millions on both radio and television daily, is entirely unique in broadcasting.

"And the Worldwide Church of God, behind these global enterprises, is altogether unique on the earth—practicing, as it does, the revealed ways of the living Creator God, and for the first time in 18½ centuries, thundering His all-important message over all continents of the earth."[1]

So wrote Mr. Armstrong in the introduction to the 1973 edition of his autobiography.

The "Work," as it was sometimes called, has been described as one of the most incredible success stories of our time. For 35 years the Work grew at an average increase of 30 percent per year. This means a doubling in size, scope and power every two and two third years, and increasing more than 4,000 times in 32 years.

Here is an organization with no product to sell but rather one to give away, free of charge, to the consumer. Did ever a commercial company, or any other enterprise even set out with such a policy, much less grow and prosper?

Mr. Armstrong took no personal credit for the success of the venture that had dominated his life for more than 50 years.

"For it is the story of what the living God can do—and has done through a very average human instrument, called and chosen by Him—one whose eyes He opened to astonishing truth—one He reduced to humble obedience, yielded in faith and dedicated to God's way! God promised to bless His own Work. And how greatly He has blessed and prospered it like the grain of mustard seed, it grew—and grew!"

A Passion for Success

Mr. Armstrong was born July 31, 1892, in Des Moines, Iowa, of respected Quaker stock. His ancestors had come from England along with William Penn.

His boyhood was a happy one and typical of many others in the United States around the turn of the century. At age 16 he obtained his first job away from home as a waiter in an Altoona hotel. It was at this point in his life that Herbert, inspired by the praise of his employer, began to consider the subject of success in life and, fired with newly acquired self-confidence and a measure of cocky ambition, began to seek out the ladder of success and started to climb it.

This desire to succeed was motivated entirely by vanity and what he was much later to define as the selfish "get" philosophy of life. It was also, however, a burning and driving passion such as only a tiny minority of human beings ever experience. For the majority of people around the world to earn a reasonable wage and to achieve a measure of physical security and comfort represents about the limit of personal ambition.

For several years he read, or, rather devoured, every book that he could obtain relating to personal success, including Benjamin Franklin's *Autobiography*, three times over.

One such work, entitled *Choosing a Vocation*, took him an important step further down the road to success. The thorough self-analysis that was advocated revealed to Mr. Armstrong that he would be most suited to the professions of journalism and advertising.

Although ambitious, he was not too proud to seek and accept career guidance from those that he respected and obtained a job selling advertising space for a newspaper.

He learned by practical experience several of the "Seven Laws of Success." A goal was fixed—to become "important" in the field of business, he educated himself towards the goal and by degrees came to an understanding of the laws that regulate good health.

Drive was developed as he drove himself forward with dynamic energy. Resourcefulness and perseverance were also employed in the relentless quest for success. The seventh law of success was not understood until many years later.

A Flair For Advertising
In 1912, Mr. Armstrong talked himself into an advertising position with *The Merchants Trade Journal* of Des Moines, despite the protests of the advertising manager that no such vacancy existed.

During his time with the *Journal* he was able to develop the crucial skills in writing effective advertisements which were to pay dividends many years later in drawing the attention of the public to his own religious orientated booklets and *The Plain Truth* magazine.

Here, under expert tuition, he learned the art of writing eye-catching and thought-provoking headlines, sub-headings that grabbed the attention and created suspense in the reader—a desire to know more. His text matter began to hold the interest and arouse desire to obtain the product offered for sale and finally an emotional appeal was designed to stir the reader to action—to go out and buy the item that had been promoted.

Within two to three years he was writing ads that brought results. The words and phrases used were plain, simple and direct; they were designed to appeal, in an effective and sincere manner, to the common man or woman, people of average educational background.

Mr. Armstrong began to develop an effective writing style: "It had to be fast-moving, vigorous, yet simple, interesting, making the message plain and understandable." All this training in communication skills, although not remotely realized at the time, was merely preparation for a life's work—which would become apparent much later.

In order to create interest, the ads were presented in a story-flow form, in which the reader felt impelled to read on to the end. They were sincere and based on the slogan *"Truth in Advertising."*

"But I was entirely sincere. Usually a bragging, conceited young lad who is cocky, is also an insincere, flippant, smart aleck. I was not. It seems I was, by nature, deeply sincere and in earnest, and although excessively self-confident, even snappy and cocky in manner, there was always with it a sense of earnestness and dignity. At least I thought I was right, and in my heart meant to be. Human nature wants to be good, but seldom does it want to do good. That natural desire in one to wish to consider himself good, I suppose, led to an attitude of sincerity."[2]

In 1913 Mr. Armstrong began touring the United States as an "Idea Man" for the *Journal*. He interviewed merchants and gathered material on successful business ideas, which he presented in article form in the *Journal*. During this period, he was forced to put a prod on himself and become an "early bird," rising at 6:00 a.m.

Work of this nature gave him the opportunity for in-depth study into the question of why some succeed in the business world and others fail. Much later in life he was to write of his findings in this field in a booklet, *The Seven Laws of Success*. Some of these laws were learned by bitter experience—Mr. Armstrong had his failures as well as successes. Although he was developing valuable expertise in his field, his own lack of maturity caused him to often sell his services at a fraction of their true value. As a piano salesman he was a dismal failure and was unable to sell a single piano.

Mr. Armstrong's real flair was for advertising. He reflected the saying, "Where there's a will there's a way." He was a man of vision and constantly conceived of ideas, involving the skillful application of advertising, which would expand and extend the businesses that received his attention.

During the course of his business career he became personally acquainted with hundreds of prominent bankers and many other leaders in the world of commerce. One of the factors that contributed to his own success was that he spent a good deal of time with men who were successful.

Marriage to Loma Dillon

In 1917, Mr. Armstrong met the woman who was to be his first wife and constant source of help and encouragement for almost 50 years. He was convinced that God, who seemingly was guiding other aspects of his life, played a definite part in the selection of Loma Dillon as the future Mrs. Armstrong.

Loma, who was a distant cousin of her husband-to-be, exuded an almost boundless energy, sparkle, sincere friendliness and outgoing personality. Herbert, himself very much a "live wire," was immediately impressed and found himself drawn towards her.

She was a girl of superior intelligence and high ideals. Although lacking in sophistication and somewhat naive, she did have strength of character and the captivating "unspoiled wholesomeness of an Iowa country girl."

They began to date, by personal contact and exchange of letters, and, over a period of several months, shared each other's views on a variety of serious subjects. Love began to blossom but marriage plans were complicated by the entry of the United States into World War I.

Mr. Armstrong, in common with many other young men, was stirred by the emotion of patriotism and applied to join the army as an officer trainee. He felt very strongly that all plans for marriage should be postponed until after the war was over. Loma, driven by the urgent yearnings of a girl in love, was of the opposite opinion and wanted them to marry without delay.

They were married on Herbert's 25th birthday, July 31, 1917.

Loma Armstrong's Dream

Shortly after the wedding Mrs. Armstrong had a most unusual dream that was so vivid that it left her in a dazed and shocked condition for several days. In the dream, she, along with her husband, was crossing a busy Chicago intersection where Broadway and Sheridan Road meet. Suddenly a dazzling spectacle of stars in the shape of a huge banner appeared in the sky. As she and her husband were looking up at the sight, the stars moved away and three angels descended and began to talk with them; Christ also spoke briefly to them.

The message that the Armstrongs received was that Christ was shortly to return to earth and that they were to have a part in preparing for this awesome event. Mr. Armstrong was embarrassed by the dream, and at the time did not ascribe to it any particular importance or significance.

Later that year, 1917, Mr. Armstrong received a draft classification of "Class IV, Noncombatant," which meant that he was not called up for Army service as he had expected. He was free to continue his promising career in advertising. Success, and along with it personal income, increased rapidly.

"Actually, during these next few years, I did not work more than four or five days a month. But, with the nine magazines and a national circulation, the commission of a half-page, or a full-page contract for one year was rather large. I did not need to have too many of the brilliant days to make a good year's income.

"From memory, my income for that year 1918 was approximately $7,300; for 1919 approximately $8,700; and for 1920 more than $11,000. When you consider what a dollar in those days was worth, those were very good incomes by today's standards."[3]

By 1920 the Armstrongs had become the proud parents of two daughters, Beverly Lucile and Dorothy Jane. The birth of the second baby, however, was accompanied by serious risk to the health of mother and baby.

"The world-famous obstetrical specialist brought in on my wife's case in Chicago, her Des Moines doctor, and my wife's uncle who was a captain in the Medical Corps in the Army, all told us that another pregnancy would mean the certain death of my wife and of the baby. Although we did not know at the time, we learned much later we were of the opposite Rh blood factor."[4]

Business Depression

The lucrative and successful advertising career that seemed to be taking Mr. Armstrong towards his goal of being "important" in the commercial world was not to last. By 1922 the depression that had rapidly swept the United States had ruined almost all of his major clients.

"Things in my business went from bad to worse. It was discouraging—frustrating. I was taking the biggest beating of my life, but hung stubbornly on. Finally, about July 1922, it became necessary to give up our apartment. My income had gone too low to support my family, and at that time we decided that Mrs. Armstrong and the girls should go to her Father's farm in Iowa, to lessen the expenses."[5]

This solution to the problem, however, proved to be no real solution at all. With too much time on his hands and lacking the support and companionship of his family, Mr. Armstrong decided to leave Chicago and join them in Iowa.

For a time Mr. Armstrong went back to selling business surveys to newspapers, but with only a limited measure of success. In 1924 the whole family set out on a trip to visit his parents in Oregon. Their transport was a "Model T" Ford.

After several interesting experiences and a host of car problems they finally reached the West Coast and settled at Portland, Oregon. It was here that a new business opportunity opened up for Herbert— writing big-space ads for a laundry. This was a new style of advertising, being largely educational in content and involved persuading women customers that the laundry would not "ruin" their clothing as some had suspected.

This new venture was successful beyond anything that he had previously tried—there were prospects of an eventual income of up to half a million dollars a year, but then "the bottom fell out" of this new business and his income was reduced to $50 per month. Mr. Armstrong and his family now experienced real poverty and hunger.

"In Chicago I had built a publisher representative business that brought me an income equivalent to $35,000 a year or more before I was thirty. The flash depression of 1920 had swept away all my major clients, and with them my business.

"Now, with a new business of much greater promise, all my clients were suddenly removed from possibility of access, through powers and forces entirely outside of my control. "It seemed, indeed, as if some invisible and mysterious hand were causing the earth to simply swallow up whatever business I started."[6]

Spiritual Turning Point

It was at about this point, in 1926, that Mr. Armstrong was to face the most momentous turning point of his life. An elderly neighbour lady, Mrs. Ora Runcorn, began to re-awaken Mrs. Armstrong's interest in religious and spiritual matters, with the result that Mrs. Armstrong became convinced that the Bible clearly stated that Saturday and not Sunday was the true Christian Sabbath.

To Mr. Armstrong, however, this "wonderful discovery" was nothing short of "rank fanaticism." The controversy became so heated that it seemed this issue could well lead to the break-up of their marriage.

"I felt I could not tolerate such humiliation. What would my friends say? What would former business acquaintances think? Nothing had ever hit me where it hurt so much—right smack in the heart of all my pride and vanity and conceit! And this mortifying blow had to fall immediately on top of confidence-crushing financial reverses.

"In desperation, I said: 'Loma, you can't tell me that all these churches have been wrong all these hundreds of years! Why, aren't these all Christ's churches?'

"'Then,' came back Mrs. Armstrong, 'why do they all disagree on so many doctrines? Why does each one teach differently than the others?'

"'But,' I still contended, 'isn't the Bible the very source of the teaching of all these Christian churches? And they all agree on observing Sunday! I'm sure the Bible says, "Thou shalt keep Sunday."'

"'Well, does it?' smiled my wife, handing me a Bible.

"'Show it to me, if it does—and I'll do what it says.'"[7]

Intense Library Studies

Mr. Armstrong, although he knew little of the Bible, agreed to conduct a thorough study into this question and to find out from the Bible which day Christians should keep holy.

Reduced to a state of virtual unemployment, and having just one advertising account left (which absorbed no more than about 30 minutes a week of his time), he was able to devote six months of his life to an intensive, in-depth study into such questions as—Does God exist?, Did life evolve—or was it created?, Which day is the Christian Sabbath? and other related topics.

This period of intense study was not to be done on a casual basis out of mere curiosity. Much of it was done at the Portland Public Library where he worked from opening to closing time. Each question was examined from every possible angle and viewpoint, often the study continued at home until the early hours of the morning.

The end result of this experience was that Mr. Armstrong found unmistakable evidence that God did exist, that the Bible, in its original form, was inspired and accurate, and that the seventh day was the only Sabbath authorized by the Bible, Christ and the apostles, that Sunday worship had been taken directly from paganism.

He also found evidence that the theory of evolution was both unproved and by its very nature unprovable. Science could offer no answers to account for the host of problems and "gaps" within the theory. The sheer complexity of the vast array of life forms on earth, and the amazing interdependency that existed between them, demanded intelligent planning and creation—blind chance and accident could never account for the varied and exquisite beauty of everything from a tiny insect and delicate flower to the mighty elephant or whale. Mr. Armstrong later wrote booklets that explain the details of his findings.

Evolution could not account for the vast gulf between animal brain and human mind—the only solution to this mystery is that there does indeed exist a "spirit in man" that separates human kind from all other life-forms on earth.

A Painful Conversion

Mr. Armstrong, now at the crucial turning point of his life, realized that God had revealed amazing truth to him. The all-important question was: would he accept it and live by it? God had already "softened" him, it seemed, by destroying every material money making enterprise that had been started. His self-confidence had been shattered.

"To accept this truth meant—so I supposed—to cut me off from my former friends, acquaintance and business acquaintances and associates. I had come to meet some of the independent 'Sabbath-keepers,' down around Salem and the Willamette Valley. Some of them were what I then, in my pride and conceit, regarded as backwoods 'hillbillies.' None were of the financial and social position of those I had associated with.

"My associations and pride had led me to 'look down upon' this class of people. I had been ambitious to hob-nob with the wealthy and the cultural.

"I saw plainly what a decision was before me. To accept this truth meant to throw in my lot for life with a class of people I had always looked on as inferior. I learned later that God looks on the heart, and these humble people were the real salt of the earth. But I was then still looking on the outward appearance. It meant being cut off completely and forever from all to which I had aspired. It meant a total crushing of vanity. It meant a total change of life!

"I counted the cost!

"But then, I had been beaten down. I had been humiliated. I had been broken in spirit, frustrated. I had come to look on this formerly esteemed self as a failure. I now took another good look at myself.

"And I acknowledged: 'I'm nothing but a burned-out old hunk of junk.'

"I realized I had been a swellheaded, egotistical jackass.

"Finally, in desperation, I threw myself on God's mercy. I said to God that I knew, now, that I was nothing but a burned-out hunk of junk. My life was worth nothing more to me. I said to God that I knew now I had nothing to offer Him—but if He would forgive me—if He could have any use whatsoever for such a worthless dreg of humanity, that He could have my life; I knew it was worthless, but if He could do anything with it, He could have it—I was willing to give this worthless self to Him—I wanted to accept JESUS CHRIST as personal Saviour!

"I meant it! It was the toughest battle I ever fought. It was a battle for LIFE. I lost that battle, as I had been recently losing all battles. I realized Jesus Christ had bought and paid for my life. I gave in. I surrendered, unconditionally.

"I told Christ He could have what was left of me! I didn't think I was worth saving!"[8]

Although the process of repentance and real conversion was, for Mr. Armstrong, an experience, painful almost beyond words, to describe, it brought with it a deep and lasting JOY that more than replaced the personal goal of being "important," that he had decided to reject.

In his continual study of the Bible, he began to come to see more and more spiritual truth, "a single doctrine at a time." Although the literature of many religious groups and churches was studied, the Bible alone remained the ultimate authority on doctrinal matters.

Mr. and Mrs. Runcorn introduced the Armstrongs to a small group of "Church of God" people at Salem and Jefferson, Oregon. They began to fellowship with these people.

The Miracle of Baptism

Having seen the clear command to new converts to "repent, and be baptized every one of you in the name of Jesus Christ" (Acts 2:38), Mr. Armstrong became baptized, by total immersion in water. Following this he found that he could now really understand the Bible.

"It was like a miracle! And indeed, it was a miracle! The very Holy Spirit of God had come into and renewed my mind. I had been baptized by the Holy Spirit into the true Body of Christ, the Church of God—but I did not realize that fact literally. I was still to search earnestly to find the one and only true Church which Jesus founded, before recognizing fully He had already placed me in it!"[9]

In August 1927, Mrs. Armstrong became dangerously ill due to an unusual chain of circumstances involving a dog bite, tonsillitis, a "backset," and blood poisoning.

Quinsy developed and her throat became swollen shut. For three days and nights she was unable to eat or drink. Lack of sleep was leading to a state of near exhaustion. The red line of the blood poisoning was streaking up the right arm on its way to the heart; Mrs. Armstrong was not expected to live another 24 hours.

At this point it was suggested to Mr. Armstrong that a man and wife come and anoint and pray for Mrs. Armstrong.

Although feeling embarrassed at the prospect, Mr. Armstrong agreed.

The couple arrived, and after answering several questions on the subject of healing from the Bible, the man anointed Mrs. Armstrong and prayed in faith to God that He, in accordance with His written promise to heal, would totally heal her of all sickness. After sleeping deeply until 11:00 a.m. the next day Mrs. Armstrong arose from bed completely healed.

For the Armstrongs the 1920s marked the beginning of more than a quarter of a century of financial hardship. Although suffering—often to the point of going hungry—the years also brought great personal happiness and joy of understanding more and more of God's truth.

"In those days we were constantly behind with our house rent. When we had a little money for food we bought beans and such food as would provide the most bulk for the least money. Often we went hungry. Yet, looking back over those days, Mrs. Armstrong was remarking just the day before this was written that we were finding happiness despite the economic plight, and we did not complain or grumble. But we did suffer.

"From the time of my conversion Mrs. Armstrong has always studied with me. We didn't realize it then but God was calling us together. We were always a team, working together in unity."[10]

Quest For the True Church

As new doctrinal truths were uncovered one at a time, it seemed only natural that Mr. Armstrong should want to share them with others that he assumed would be overjoyed to receive them. He was sadly disillusioned to find that where obedience to God and His Word is involved few indeed had the motivation of faith to go against commonly held views. Even the "man of God" who had been used in the healing of Mrs. Armstrong was unwilling to accept a point of new truth that Mr. Armstrong had wished to share with him. The sad result was that God took away from him the wonderful "gift of healing" that he had up to that point been using.

Mr. Armstrong was also to learn by bitter experience that he was utterly unable to "get our families converted." The unconverted mind simply cannot understand spiritual things. No person can come to Christ unless God, through the Holy Spirit, "draws" the person.

A question that greatly concerned and perplexed Mr. Armstrong was—where is God's true Church today? Which of the many hundreds of differing sects and churches—if any—constituted the real "Church of God" that Jesus established?

"My shocking, disappointing, eye-opening discovery, upon looking into the Bible for myself, had revealed in stark plainness that the teachings of traditional Christianity were, in most basic points, the very opposite of the teachings of Christ, of Paul, and of the original true Church!

"Could the original and only true Church have disintegrated and disappeared? Could it have ceased to exist? No, for I read where Jesus said the gates of the grave would never prevail against it. Also He said to His disciples who formed His Church, 'Lo, I am with you always.'"[11]

This quest to find the true Church finally led Mr. Armstrong to a small almost unheard of group calling itself "The Church of God," which ran a publishing house at Stanberry, Missouri. Part of the history of this group has been covered in an earlier chapter of this book.

Although it had the right name and obeyed the commandments of God (Revelation 12:17), it numbered only about 2,000 members and seemed to be almost totally lacking in real power and works. As it had more Bible truth than any other group, the Armstrongs began to fellowship with some of its scattered members in Oregon.

Some of the fruits of Mr. Armstrong's research were presented to the church in article form, and several such articles were published in the *Bible Advocate*. Other material, however, although privately endorsed as "new truth" by some of the leaders of the church, was not publicly proclaimed for fear that some members might become offended and withdraw financial support.

First Sermon on the Sabbath

In 1928, after much urging by local church members, Mr. Armstrong preached his first "sermon" to a small congregation near Salem. His subject was the Sabbath Covenant. Leaders within the church began to show signs of concern and suspicion over the members; and opposition, which was to last for several years, began to develop.

That year, 1928, saw the birth of a son to the Armstrongs, Richard David. A year and four months later Garner Ted was born.

This period was one of severe financial hardship for the Armstrongs, but also one of real growth spiritually; a time when humility was developed and when they were forced to rely on God for many of the essentials of life.

Shortly before the birth of Garner Ted in 1930, the family suffered a severe trial. Mrs. Armstrong was anaemic and her condition, which was caused by a serious iron deficiency, threatened the safe delivery of the unborn child. No money was available for hospital bills—even the bill relating to the delivery of Richard David had not yet been paid.

Mr. Armstrong was virtually driven to seek the solution to the problem by fasting and prayer. This period of self-examination to discover where he was wrong, led him to realize that a business project had been absorbing his mind to the detriment of a close relationship with God. He repented of this and within a very short space of time an amazing series of incidents resulted in all of their immediate material needs being satisfied.

"And, Ted, too, was born as a result of an almost incredible miracle of healing only three weeks before his birth! But God had need of these two sons.

"We dedicated them, of course, to God from birth—for Him to use as He had need."[12]

Ordained to the Ministry

In June 1931, after some three years of preaching experience, Mr. Armstrong was ordained a minister—not by the Stanberry, Missouri headquarters, but by the separately incorporated "Oregon Conference" of the Church of God. Not everyone welcomed this ordination.

"From the first, and for some time, I was treated by the ministers as the green-horn tail-ender among them. They used every practice and device constantly to humiliate me and belittle me in the eyes of the brethren. I needed this—and I knew God knew I needed it! Aware of my need of humility, I felt, myself, that I was the 'least of the ministers.' However, the brethren loved me and continued looking to me for leadership. The only 'fruit' being borne resulted from my efforts. This, naturally, was the very reason for the opposition and persecution."[13]

For a time, Mr. Armstrong worked with various ministers of the "Sardis" era, and participated in several evangelistic campaigns. He was employed by the Oregon Conference at a salary of $3 per week. Members also provided the Armstrongs with sacks of flour, beans and other foodstuffs.

Mr. Armstrong came to an understanding of tithing during this period, and found out from experience that it really worked.

The Incredible History of God's True Church

By 1933, opposition and persecution from those within the ministry had reached such a level that Mr. Armstrong felt compelled to reject the $3 salary in order to be free to preach the word of God without restriction. Pressure had been growing within the ministry to dictate what should be preached. Although it was not realized at the time, this rejection of financial support from those who did not support Mr. Armstrong's work, marked the beginning of the "Philadelphia" era of the Church of God, as described in Revelation 3.

A Fruitful Work Begins

"But, from that moment when we began to rely solely on God for financial support not only, but also for guidance, direction, and results, the Work began a phenomenal yearly increase of 30 percent for the next 35 years."[14]

For six weeks during the summer of that year, 1933, Mr. Armstrong spoke at a series of meetings held at the Firbutte schoolhouse near Eugene, Oregon. A new Sabbath-keeping congregation of more than 20 members was established as a result of this.

In September of that year an opportunity presented itself for Mr. Armstrong to speak on a local 100-watt radio station, KORE of Eugene. It was a morning devotional program lasting for 15 minutes and was available, free of charge, to local ministers.

The first program brought a surprising response; 14 letters and telephone calls were received by the station asking for written copies of the message. This was the first time that such a response had been received by a program of this type, and Mr. Frank Hill, the station owner, invited Mr. Armstrong to present a regular half-hour Sunday morning church service, for which a small charge of $2.50 per broadcast would be made.

Mr. Armstrong became aware that God was opening before him, in a small way to begin with, the door of mass evangelism. He had faith that God would provide the financial means by which the broadcast could be sustained.

"And, to finance what He opened before me, He added, slowly, gradually, but consistently to the little family of Co-workers who voluntarily wanted to have a part in God's WORK—in changing hearts, changing human nature, preparing for Christ's coming to CHANGE AND SAVE THE WORLD! But I could not invite people to become

Co-workers. I could welcome them with gratitude when God caused them voluntarily to become Co-workers with Christ—but until they took the initiative I could not ask them. No other activity on earth is operated like this—and perhaps none has grown so surely."[15]

The radio program was first called "Radio Church of God,"[15] and was indeed a church service, including music provided by a mixed quartet. Later, when it was realized that the audience was drawn by the message of a speech-type program, the title was changed to *The World Tomorrow* and the format also gradually changed.

On the first Sunday in 1934, *The Plain Truth* magazine was first introduced to the public through the broadcast. That first issue was "a pretty amateurish, home-made looking sort of thing." About 250 copies were produced by hand on a mimeograph.

The aim was to publish a magazine going to the general public, not primarily church members, to make plain God's truth—the true gospel of God's coming kingdom. For several years all articles were written by Mr. Armstrong.

Like the proverbial grain of mustard seed, the magazine was to grow, and grow, and grow in quality and circulation. By 1973 it had become a high quality, professional appearing, 52–page magazine with a circulation of more than three million.

The Three-Point Campaign

A "three-point campaign" was started, which used the broadcast, magazine, and personal public meetings. Although some believed that people would never support this campaign because "you are preaching exactly what the Bible says—people don't want to be told they are wrong," it was the critics who were proved wrong.

One crucial factor that few understand, or are willing to accept is that "there has been vision behind the planning and phenomenal growth of this great work. But this is the Work of God, not of man."[16]

The early public meetings drew crowds of about 100, but a measure of persecution and opposition was received from local religious sources.

For some years Mr. Armstrong and the little group that looked to him for leadership cooperated with the "Sardis" church but did not "join" it in the sense of coming under its authority.

Although the cost of producing *The Plain Truth* and radio broadcast in 1934 was almost unbelievably small by modern standards, members and co-workers seemed almost never to be able to provide those funds in full. At one point contributions fell short by $4.33 per month.

"I had no idea, then, where that additional $4.33 per month was to come from! But I felt positively assured that God had opened this door of radio, and expected me to walk on through it! And I relied implicitly on the PROMISE in Scripture that 'my God shall supply all your need according to His riches in glory by Christ Jesus.' And although God has allowed many severe tests of faith, that promise has always been kept!"[17]

Walking By Faith

Progress continued to be made, but not without effort and real sacrifice on the part of the Armstrongs and their little band of co-workers. The struggle was "uphill all the way." By August 1935, the radio audience had grown to an estimated 10,000. The number of people attending the public meetings also gradually increased. By 1936 some meetings attracted 200 or more people.

It took time to learn that the Work was to move ahead on faith. When Mr. Armstrong began to rely on the promises of people rather than to simply walk through the doors that God was opening—relying on God to provide the means—at such times the doors remained closed until faith was exercised. By the end of 1936 the broadcast was being carried by the three radio stations of the Oregon Network.

For a two-and-a-half year period, from August 1935 to January 1938, *The Plain Truth* ceased publication entirely. This was later seen by Mr. Armstrong as a punishment and means of correction resulting from his own lack of faith.

During 1937, steady progress was made towards "our goal of 100,000" radio listeners. Looking back on that period, Mr. Armstrong reflected: "WHAT A GOAL! That looked mighty BIG, then! Yet to-day (1973) our listening audience is estimated at some one hundred and fifty MILLION people per week."[18]

Despite persecution, and even attempts by some opposing ministers to stop the broadcast altogether, the Work continued and prospered. Soon it was being heard not only in most of Oregon, but also parts of Washington. Financial contributions, however, as usual seemed woefully inadequate—many were willing to listen to the message but few were willing to provide financial support to help promulgate it.

The Plain Truth was revived in January 1938. Funds were still not available for it to be printed, however, and, as before, it was hand-produced on the mimeograph. The task of producing and sending out the magazine was handled by Helen Starkey, Mr. and Mrs. Armstrong, and a few volunteer helpers. By this time the mailing list had risen to 1,050.

Expenses for the Work (including living costs for the Armstrongs) had by that year reached $300 per month. The financial pressures were such that at one point Mr. and Mrs. Armstrong came close to losing their small home. They struggled on, and, by combining the May-June issue of the magazine in 1938, were able to present the first printed issue. It included, for the first time, the slogan, *"A Magazine of Understanding."*

A Fledgling Work

Although reaching an increasingly large audience, many aspects of the "Work" at this time could only be described as crude: the "office" was no more than a small, inside, unventilated room. There were no filing cabinets—just cardboard cartons, no addressing machine, mail was addressed by hand—even the office desk was an old scarred table.

As war raged in Europe, and the Battle of Britain reached its climax, the broadcast started on KRSC, in Seattle, September 15, 1940. This gave good coverage of the Pacific Northwest.

The Plain Truth at that time was speaking out boldly on world news subjects, as they related to Bible prophecy. The August-September 1940 issue announced that "the invasion of the British Isles is awaited hourly—may be in actual progress before this paper is in your hands—may, possibly, not come at all."

By the end of the year the subscription list to the magazine had reached 3,000, and the estimated listening audience to the broadcast stood at 150,000. Publishing and mailing costs were in the region of $100 per issue of the magazine.

A growing number of listeners to the program were coming to recognize that they were hearing "God's very own message." A small number even began sending financial contributions. Letters were received indicating that an increasing number of lives were being changed by the broadcasts—atheists converted, a suicide prevented, and many after searching for years were now finding a real purpose in their lives.

1941 was a year of rapid growth. The weekly listening audience from the three stations in Eugene and Portland, Oregon, and Seattle, Washington, grew to a quarter of a million. *The Plain Truth* circulation reached 5,000 and by this time it had become a printed 16–page magazine.

Real "growing pains" were experienced about this time. The dismal, cramped "office" with its antiquated equipment became quite inadequate to handle the increasing volume of mail.

In May of that year a larger, sun-lit office became available in the I.O.O.F. building in Eugene. Newer and more suitable office equipment was gradually purchased for a Work that was "growing up."

Mr. Armstrong became filled with an increasing sense of urgency to send out a powerful warning message to modern "Israel," the United States, Britain and other nations of northwestern Europe. Not just his message, of course, but God's.

The *World Tomorrow* Changes Gear

In 1942 the church-service type program (with its singing of hymns prior to the message) was dropped, and the format that became so well known to *World Tomorrow* listeners was adopted. The name of the program was also changed to *The World Tomorrow*. With its increasingly professional presentation, the program became more acceptable to really "big-time" radio stations. A major step forward occurred when it was accepted by station KMTR, located in Hollywood.

Art Gilmore, who was a well-known coast-to-coast announcer, was employed to introduce and sign off the broadcast. The fact that Hollywood was the radio headquarters of the nation was a great advantage, as the Work was able to have access to top quality recording equipment.

Putting *The World Tomorrow* on a Hollywood radio station represented a big leap forward for the Work. It resulted in a doubling of the listening audience.

When an opportunity came to begin daily broadcasting over station KMTR, Mr. Armstrong accepted the offer as a matter of faith—there were no indications at the time as to how the sudden jump in expenses—a doubling in fact—would be met. By now he had learned that when a door opened before him he had to walk through it in faith—relying on God to provide the needed finance. The check for the first week's broadcast took "every dollar we had in the bank."

The response to daily broadcasting was immediate and tremendous, the sudden big increase in financial contributions was sufficient to ensure that the broadcasts could continue. Faith was rewarded—God did supply the funds as and when they were needed. The broadcast was now heard seven days a week in Southern California. It went out at 5:30 p.m. on weekdays and 9:30 a.m. Sunday mornings.

Such was the impact of the broadcast that when the Biltmore Theatre, Los Angeles, was hired for a Sunday afternoon personal appearance campaign by Mr. Armstrong, 1,750 people attended. After the meeting, when the two offering boxes were opened, they were found to contain, to within one cent, the exact sum needed to cover the expenses of hiring the building.

By 1943, the radio broadcast was being heard in every state. Stations had been added in Spokane and San Diego. Later the first superpower clear-channel station could be picked up in every state; one broadcast alone brought in 2,200 letters from listeners.

Shortly afterwards, a second exclusive channel station, the 50,000 watt WOAI, San Antonio, accepted the program; it went out at 11:00 p.m. on Sundays.

During this period, strong persecution was received from organized religious sources, much of it coming from New York—there were many it seems who wanted the *World Tomorrow* broadcast put off the air.

Growth at a Price

As a result of evangelistic services held in the Chamber of Commerce auditorium in Seattle and smaller services at Everett, Washington, a small church congregation was established in that area.

By the end of 1943, *The Plain Truth* was able to list ten stations that carried the broadcast. One small Texas station even offered, without being approached by Mr. Armstrong, to carry the program. In 1944 the mail response indicated that the radio audience had risen to more than half a million and *The Plain Truth* circulation reached 35,000 copies per month, sent out at a cost of $1,000 per issue. Each copy, at this time, had gone down from 16 to only 12 pages.

During the decade between 1934 and 1944 the radio power used by the church rose from 100 watts per week to 91,000 watts. By 1962 it had reached more than 22 million watts per week.

Prior to the founding of Ambassador College, Mr. Armstrong was the only converted and ordained minister in what was then the Radio Church of God (the name was later changed to Worldwide Church of God). As small church congregations were raised up from the growing radio audience, no qualified and dedicated ministers were available to pastor these congregations.

The result was that "fierce wolves" began to enter in, "devouring the flock." This was one of the prime reasons that led Mr. Armstrong to establish the college. Qualified and loyal ministers were desperately needed by the growing Work of God.

In 1944 a major financial crisis developed for the Work. Ten thousand booklet requests went unsatisfied as funds were not available to print and send them out. Prospects of having the broadcast forever off the air induced the Armstrongs to sell their small home. They were determined to keep the Work going, even if "it took our all." For the time being the Work was saved. For Mr. and Mrs. Armstrong, however, the sale of their home meant three frustrating years with no permanent home. They, along with their unmarried children, were forced to move, every few days or weeks, from one temporary home to another.

By this time, they placed no great importance on material prosperity or security. The tremendous spiritual blessings they had come to enjoy, and the privilege of serving in God's Work, far outweighed the loss of worldly acquisitions.

During this period, the radio program was aired by means of electrical transcriptions. Programs were received on large size semi-soft acetate phonograph discs. Each disc recorded 15 minutes and was 15 inches in diameter. Most of the recording was carried out at a professional recording studio at Portland, Oregon. Where possible, Mr. Armstrong visited radio stations, especially the 50,000 watt ones, in order to speak to the listening audience "live."

The next big step forward for the Work came when *The World Tomorrow* was accepted by the 100,000-watt station XELO, of Juares,

Mexico. This station had twice the power of any station in the United States and had an exclusive clear channel. It was heard across the United States and even into Canada. The program was aired at the prime time of 8:00 p.m. on Sunday.

The response was described by Mr. Armstrong as "fantastic," and resulted in a steady increase in circulation for *The Plain Truth* magazine.

In 1945, Mr. Armstrong, as a fully accredited press representative, accompanied by his wife, had the opportunity of attending the San Francisco Conference at which the United Nations Charter was drawn up. He was able to listen to many speeches given by world leaders in which they spoke of civilization's "last hope."

That year also saw *The World Tomorrow* broadcast on a daily basis, coast-to-coast. A major theme that Mr. Armstrong stressed at this time was that Germany, then conquered and devastated, would rise again to head a powerful and prophesied United States of Europe.

An even bigger door was opened to the Work when the broadcast was aired by station XEG, with 150,000 watts at 8:00 p.m., six nights a week. This was in addition to the Mexican station XELO which was also carrying the broadcast six nights a week. The Work during this period experienced rapid growth, circulation for *The Plain Truth* reached 75,000 copies per month.

The Work Grows Up

It has been said that 1946 "marked the very beginning of the organized Work of God in these last days." Until this time it had been virtually a one-man operation, but one man, with the aid of his wife, simply lacked the time and opportunity to handle all the needs of a rapidly growing Work.

Mr. Armstrong had learned by bitter experience that not every person or minister to whom he had entrusted responsibility was as capable or dedicated as the position required. A college was clearly needed, where suitable people could be properly trained and tested before being given ministerial or other important responsibilities. For some time while recording programs at the Hollywood recording studios, Mr. Armstrong searched the Pasadena area for suitable college premises. Several possible sites were examined but the big problem always remained that of raising sufficient funds to make a purchase.

About this time it was decided that the Armstrongs should conduct a nation-wide baptizing tour. Scores of listeners had written from many parts of the United States requesting baptism, and Mr. Armstrong was able to baptize several in local rivers, lakes or streams; some were even baptized in a bathtub.

After the tour it was discovered that a small mansion had come onto the market in Pasadena. It contained some 18 rooms and was located on Grove Street, just off of South Orange Grove Boulevard—Pasadena's "Millionaire's Row."

The building was set in magnificently landscaped grounds, which had become somewhat neglected over recent years—it seemed an ideal setting for a college designed to instill culture and character-building qualities in the students. The one big problem was that it cost $100,000.

A contract was agreed with the owner in which Mr. Armstrong was to pay $1,000 per month until $25,000 had been paid; this would then be counted as a down-payment and then an option to purchase would be exercised leading to the eventual ownership of the property.

Walter E. Dillon, Mr. Armstrong's brother-in-law, agreed to inspect the college and afterwards accepted an invitation to become its first President. He held a Masters degree and had many years' experience in teaching and college administration.

In order to recruit students, the college was advertised in the January-February 1947 *Plain Truth*. The article announced that "Ambassador offers superior advantages in location, beauty of campus, nature of courses of study, high academic standards—advantages in our special recreational and social program, cultural advantages, physical education, as well as in religious instruction."

Ambassador College was not to be a Bible School or Ministerial College, but a general liberal arts institution. It was recognized that one must be called of God to the ministry; a person cannot select it of his own volition, as a career. At the same time, it was expected that God would call a proportion of students and that such would be evident by the "fruits" of their lives.

The college was to be a revolutionary new type of institution, progressive and forward looking, built on sound academic and Biblical principles.

In February 1947, several months before the first Ambassador College was to open, Mr. Armstrong was told of another property that might be available in Switzerland. Stirred by the prospect of a second college where students would have an ideal opportunity to learn European languages, Mr. and Mrs. Armstrong set off at very short notice on the Cunard liner Queen Elizabeth.

Starting Ambassador Colleges

During this trip to Britain and Europe, Mr. Armstrong came to see that the Work needed to expand beyond the confines of the United States. "WE MUST REACH EUROPE, AND ENGLAND, as well as America! Our work is just STARTING!"

From Lugano Mr. Armstrong wrote to those at home, "I have decided DEFINITELY and FINALLY on the Swiss branch of Ambassador." This was not to be, however. "I was to learn, later, that CHRIST had decided DEFINITELY and FINALLY otherwise."

A second college was established, 13 years later, in 1960, not in Switzerland, but in England, not far from London. On the return journey to the United States, a hurricane was experienced in mid-Atlantic. The ship was in "mortal danger." Mr. Armstrong, remembering God's promise in Psalm 107:23–30 regarding those in peril on the sea, prayed in faith, with his wife, that God would calm the storm. Early next morning he awoke to find a calm sea.

Immense problems surrounded the founding of the College at Pasadena. Looking back on those events many years later, Mr. Armstrong was to write that "it became crystal clear, now, why even Satan was so concerned that he threw at us everything possible to stop the founding of the Ambassador Colleges."[19]

The former owner, a Dr. Bennett, seemed to have no intention of moving out or turning over possession of the property. Subtle tactics were used to finally gain possession.

Opposition to the founding of the College was also experienced from within the church.

"But some in the Church did not like the idea of my moving to Pasadena to start a college. Several were becoming self-centered and local-minded.

"...Those who disagreed with the wisdom of founding the College— who could not see God's hand in the College found sympathizers siding with them, until about half the Church members became antagonistic. They left it for Mrs. Armstrong and me to go it alone, in the struggle to found the College. But we were not alone. The living CHRIST never forsook HIS work!"[20]

As if this were not trial enough, the College next faced a $30,000 "headache." Building inspectors found that the College building did not reach the standard required of a classroom building. All walls and ceilings needed to be torn out and replaced with a one-hour-fire resistant construction.

The financial pressures became almost unbearable. Everyone, it seems, apart from the Armstrongs, "knew" that the College would "fold up" even before it opened its doors to the first students. Once again, however, faith was rewarded and donations covered the extra expenses.

The Pasadena College Opens

The College did finally open on October 8, 1947, with four students and a faculty of eight. Like other aspects of the Work the College also started as small as the proverbial grain of mustard seed.

Another problem Mr. Armstrong discovered was that the vision he had of the type of education which the college was to provide was not shared by the first members of the faculty. They never seemed able to grasp that the College was to be neither a "religious" school nor a rubber stamp of other secular institutions. It was intended to be a liberal arts, co-educational institution—but based on God's revealed knowledge.

After leaving curricula-planning to the leading faculty members, Mr. Armstrong was dismayed to discover that his own theology course had been reduced to a two-hour minor subject. From then on he insisted that all students and faculty members attend his lecture. Everyone was to know what he and the College stood for—even if not all accepted these precepts. Some attempts were made to inject atheistic and other views that were contrary to the policy that the Bible was to be the starting point in attaining knowledge. Such problems gradually faded out when converted Christians were added to the faculty.

Financial pressures, resulting from attempting to operate a College and radio broadcast with inadequate funds, led to a reduction in the program schedule and a "half-time" college for which teachers received half pay during 1948. Three female teachers failed to return to college after the end of the first college year.

Photo Credit: Misty Crowe

Ambassador College, Pasadena Campus
Herbert Armstrong's vision became a reality.

At the end of 1948 a "supreme crisis" loomed for the Work. A lump sum of about $17,000 had to be paid on December 27, to cover taxes, insurance and interest relating to the College; this, of course, was in addition to all the other expenses and costs of running the Work. An amazing thing then happened. The normal daily income at that time was $500 to $600; for 15 days during the first half of December, as if by a miracle, the income soared to about $3,000. The result was that all outstanding debts were paid on time and the College survived.

During 1949 and 1950 the Work continued to experience a tight financial squeeze. Only four issues of *The Plain Truth* were printed in 1950, each copy reduced to just eight pages.

Firstfruits of the College
In 1951 the first two students to graduate, Herman Hoeh and Betty Bates, received their degrees. Additional property and land was purchased, which provided the small but growing College with an athletic field and dormitories.

The first "fruits" of the new College were produced in that year. The young Mr. Hoeh began to assist Mr. Armstrong with the teaching schedule. He handled some of the Bible courses. His articles also began appearing at about this time—first in the publication for Church members only—*The Good News*—and later in *The Plain Truth*. Up to this time Mr. Armstrong had written all articles in church publications.

Another student, Raymond Cole, took over the duties of pastor of the Portland, Oregon church for several months during 1951. Mr. Cole, Dick Armstrong and Roderick Meredith comprised the Ambassador College graduating class of June 1952. Along with Mr. Hoeh, Mr. Meredith began assisting Mr. Armstrong with writing and editing both *The Plain Truth* and *The Good News* magazines.

During 1953 *The Plain Truth* increased its size back up to 16 pages, and was published on a monthly basis. Up to this time it appeared only when funds permitted, often no more than three or four copies a year. As time passed the College produced trained editorial staff, who relieved Mr. Armstrong from some of his crushing responsibilities.

Richard D. Armstrong and Herman L. Hoeh took a trip to Europe in 1952. Their report was published in *The Plain Truth*, its very first material that had not been written by Mr. Armstrong. From that time on Ambassador College strove to produce students who are able to speak foreign languages "like a native."

Mr. Armstrong's radio broadcast was heard on eleven stations in 1953, and this year marked the beginning of what came to be known as the "Foreign Work." On January 1, on the nineteenth anniversary of the *World Tomorrow* broadcast, the program was first aired over Radio Luxembourg, the most powerful radio station on earth.

In October of that year the Work took a great leap forward when the radio program went onto the ABC, coast to coast, national radio network. It meant millions of new listeners every week and tremendous prestige. This move put the broadcast on some 90 additional radio stations every Sunday.

The Work Starts in Britain
Shortly after the broadcast began on Radio Luxembourg, it became necessary to open an office in Britain to handle the mail response. In February 1953, Dick Armstrong flew to London and arranged a mail address—B.C.M. Ambassador, London, W. C. 1. He remained in Britain for several months, handling the mail.

Herbert and Loma Armstrong
Graduation Day, Bricket Wood, 1966

For a time after this the British Monomark office forwarded the mail direct to Pasadena, but this proved an unsatisfactory, short term arrangement. It became essential that a permanent office be established in London, and that Mr. Armstrong should see for himself the plans that needed to be made to take care of the small but growing European Work.

Public meetings were held during 1954 in Belfast, Glasgow, Manchester and London, which gave Mr. Armstrong an opportunity to meet and address some of the *World Tomorrow* radio audience. Mr. and Mrs. Armstrong, along with their son Dick and Roderick Meredith, were able to do a little "sight seeing" in Britain and Europe as well as making arrangements for the promotion of the Work in those areas.

The public meetings in Britain drew crowds of up to 750 people, and the theme of the lectures was *"What's Prophesied for Britain."* During the visit Mrs. Edna Palin of Crewe was baptized by Dick Armstrong the first baptized Church member in Britain.

Very slowly the Work in Britain began to grow. A small church was established in London during 1956. As the radio program went out at 11:30 p.m. (later changed to 6:00 p.m.), the response was poor. During 1957 a lecture series conducted by Roderick Meredith, and followed up by a period of intensive preaching and counselling, resulted in an increase in the church congregation to 30 people.

The task of feeding this little flock was taken over by Gerald Waterhouse in 1958, and steady growth continued. By the end of that year the circulation of *The Plain Truth* in Britain had reached about 12,000, and the fledgling church had increased to 75 members.

The dedicated ministry of Mr. Waterhouse produced steady growth. By July 1958, when he left to take an assignment in the United States, the church congregation of London averaged about 45 each Sabbath. Mr. Raymond F. McNair arrived with his family that same month to assume responsibility for the Work in Britain.

During the summer of 1958, Mr. McNair, assisted by George Meeker, conducted a full-scale baptizing tour of England, Scotland, Ireland and Wales. About 60 people were baptized.

Between 1958 and 1966 a spectacular growth-rate in Britain took the membership figures from 30 to 1,030.

In 1959 Mr. McNair began conducting Bible Studies in Bristol and Birmingham. The Bristol meetings were held in the home of a local member, and attendance averaged 18. Early in 1960, Sabbath services began in the Grand Hotel, located in the centre of Bristol.

Mr. McNair, looking back on those days, reflected: "We averaged about 20 each Sabbath—if I counted myself!"

The British Work Expands

An evangelistic campaign conducted in the summer of 1960 doubled the numbers of this struggling little congregation to 40 members.

The Plain Truth for June 1960 carried an *"Important Announcement to Our British Readers"* from Mr. Armstrong.

"I have important news for you! We are opening a campaign of dynamic evangelistic meetings in Bristol—starting Monday night, June 20.

"Never has Bristol and its surrounding area heard the shocking, sobering facts that are going to be disclosed during this lively campaign—facts I cannot give over the air!"

The theme of these meetings was: what lies ahead for Britain and the world in the immediate future, as described in Bible prophecy. Roderick C. Meredith was the speaker.

"Mr. Meredith is fully consecrated, utterly sincere and in earnest, stirringly dynamic. He knows what he is talking about! And he is going to talk! He is going to tell you things you can't hear from any other source! He is coming in the power of the living Christ, supercharged by his Holy Spirit!"

Bricket Wood

The Bricket Wood campus of Ambassador College, outside London, operated from 1961 to 1974 and was the primary international training college for the Church. Situated a short distance from St. Albans where the Apostles Peter and Paul are believed to have brought the gospel to England 1,900 years prior.

Potential listeners were warned: "Yes, you'll be shocked, surprised—you'll hear more real truth in one night in these meetings than most people learn in years of the preaching of our day!"

The lectures were held five nights a week at the Y.M.C.A., Colston St., Bristol.

Later that year, campaigns were held in Birmingham and Manchester. Church congregations of some 45 to 50 people were established at these locations.

During this period, advertisements were placed in the British editions of *Reader's Digest* magazine, which were said to have had "a terrific effect," with about 10,000 people requesting literature as a result.

On October 14, 1960, a second Ambassador College campus opened its doors at Bricket Wood, Hertfordshire, not far from London.

By 1966, several additional church congregations had been established in Britain. Attendance figures for that year were as follows: Bricket Wood, 300; London, 220; Warrington, 120; Birmingham, 120; Belfast, 115; Bristol, 78; Leeds, 57; Glasgow, 70; Newcastle, 45.

During the period of 1965–67, the British Work received a tremendous boost when *The World Tomorrow* was accepted by several commercial radio stations. These so-called "pirate" stations were located on ships, off the coast of Britain, and a powerful "witness" was beamed across the nation. Garner Ted Armstrong, who was the main speaker at the time, expressed his delight when he heard his own voice coming from several car radios as he was held up for a few minutes in a London traffic jam.

Although the Bricket Wood campus was forced to close down in 1974 due to financial pressures within the Work, a vigorous public lecture campaign, along with advertising *The Plain Truth*, kept the British public aware of the Work, and a steady growth rate continued.

The British press had in general a somewhat negative approach to the Work; its main concern was over the question "Where does the money come from?" A measure of unrest was generated in 1976 when three of the top men in the British Work were disfellowshipped. Following that, however, the Work in Britain enjoyed a healthy increase in its income, and the policy of advertising *The Plain Truth* and booklets in newspapers and magazines brought a response from several thousand new readers.

Into All the World

In 1955, the *World Tomorrow* broadcast was beamed to the vast Indian sub-continent over Radio Ceylon. The following year saw it going out over an Australian network of eight stations. An office was opened in Sydney during 1959, and within a short time a number of churches were started in the land "down under." An advertising campaign in the Australian and New Zealand editions of the Reader's Digest gave an additional boost to the Work in that region. Many radio stations were added, and by 1968 the broadcast could be heard in most parts of the island continent. A number of Garner Ted Armstrong hour-long television specials and selected half-hour programs were later shown on Australian television. Thousands of Australians began to attend regular "Worldwide Church of God" Sabbath services.

The following 20 years saw rapid growth for the Work in the Philippines, Malaysia, Burma, India and other parts of Asia. In 1974, Mr. Armstrong was received as an honoured guest by Philippine President Marcos. He also conducted several personal appearance campaigns, which drew crowds of many thousands of local Filipino people. Church membership increased rapidly in the area during the following years.

In 1960 the broadcast was carried on three Canadian radio stations, and a year later the Work opened an office in Vancouver, under the management of Mr. Dennis Prather. The modest two-room office suite was to soon prove inadequate for the soaring growth-rate of the Canadian Work. By 1974 the total mailing list for *The Plain Truth* had passed the 200,000 mark. The magazine was available in both the English and French languages.

Mr. Armstrong launched the *Tomorrow's World* magazine in June 1969 with Roderick C. Meredith and Herman L. Hoeh serving as writers and senior editors. Adding to the Church's already long-running *The Plain Truth* and *Good News* magazines, Mr. Armstrong wrote about the purpose of the new *Tomorrow's World* magazine, "Consequently, we get this GOOD NEWS to the world in the world's language. *The Plain Truth* magazine makes that Truth plain—in a language this world understands, and will accept. But now comes *Tomorrow's World*, for those who accept the one Source where this Truth may be found—those who wish to go *deeper* into this precious gold mine of Truth, IN ITS OWN LANGUAGE!"

In addition to the radio broadcast, by the mid 1970s, some 265 Canadian television stations carried the Work's telecast. By this period there were also more than 8,000 people attending Church services around the globe.

From 1954, the *World Tomorrow* broadcast was carried by a number of radio stations in Africa that stimulated a demand for Church publications far in excess of the available supply. In 1970 a major baptising tour of East, Central and West Africa was undertaken that resulted in additional membership. Mr. Harold Jackson ministered to the spiritual needs of people in this area.

The Work was able to use the tools of radio, television and publishing to send out a witness in South Africa and Rhodesia. Mr. Armstrong's meetings with political leaders in South Africa and South West Africa gave the Work increased prestige and Church membership rose steadily.

For many years the *World Tomorrow* broadcast had been going out in the French, German and Spanish languages, not only to European nations but also to areas such as Canada, South America, and the West Indies where a significant proportion of the local populations spoke such languages. It can truly be said that, "The sun never sets on the worldwide work of the Worldwide Church of God!" *The Plain Truth* and other literature, including booklets on a host of subjects, became available in an increasing number of foreign languages.

A Very Fruitful Work

The true gospel was indeed being preached, and published, in all the world for a witness unto all nations (Matthew 24:14; Mark 13:10).

In terms of figures and statistics, the output of the Work during its 45-year life had been truly amazing. By 1979 it had produced 4,891 radio programs and 768 television programs. The total amount of literature mailed out added up to 288 million pieces, 224 million copies of *The Plain Truth*, 12 million copies of *Tomorrow's World* and 12 million copies of *The Good News*; a staggering overall total of 536 million items.

The Work by 1979 had received 37 million letters, which if put in a stack would reach 14 miles high. Since 1973 it had received 2,090,000 telephone calls via the WATS telephone service. A total of 565 church congregations met in various parts of the world, the 71,003 members were served by about 1,000 ordained ministers. Some 100,000 members and others gathered for the annual Fall Festival, kept in 75 locations around the world.[21]

The Worldwide Church of God recognized that it needed to play a part in serving the physical and cultural needs of the world, in addition to its important spiritual role. In 1975 the Ambassador International Cultural Foundation (AICF) was founded. It was dedicated to serving mankind, of helping people to realize and fulfill their individual and collective potentials. To achieve this objective a number of humanitarian, cultural and educational projects and programs were instituted throughout the world.

These activities included assisting handicapped children, promoting major cultural events, and sponsoring archaeological excavations. The elegant Ambassador Auditorium was used as a beautiful setting for AICF-sponsored concerts at which world-renowned singers, musicians, dancers and entertainers delighted the audience and raised funds for charitable concerns. The prestige of the Church was also enhanced by such "good works."

Perhaps the most unexpected and inspiring aspect of the Work in the 1970s was the personal meetings that took place between Mr. Armstrong and a host of world leaders, which included the emperors of Ethiopia and Japan, in addition to the kings, presidents and prime ministers of many nations around the world.

Many world leaders recognized Mr. Armstrong as a leading educator, spiritual leader, and as an "ambassador for world peace." He spoke to them of the "missing dimension" in world history, and of the fact that "a strong hand from someplace" would soon restore peace and set up a world government.

In December 1979, Mr. Armstrong made a very significant visit to the People's Republic of China—the first such visit of a leader from the world of Christianity since Communists came to power in that country.

Chinese leaders greeted Mr. Armstrong with friendliness and the level of official honour that is reserved for high-ranking political visitors from foreign countries.

Mr. Armstrong and his party were housed in the government guest State House of Beijing. They were able to visit the Great Wall of China, the Forbidden City, and other places of interest.

Mr. Armstrong was the guest of honour at several official banquets attended by high-ranking Chinese leaders and also diplomats and ambassadors from 57 other nations.

In his address to such important gatherings, he was not lacking in the skills of a diplomat himself. In this atheistic nation he spoke of the return of Christ in the terminology of the intervention of a "strong unseen hand from someplace" that would usher in a time of world peace. Even some of the inscrutable Chinese seemed to be impressed by Mr. Armstrong's theme of the "give" and "get" philosophy of life.

A one-hour meeting was held with Vice Chairman Tan Zhen-Lin, one of the top men in the Chinese government. This man and his colleagues were responsible for moulding the thinking of one billion people (one thousand million), a quarter of the earth's population.

Invitations were received for Mr. Armstrong to visit leaders in the Soviet Union, Poland, North Korea, and several other nations.

At an age when most men or women would be content with a quiet and dignified retirement, Mr. Armstrong, and the Church he represented, seemed intent on ensuring that the prophesied witness of Christ's return and the setting up of the Kingdom of God would without fail be "preached throughout the whole world."

Chapter Summary
The Church in the twentieth century. The life and work of Mr. Herbert W. Armstrong, one of the most prominent religious leaders and televangelists of the twentieth century. A worldwide work of taking the true Gospel to all nations.

Chapter 15

A PLOT IS THWARTED

*"Do you condemn people as children of the devil just because they keep
the fourth commandment on the wrong day? To keep the Sabbath on
Sunday... is not the same thing as being in rebellion against God"*
(Joseph W. Tkach, Letter to a minister, 1994).

*"But I fear, lest somehow, as the serpent deceived Eve by his craftiness,
so your minds may be corrupted from the simplicity that is in Christ"*
(2 Corinthians 11:3).

The 1980s proved to be one of the most traumatic decades in
the entire history of the Church of God. Mr. Armstrong's
policy of putting the Church "back on the track" doctrinally,
following the liberal years of the previous decade was producing
good fruit. Church membership and income increased steadily and
opportunities for Mr. Armstrong to visit world leaders continued. In
late 1980 he was able to meet President Anwar Sadat of Egypt.

During the following year he was able to hold important meetings
in Japan and the Philippines. In a co-worker letter dated February 8,
1981, Mr. Armstrong reported "in Tokyo I spoke a vigorous message
on the soon coming Kingdom of God at a banquet of some 400
important and leading people of that energetic and upcoming nation.
Then I spoke on the Sabbath afternoon to 100 Japanese subscribers
to *The Plain Truth*, mostly college students and professors"
(*Autobiography of Herbert W. Armstrong*, Vol. 2, p. 618).

Church television programs from this period often showed
material that had been taped during these foreign visits. 1982 became
the most successful year to date for God's Work. *The Plain Truth*
circulation reached more than 5 million copies a month. The number
of television stations that showed the telecast also increased.

Bible prophecy was the theme of many magazine articles; one
subject to receive regular coverage was the coming "United States of
Europe." During 1984 Mr. Armstrong visited the Church sponsored
Youth Camps in New Zealand and Australia. He received an enthusi-
astic response from several hundred young people.

Towards the end of that year, Mr. Armstrong conducted a five-week tour of the Far East. In Bangladesh he was deeply moved by the living conditions of this country with a population of more than 100 million people. It is one of the poorest countries on earth. Areas such as this show the desperate need for Christ to return and set up the Kingdom of God.

Probably the most important event in Mr. Armstrong's life during 1985 was the writing and publication of *Mystery of the Ages*, which he considered to be "the largest and most important book of my life."

By the final weeks of that year, however, it was becoming clear to Mr. Armstrong that his life was drawing to a close. In a letter to the brethren dated November 25, 1985, he mentions "I have been suffering a serious illness that started from a flu bug in August. Since then I have been confined to my home... I have been unable to rid myself of a fever that has left me with low blood levels and very little strength."

On January 10, 1986, Mr. Armstrong wrote his final letter. "This is my first letter to you in 1986, and could very well be my last. Now in my 94th year I am in a very physically weakened state enduring severe pain and with virtually no strength whatsoever." He also mentioned that Mr. Joseph W. Tkach had been appointed Deputy Pastor General. He would take over the position of Pastor General in the event of Mr. Armstrong's death.

Six days later, on January 16, 1986, Mr. Armstrong died. So ended the life of perhaps one of the most important and influential leaders in the Church of God since the first century.

The New Administration

For a time the Work of God continued to grow and prosper under Mr. Tkach's leadership. On March 6, 1987 he was able to report, with confidence, that "the Work of God is certainly continuing to grow!"

The growth figures for the previous year were very impressive. Telecast related phone calls were up 46.6 percent. Many individual telecasts produced more than 26,000 responses. *The Plain Truth* circulation figures reached around 8 million copies per month. In 1986, 100 million pieces of literature were sent out. By 1987, Church income had reached a record level of $192 million. The following year it had reached an all-time high of $201 million. Church membership figures reached 88,455 by the end of 1987.

That year of 1987, however, was a pivotal one in the history of the

Church. A new booklet on the subject of healing was published and the first of many doctrinal changes or "clarifications" was introduced. This first "clarification" specifically related to the Passover, divine healing and the medical profession, and was the beginning of a veritable avalanche of changes that one minister described as "living through a doctrinal tidal wave." But by no means could it be said that all of the changes were in total harmony with the Scriptures.

The end result of this process was that within about 10 years, the Worldwide Church of God had abandoned most of the Bible-based doctrines it had received under Mr. Armstrong's leadership and had returned to mainstream Christianity.

Even writers on religious issues who had no connection with the Church of God were amazed at such a radical and comprehensive turnaround in doctrinal belief over such a short time, which is almost without precedent throughout Christian history.

Author Anne Sanderson, a former Jehovah's Witness, in her book *Fearless Love*, comments (p. 238) that: "in view of the astounding about turn—which started around 1987 with the Worldwide Church of God (founded by Herbert Armstrong and known by its free magazine, *The Plain Truth*, which was first published in 1934), it is just possible that a similar change might take place within the Watchtower Society."

In his perceptive and well-researched 2013 book *The Fragmentation of a Sect—Schism in the Worldwide Church of God*, author David V. Barrett mentions the "cognitively dissonant elements" or confusion created by attempting to reconcile two very different and contradictory opinions.

In his lengthy sermon of late December 1994, Mr. Tkach rejected many of the most fundamental teachings that the WCG had held during the Armstrong era. For those with eyes to see, WCG was now clearly heading back into mainstream Christianity.

For author Barrett, who is writing from the perspective of a sociologist, rather than that of a theologian, the ramifications of this astonishing sermon are all too obvious. He writes on page 94 of his book:

"The old Worldwide, with all its distinctive doctrines, was now officially dead, replaced by the new Worldwide, almost indistinguishable from standard Evangelical Christianity."

In effect, members were being told that Mr. Armstrong's teachings, upon which they had based their lives probably for several decades, were all wrong. Mainstream Christianity had been right all along.

Could any sermon have had a more dramatic impact on its hearers? According to Mr. Joseph Tkach Jr., within a year membership had fallen from 109,600 to 66,400!

In 1998, a senior leader of WCG, Greg Albrecht, described Mr. Armstrong as a false prophet and heretic. By 2009 the Worldwide Church of God had even abandoned its name and became "Grace Communion International."

For Certain Men Have Crept In Unawares

The New Testament contains several strong warnings about Satan, the tireless enemy of the church. His aim is to infiltrate the Church of God and destroy it from within. His agents or ministers (2 Corinthians 11:14–15) seek to gain positions of prominence or influence and then destroy the truth of God, and along with it the converted membership.

Jude, in his letter to the church (written circa 80 A.D.) warns that "...I find it necessary to write to you exhorting you to contend earnestly for the faith which was once for all delivered to the saints. For certain men have crept in unnoticed, who long ago were marked out for this condemnation, ungodly men, who turn the grace of our God into lewdness and deny the only Lord God and our Lord Jesus Christ" (vv. 3–4).

The Apostle Paul, writing some 20 years earlier, mentions the same problem, "But I fear, lest somehow, as the serpent deceived Eve by his craftiness, so your minds may be corrupted from the simplicity that is in Christ. For if he who comes preaches another Jesus whom we have not preached, or if you receive a different spirit, which you have not received, or a different gospel, which you have not accepted—you may well put up with it" (2 Corinthians 11:3–4).

Earlier in this letter Paul mentions the process that leads to conversion. Quoting a passage from Isaiah, he urges Christians to... "come out from among them and be separate, says the Lord. Do not touch what is unclean, and I will receive you" (2 Corinthians 6:17).

The Apostle Paul, about to depart from Ephesus, warned the church elders to beware of false teachers. "Therefore take heed to yourselves and to all the flock, among which the Holy Spirit has made you overseers, to shepherd the church of God which He purchased with His own blood. For I know this, that after my departure savage wolves will come in among you, not sparing the flock. Also from among yourselves men will rise up, speaking perverse things, to draw away disciples after themselves" (Acts 20:28–30).

The entire process of conversion involves coming out of the world, spiritually, and being separate from it. Satan, operating through those leaders that he can influence, preaches a message, often under the guise of "new truth," which involves rejecting the real truth of God and returning to the world—Satan's world—that they have been called out of. This, in effect, is a reversal of the conversion process.

Such teachings often promise an easier lifestyle; they appeal to human nature. We all want to fit in with our local community. Nobody wants to appear different or odd. We want to be accepted by people around us.

The WCG doctrinal changes were not introduced all at once, but over a period of time. This reminds us of the well-known analogy of the frog in the pan. If a frog is put into a pan of hot or boiling water it quickly jumps out because it recognises the danger it is in. If, however, the heat is increased slowly and gradually, the frog does not realise what is happening until it is too late.

Amazingly, most within the Worldwide Church of God, perhaps as many as two thirds, failed to grasp the spiritual danger they were in. Some accepted the changes and others became upset, confused and left the church. Let us hope, in time, that many such people will, like the prodigal son of the parable, "come to themselves," repent and return to God and His truth.

The Changes

Depending on how one defines a change in doctrine or policy, it could be said that the Worldwide Church of God introduced dozens or even hundreds of changes during the final years of the twentieth century. It would require an entire book to cover all of these in detail, so I will just deal with some of the most important changes here.

United States and Britain in Prophecy

One of the most important and frequently requested of Mr.

Armstrong's books was *The United States and Britain in Prophecy*. This book uses Bible prophecy and history to explain what happened to the so-called "lost" ten tribes of Israel. The focus of much end-time prophecy relates to the modern descendants of ancient Israel, so we need to know who these people are and where they now live.

By 1992 the Worldwide Church of God was well on its way to phasing out this important teaching. Joseph Tkach Jr., in a letter to another WCG minister, stated: "when you stop and consider the significance of Acts 4:12, the teaching about the US & BC has NO SIGNIFICANCE." He later added that "all of our traditional proofs are based upon folklore, legend, myth and superstition" (letter dated August 10, 1992).

The quoted Bible verse states: "Nor is there salvation in any other, for there is no other name under heaven given among men by which we must be saved."

The subjects of personal salvation and Israel in prophecy, though having some connection, are not talking about the same thing. We cannot say that one negates or contradicts the other. Given that the modern Church of God has a duty to warn the modern descendants of ancient Israel of what lies ahead for them unless they repent, it is simply incorrect to call the *The United States and Britain in Prophecy* of "no significance." In 1993 Mr. Armstrong's book was removed from circulation.

Tithing

The people of God, from ancient times, even as early as the time of Abraham, paid tithes, along with offerings. In ancient Israel, it was the Levites who received the tithes of the people. From the time of Christ, tithes were to be given to the Church, as the continuation of Israel and the representatives of Jesus Christ as our High Priest (Galatians 6:16; Hebrews 7:8–17). Tithes and offerings, commanded by God (Malachi 3:8–11), are used by the church as a means of fulfilling its commission to preach the gospel and look after the flock.

Mr. Armstrong, in his booklet entitled *Ending Your Financial Worries*, makes the very bold statement: "so tithing, far from being abolished is NEW TESTAMENT law."

The new WCG administration later decided "under the New Covenant the tithe is voluntary..." (Joseph W. Tkach, *Pastor General's*

Report, January 5, 1995). Yet Jesus Christ said that we should live by every word of God (Matthew 4:4) and there is no indication that tithing should be discontinued under the New Covenant.

As one might have expected, some members were quick to take advantage of this new personal "freedom" and WCG experienced a catastrophic loss of income during the 1990s.

In just 5 years from 1990–1995, income plummeted from $211 million to $103 million. This was only partly due to the changes made to tithing. Many of the other doctrinal changes would also have an impact on church income. By 1997 church membership had dwindled to around 58,000, a fall of about 60 percent from its peak of an estimated 150,000 less than ten years earlier. Church income continued its sharp decline.

The Trinity

The doctrine of the Trinity, the concept of a triune God—one God consisting of three persons—is accepted by most church authorities as the "litmus test" of genuine Christianity.

The Trinity doctrine, however, though a common concept in many ancient pagan beliefs, is not found in the Bible. Some might be tempted to turn to 1 John 5:7 to disprove this, believing that this verse supports the trinity. It reads (in the *King James Version*): "For there are three that bear witness in heaven: the Father, the Word, and the Holy Spirit: and these three are one."

The problem here is that the Apostle John never wrote this. Many Bible translations point out that this verse is not found in any early Greek manuscripts written before the fifth century. It is almost certainly a fifth-century addition to the text. No early Greek or Latin writers quote this verse, even if they themselves support the Trinity concept. The first person to quote it was Virgilius Tapsensis, towards the end of the fifth century.

One of Mr. Armstrong's most important teachings was that God is not a Trinity, but rather, a *family*, into which all true Christians will eventually be born. And with this the Scriptures agree. For example, Hebrews 2:11 in the *New International Version* says "Both the one who makes people holy and those who are made holy are of the same family. So Jesus is not ashamed to call them brothers and sisters."

271

Mr. Armstrong wrote: "IN OTHER WORDS, GOD IS NOW A FAMILY of Persons, composed so far of only the TWO—God the Father and Christ the Son. But IF the Holy Spirit of God dwells in someone... at the time of Christ's return to earth... then all being filled and led by God's Spirit shall become BORN sons of God." He later adds: "the Trinity doctrine *limits* God to a supposed three Persons. It DESTROYS the very gospel of Jesus Christ!" (*Mystery of the Ages*, pp. 50–51).

Just a few years later, WCG in its 1995 *Statement of Beliefs* declared: "God, by the testimony of Scripture, is one divine Being in three eternal, co-essential, yet distinct persons, Father, Son and Holy Spirit."

The Ten Commandments

One of the most dramatic and moving events in the Bible was Moses receiving the Ten Commandments directly from God at Mount Sinai (Exodus 20). So important are these laws to God that He considers the breaking of any one of them as sin (1 John 3:4; James 2:10–11). Paul mentions that this sin (un-repented of)—or law breaking—incurs the death penalty. "For the wages of sin is death..." (Romans 6:23). In Hebrews 9:15, we are informed that all of those who are "called" are redeemed by Christ's blood from "transgressions under the first covenant," the heart of which is the Ten Commandments.

The Church of God has, unsurprisingly, long regarded the keeping of these commandments as a fundamental part of the lifestyle of all true Christians.

"There is one root CAUSE for all the troubles this world is suffering—transgression of our Maker's WAY OF LIFE—that WAY expressed in principle by the Ten Commandments" (Herbert W. Armstrong. *The Good News*, October/November 1984).

One might assume that any person who claims to be a Christian would agree with this, but let us read something from Mr. Joseph W. Tkach, written in 1992.

"It is a common mistake to assume, 'if everybody would just keep the Ten Commandments, what a nice world we would have.' Christians should consider that the Ten Commandments do not require kindness, mercy, compassion, generosity, sacrifice for others, impartiality, patience or love. Nor do the Ten Commandments specifically forbid conceit, envy, hatred, rage or selfish ambition.

The Ten Commandments are important but they are not enough"
(Joseph W. Tkach, May 27, 1992 Co-Worker letter).

Shortly afterwards, in a sermon given on June 7, 1992, Mr. Michael
Feazell stated: "Brethren, we need to understand that the Ten
Commandments are like one straw, in one brick, in a huge edifice of
obedience before God."

But Jesus Christ never compared these laws to a tiny part of a
single brick. He described them as the very key to eternal life! When
questioned about the subject, Christ told a rich young man, "But
if you want to enter into life, keep the commandments" (Matthew
19:17). He then clarified His point by explaining that He was talking
about the Ten Commandments.

The Sabbath and Sunday
One of the main doctrines that separates the Church of God from
other church groups is its observance of the seventh-day Sabbath
(sundown Friday to sundown Saturday). Most church groups follow
the mistaken notion that Christ was resurrected on a Sunday, and
keep Sunday as their day of worship.

Mr. Armstrong made some very strong statements on this subject:

"As the Sabbath is the identifying sign of the people of God (Jew,
Gentile or any race), so Sunday is the mark that identifies the AU-
THORITY of false Christianity—'BABYLON THE GREAT, THE MOTHER
OF HARLOTS. Because Sunday carries no other authority. The substi-
tution of the pagan Sunday to counterfeit God's Sabbath, is a primary
stratagem of Satan in deceiving all nations and counterfeiting God's
TRUTH as well as God's Church" (Herbert W. Armstrong, *Where Is the
True Church?*, p. 24).

By 1994, Mr. Tkach had established a very different perspective on
this subject. In a letter written to a fellow minister, early in that year,
he remarks:

"Do you condemn people as children of the devil just because
they keep the fourth commandment on the wrong day? To keep
the Sabbath on Sunday... is not the same thing as being in rebellion
against God... It is obvious from the fruits, that some Sunday keeping
Christians have the Holy Spirit. It is simply not right to say that their
lack of understanding about the day of Sabbath-keeping means they
are in utter rebellion against God..."

In the New Testament (Mark 2:27) Jesus upheld the keeping of the Sabbath *for everyone*: "The Sabbath was made for man" [Greek *anthropos*, mankind].

Christmas and Easter

One of the most prominent features of Church of God worship has been the observance of the biblical Holy Days (see Leviticus 23). These days, when kept with a correct understanding of their meaning, reveal God's wonderful plan and purpose for humanity.

Mr. Armstrong always strongly supported the keeping of these days, along with the rejection of worldly religious festivals such as Christmas and Easter, whose roots go back to paganism.

He mentions in his booklet *The Plain Truth About Christmas*, pp. 11–12: "The people of the Roman world began to accept this now-popular Christianity by the hundreds of thousands... But remember, these people had grown up in pagan customs, chief of which was this idolatrous festival of December 25 (Saturnalia)... and... the influence of the pagan Manichaeism, which identified the SON of God with the physical SUN, gave these pagans of the fourth century... their excuse for calling their pagan festival date of December 25, the birthday of the SON of God.... And that is how 'Christmas' became fastened on our Western World!"

After revealing similar background information about Easter, Mr. Armstrong concludes that: "Yes, deceived into believing this is Christian, millions practice every Easter the identical form of the ancient sun worship of the sun god Baal! Throughout the Bible this is revealed as the most abominable of all idolatry in the sight of the Eternal Creator!" (*The Plain Truth About Easter*, pp. 10–11).

In an astonishing reversal of this teaching, Joseph Tkach Jr, in the January 11, 1994 *Pastor General's Report*, mentioned that: "We have especially fallen short of Paul's priorities in how to proclaim Christ by using the terms pagan and paganism as verbal bludgeons. A symbol or practice deemed less than fully Christian (including the cross, national or religious holidays and medications) would quickly be branded 'pagan' in the past. Let's ask God to help us grow in love sufficiently to eliminate this false paradigm from the Church."

The blending together of pagan and Christian forms of worship are expressly what God does *not* want His people to do (Deuteronomy 12:28–32).

These are just a few of the major doctrinal changes that were introduced over a period of little more than ten years.

An obvious question that one might ask at this point is: If God really is all-powerful, loves His Church and still wants His truth proclaimed to the world, why did He allow it to be taken over by an administration that led it away from the truth?

We may never know the full answer in this life. What we do know though, is that those who are called of God are being trained and prepared for awesome positions of power and glory in His coming Kingdom. So God must be certain that such people will be obedient, dedicated and loyal to Him through eternity. They must undergo trials and testing, often under severe and traumatic conditions, to ensure that they will always be loyal to God, and will never compromise with the truth, regardless of the pressures they come under.

Although many in WCG were content to remain with the new administration and the changes that were being made, thousands of members, along with many ministers, were moved to embark upon a different path.

They separated themselves from WCG in order to retain the truth of God. Many came together in order to form groups that would continue to do God's Work and preach the true gospel of the Kingdom of God to the world. And although few in number, the story of Gideon (Judges 7) shows that God is not greatly concerned about numbers. He can achieve His purpose just as easily with 300 men as with 32,000.

Many New Church Groups
It has been estimated that several hundred new Church of God groups have been formed since Mr. Armstrong's death. It would be a monumental task to chart the history and teachings of all of these groups but let us now take a brief look at some of the largest and most well-known.

The Philadelphia Church of God
In late 1989 Gerald Flurry and John Amos were disfellowshipped from WCG, due to their rejection of the new teachings. They established the Philadelphia Church of God (PCG) and began to publish a professional-quality monthly magazine named *The Philadelphia*

Trumpet. They also send out a variety of booklets. Mr. Flurry established an international telecast entitled *The Key of David,* and over a period of time their membership grew to 5,000–7,000. During recent years this group established its own college patterned after Ambassador College.

Proclaiming their very high regard for the teachings and writings of Mr. Armstrong, the group began to republish many of his books and booklets. As the WCG held the copyright on this material and did not want it to be republished, they took legal action against PCG. The case dragged on for a grueling six years, at the end of which WCG sold the legal right to PCG to republish the material. Legal fees and settlement costs reached $5 million. Mr. Flurry regards himself as a latter day prophet. However, his seemingly harsh and exclusive approach to other Church of God people is often viewed as off-putting to many.

The United Church of God

In 1995, some 20,000 people left WCG to form the United Church of God (UCG). They rapidly undertook a comprehensive media publishing effort based on a monthly magazine, *The Good News.* They also produce a *Bible Correspondence Course*, many booklets on biblical topics, and a television program. Right from the start the intention was to pursue a different form of Church government with power more evenly distributed throughout the ministry. This form of government unwittingly opened the door to disagreement and disunity. Three years later some 10 percent of the group split off, under the leadership of Mr. David Hulme, to establish the Church of God—an International Community (COGaIC).

When UCG was founded in 1995, Mr. Hulme had become both its chairman and its president. The system of Church government required decisions on policy and doctrine to be made by the UCG ministry as a whole (through the process of balloting or voting), rather than by a single leader.

The Church of God aIC

Over a three-year period, however, disagreements in UCG arose about how this system of government was to function in practice. This eventually led to an acrimonious split with Mr. Hulme and those who were like-minded.

Mr. Hulme conducted a study of Mr. Armstrong's teachings on Church government and concluded that it should be a top-down government. Mr. Armstrong had learned by experience that no other system of government would work properly. Mr. Hulme consequently placed himself securely in the top spot.

The new group led by Mr. Hulme was small and had limited resources. They established a high quality journal called *Vision* that was designed to break the mold of typical Church of God publications, complemented by a professionally produced Web site. The journal's appeal turned out to be rather narrow, appealing to a more intellectually sophisticated readership.

One of David Hulme's many talents was as a television presenter. He produced several on-the-spot, high-quality, award-winning, documentary-type telecasts, filmed in such locations as Greece, Turkey and the island of Patmos. These were based on biblical themes such as the journeys of the Apostle Paul and the seven churches of Revelation.

Unlike other Church of God groups, Mr. Hulme showed no interest in teaching the "America and Britain in Prophecy" doctrine or, for that matter, many other aspects of prophecy. COGaIC falls into the common error of believing that God is working only through them, yet at the same time seems reluctant to proclaim the Gospel message openly and effectively. Dogged by lack of fruitfulness, this organization, at the time of writing, showed signs of further schism with ministers and members leaving in an attempt to become more fruitful elsewhere.

Church of God, a Worldwide Association

Sadly, in more recent years, UCG has continued to demonstrate that it is not as united as its name would imply. A significant number of ministers and members left the group to set up yet another rival organization (Church of God, a Worldwide Association—COGWA) in December 2010.

Restored Church of God

In May 1999, David C. Pack, a former WCG minister who had been with the Global Church of God, founded the Restored Church of God. As the name implies, this group seeks to restore the Church to the doctrinal position that it had under Mr. Armstrong.

Like Gerald Flurry, Mr. Pack wanted to republish Mr. Armstrong's literature. Being aware, however, that this could lead to costly legal problems over copyright, he decided to re-write in his own words almost all of Mr. Armstrong's books and booklets, in addition to many of his own. His diligent and dedicated wife, Shirley, agreed to type out this vast amount of written material.

This group produces a glossy and well-written monthly magazine. A large and impressive new headquarters complex is being constructed in Wadsworth, Ohio. Mr. Pack is not popular with other Church of God groups due to his very aggressive marketing of his publications, his self-proclamation that he is an "apostle," and his view that all other churches are "splinter groups" and "Laodiceans."

Chapter Summary

The post-Armstrong era. After Mr. Armstrong died in 1986, a new administration, under the leadership of Joseph W. Tkach, took over the Worldwide Church of God. Shortly after this, a series of 'clarifications' or doctrinal changes were introduced. Amazingly, within less than ten years, virtually all of the Bible-based teachings of Mr. Armstrong were abandoned and the church was taken back to mainstream Christianity.

Chapter 16

THE SPEARPOINT

"I have not left the church—the church has left me"
(*Global Church News*, March 1993).

"My flock was scattered over the whole face of the earth,
and no-one was seeking or searching for them"
(Ezekiel 34:6).

A t the end of 1992, Dr. Roderick C Meredith left the Worldwide Church of God and established the Global Church of God. Dr. Meredith had been one of Mr. Armstrong's first students and evangelists. Over a long and distinguished career he had served in many influential positions, directly assisting Mr. Armstrong in his work.

As Dr. Meredith refused to accept and teach the new doctrines introduced by WCG, he was marginalized by the new administration. Although for many years a prolific writer, speaker and administrator, all these roles were quickly closed off to him. In effect, he became "less than an elder" and his only real option appeared to be that he should "retire."

Although some in that situation may have opted for a quiet, stress-free life in retirement, Dr. Meredith was ever mindful of God's Work and the plight of many thousands of faithful and dedicated Church of God members. Were all these spiritual "sheep" now to be left without a human shepherd?

God is deeply concerned for the fate of His "flock" when the human shepherds fail in their duty of care. Ezekiel 34:5–6 tells us that "they were scattered because there was no shepherd and they became food for all the beasts of the field where they were scattered. My sheep wandered through all the mountains and on every high hill, yes, My flock was scattered over the whole face of the earth, and no-one was seeking or searching for them."

In earlier times of apostasy God's true ministers were often prevented from functioning in the way that God was leading them. "I wrote to the church," says the Apostle John, "but Diotrephes, who loves to have the pre-eminence among them, does not receive us. Therefore, if I come, I will call to mind his deeds which he does, prating against us with malicious words. And not content with that, he himself does not receive the brethren, and forbids those who wish to, putting them out of the church" (3 John 9–10).

Roderick C. Meredith

Roderick C. Meredith was one of the first evangelists to be ordained by Herbert Armstrong in 1953. He served in several positions including the Director of the Ministry of the Worldwide Church of God and Deputy-Chancellor of the Bricket Wood and Big Sandy campuses of Ambassador College. He was the founding evangelist of both Global Church of God and Living Church of God.

In his 1997 book *Transformed by Truth*, WCG leader Joseph Tkach Jr. makes it very plain that he has rejected almost all of Mr. Armstrong's teachings and is intent on replacing them with the traditional teachings of Protestant theology. Even five years earlier, in 1992, it was plain to Dr. Meredith and others that the writing was on the wall, so to speak, and that WCG would never return to its earlier biblical teachings. He reluctantly saw that he had little choice but to establish a new organization that would continue to preach the Gospel and care for its members.

Global Church of God

On December 31, 1992, Dr. Meredith wrote his first letter as leader

280

of the newly established Global Church of God to brethren and co-workers:

"Greetings from Pasadena! I want to send this letter to all of you who have so enthusiastically responded to us over the past two weeks. Truly, there has been an outpouring of support from all over North America, plus Britain and Europe, and we appreciate this very much. Thank you!"

He then listed twelve of the "truly massive doctrinal changes" introduced by WCG. He explained that he had no plans to "retire" and keep silent about what was happening and that he was intending to publish a "Newsletter" the following month, followed by a regular magazine later. As finances permitted, the true Gospel would again be preached over radio and television. By the time of the first Sabbath service conducted by Global, there were 42 people in attendance.

Dr. Meredith's sermon on January 16, 1993, a few weeks after Global had started, was on the subject of faith and healing, using biblical passages and Mr. Armstrong's teachings. He sought to establish a correct balance on this sometimes-controversial subject. He also saw a clear need to build more faith in the church.

As word spread about the new group, more ministers and members were drawn to Global. One "pioneer" minister and evangelist wrote the following:

"It became increasingly clear to us that many of the new 'theological changes' were in fact directly taken from Protestant theology. It is a well known fact that several of the men changing the new theology of the Worldwide Church of God had gone to the theologians of the colleges of this world and had drunk deeply of this world's protestant theology..."

"It became painfully clear to us that the time would soon come when some of the faithful 'pioneer' ministers who had been trained by Mr. Armstrong himself for over 40 years would have to take a firm stand to defend the truths which were increasingly being cast aside..."

"Recently, God has led Mr. Roderick Meredith, assisted by numerous other co-workers, to form the Global Church of God. This new branch of God's church has been organized for the express purpose of reviving the true doctrines and the work of the living God."

The March 1993 *Global Church News* reported some dramatic

growth. Membership had reached around 300 with 13 new congregations. Six radio stations were now broadcasting *The World Ahead* radio program. Three new Feast sites were in the planning stages.

The decision to join Global for many ministers and members was not an easy one. The concept of "leaving the church" (WCG) was often traumatic and involved peer pressure from family and friends. As one person explained, "I have not left the church—the church has left me." With the church in a scattered but growing condition, many new "video groups" were forming.

By May 1993 the Work was becoming international in its scope. In Belgium, 175 members were attending under the leadership of Mr. Jean Carion. In spite of persecution, the Work was growing.

The following month ministers were given what might seem a strange announcement: "And our recent BIG news is that Mr. John Ogwyn was fired the morning after Pentecost!" Of course this meant he was now free to join Global. More radio stations were opening to *The World Ahead* and the broadcast was also starting to reach into Canada.

Growth brought more persecution, including the false rumor that Global was going back into "Jewish Legalism." Later that summer, Mr. Raymond McNair began work on a new booklet called *America and Britain in Prophecy*.

In July 1993 Global held its first ministerial conference. This included a strong focus on "servant leadership." Work also began on the first issue of a full color *World Ahead* magazine.

Later that year video groups were started in Canada, Britain, Belgium and Australia. An article in the *Global Church News* examined the common argument used by many who felt compelled to remain in WCG: "I just could not leave the Church no matter what. This is the Church that God called me into, so I must not leave it." To which one might well respond, "Should I remain with a group that has rejected the truth of God?"

Global Surges Ahead

The first issue of the 1994 *Global Church News* reported an astonishing surge in monthly income during 1993—from just over $15,000 to $263,000. Subscribers to the *World Ahead* magazine reached around 7,000 and continuing changes in WCG during 1994 prompted more and more ministers and members to take the step of "going Global." This year also saw the first Global radio broadcast in Spanish, offering the first Spanish language booklet *What Is a True Christian?*.

Mr. Bruce Tyler was appointed to administer the growing Global work in Australia. Church magazines regularly reported on the tragic state of world conditions; for example, a story of the war in Bosnia, citing the experience of one young woman who suffered the horrors of widowhood, rape, imprisonment and starvation, finally being reduced to begging for food. Tragic stories like this highlighted the urgent need for Christ's return to solve the world's problems.

By the end of 1994 plans were in place for the church to go on television. Another "first" was the beginning of a French language broadcast by Mr. Jean Carion over Radio-Television Luxembourg; its potential listening audience was around 65 million people.

Early the following year, two evangelists, Mr. Colin Adair and Mr. Dibar Apartian, became part of Global. In addition to this, several other ministers moved to Global, including Mr. Gerald Weston, then pastor of the Kansas City congregation, together with some 200 members of his congregation. There were also some ordinations of men to serve in the growing congregations.

God's Work was having a growing impact and hundreds of brethren were seeing clearly that "this is obviously where God is now working," and "this is where the real truth is still being preached."

In a letter to brethren dated March 24, 1995, Dr. Meredith urged brethren to "please pray fervently for thousands of our separated brethren who are hurt, disillusioned, confused and need God's special help and guidance at this time."

In April, the new *World Ahead* television programme was accepted by the Vision Cable Network of Canada—a channel watched by millions. This period also saw the program go on several new television channels in the United States.

An article in the Jan/Feb 1995 *Global Church News* reported that "During a short two-year period, the Global Church of God has grown to over 62 churches and served by 64 ministers, including four evangelists: Roderick Meredith, Carl McNair, Larry Salyer and Raymond McNair..."

"Besides God's full time ministers, those 62 churches are also served by nearly 100 deacons and over 30 deaconesses. All told, nearly 4,000 now attend weekly Sabbath services of the Global Church of God. A further 3,000 people attended video groups."

Satan Stirs Up Trouble

Global, however, was not without its own internal problems. A letter sent to the brethren on April 19, 1996 called for a church-wide fast to pray for unity. Some members were becoming angry, upset or confused over a variety of minor issues. "We hear that a number of brethren are accusing each other. Others are upset or accusing their local elders or hosts. Others are upset or accusing our leadership here in San Diego of being 'liberal' or misguided in various ways."

Satan, ever the enemy of God's truth, was angry because of the growth and impact of Global and was seeking to stir up trouble with a policy of divide and conquer.

By May of that year circulation of the *World Ahead* magazine had reached 50,000 copies. Financial pressures, however, caused the church to stop broadcasting over two television channels. Despite setbacks, growth continued and several new congregations were established in various parts of Africa, in the Philippines and in the West Indies. And the church did not neglect its young people—Global Youth Camps were held in several areas.

New technology was embraced and enthusiastically put to work. The newsletter of March 10, 1997 reported that "the Global website knows no bounds! Since we last reported on the effectiveness of the Internet, surfers have been flocking to our webpage in ever increasing numbers. The hits (the number of times our website has been looked at) total an outstanding 201,176 for the twelve-month period ending in February 1997."

The *World Ahead* for November-December 1997 carried a stunning cover picture and article entitled *Goodbye England's Rose,* covering the life and tragic death of Princess Diana. It was the fairy tale story of the girl who fell in love with the heir to the English throne that finished when extra-marital relationships ended both the marriage and life of this beautiful and iconic lady.

By this time millions were able to watch Global's television program that was now going out in several languages. Annual income had reached $9 million. By early 1998, Global had sent out 2.1 million magazines, tapes, booklets and other literature. The telecast had received 107,000 replies since it started.

Global Implodes

The internal state of Global, however, was not all that it seemed. Dissatisfaction and discontent among some few was bubbling to the surface; some in the leadership were unhappy with Dr. Meredith's leadership and wanted him to resign.

In late November 1998 members of the Global Church of God received a letter that to most would have seemed astonishing and almost incomprehensible. The letter came, not from Dr. Meredith, but from four members of the Board of Directors: Raymond F. McNair, Larry R. Salyer, J. Edwin Pope and Norbert Link. In part it read:

> "We are very grieved and saddened to inform you that Dr. Roderick C. Meredith has chosen to leave the Global Church of God and strike out on his own. After he had already reached this decision, the Board of Directors formalized his departure by terminating his employment following his refusal to resign. Some of his reasons are known only to him and to God, but it is apparent to us that the "primary" reason is a compelling need to be pre-eminent in every way above the brethren and the rest of the ministry."

Two days later members received a very different version of events from Dr. Meredith. He wrote, in part:

> "After I rejected a few unsatisfactory offers they made to get me to stay, they fired me as the President and Chairman of the Board! These men who I had brought in to help were finally able to oust me. In the final Board meeting they began to accuse me of doing horrible things "as President of the Church and as an authorized signer of our corporate checks." I signed those checks to repay three individuals the loans they had made to Global Church of God. One of the loans to be repaid was to a

> 74-year-old widow who will really need this money to ensure her future. None of the money was for me personally, or for relatives of mine."

It quickly became clear that the vast majority of members and the ministry supported Dr. Meredith in this situation; very few accepted the accusations made by the four Board members.

Dr. Jeff Fall, a United States-based minister, wrote the following: "The basic facts are quite clear. There is not a single example in the entire Bible of this type of overthrow. God has used Mr. Meredith to revive this phase of God's work to preach the Gospel to the world. Mr. Meredith has not changed doctrinally nor has he stopped the work of God... There is not one shred of evidence that God would bless a revolt against the man whom God has used to start his end time Work. This group of four may have legal control of the Board of Global, but we have a higher moral authority..."

An Australian minister, Mr. Michael Gill, wrote to Larry Salyer: "We are deeply disappointed with your actions and especially your accusatory attitude so clearly evident in your letter. Mr. Salyer, I want you to know that God's people here in Australia want to forgive you and your colleagues.

"Mr. Meredith is one that God chose to raise up the Global Church of God and has shown by his fruits that Jesus Christ is using him to eventually do a great work. The Board may have made a company decision but you will soon understand that Jesus Christ is the One that decides the human leadership of His Church."

Living Church of God

By the end of 1998, the newly established Living Church of God was making rapid progress, while the organization of those who had tried to oust him languished. In a member letter dated December 1998, Dr. Meredith mentions that:

"We are now moving forward to do the work in a more powerful and unified way than ever before! Mr. Richard Ames made two television programs a few days ago—and he and I both shot some introductory sequences as well. On January 6, Mr. Ames and I will both make television programs and Mr. Mario Hernandez will also make a program in the Spanish language. Mr. Dibar Apartian is continuing to produce radio programs for our French-speaking audience and will soon travel to Martinique to encourage brethren there."

"At this point, after careful checking, it appears that about 75 percent of all U.S. brethren [of Global] have come with us in the Living Church of God, about 75 percent of the United States full-time ministry and about 80–85 percent of the local church elders are here."

Among those who moved from Global to Living was Mr. Gerald Weston who was appointed to the new Council of Elders and made Midwest Regional Director. He later also took on the roles of Youth Development Director and Camp Director of the Church youth summer camp.

Early 1999 saw the Work shifting its office facilities, and several new television channels and cable networks became available to the church. This period also saw the launch of the new *Living Church News* magazine and a new booklet on marriage. The main magazine received a new title, *Tomorrow's World,* to match the new title of the television program. The church also reported on the sad deaths of evangelist Colin Adair and Robin Hulme, wife of evangelist David Hulme (COGaIC).

The End of Global

As might have been expected, the massive loss of members and income placed Global in a desperate situation. A letter from Larry Salyer, dated September 17, 1999, broke the astonishing news that:

"As of Friday evening, at 5 pm Pacific standard time, the Global Church of God closed its offices and entered into a voluntary agreement to liquidate all assets in a legal procedure known as ABC, which stands for Assignment for the Benefit of Creditors. This is not a bankruptcy declaration but it has the same effect."

Back in Living, Church income for the year reached over $6 million. And an article by New Zealand minister Kinnear Penman, describing a visit to Papua New Guinea with Regional Director Bruce Tyler, showed that there was interest in the Church even in remote and exotic parts of the world.

During the summer of 2000, Dr. Meredith was able to visit Canada, Europe and Britain. By the end of that year there were more than 270 church congregations located in some 35 countries.

In addition, the church did not seek to avoid controversial issues in its magazines. An article written by Dr. Douglas S. Winnail in the May-June 2001 issue of the *Living Church News* looked at the changing roles of men and women in society. He wrote:

"Gender confusion has blossomed as traditional roles have been trashed. Homosexuality is blatantly promoted as an acceptable lifestyle. Women have become more aggressive and men more passive. Deprived of clearly identified roles, more people are seeking psychological help to discover a purpose in life and a meaningful identity."

In the same issue of the magazine it was reported that the *Tomorrow's World* telecast could be seen on 100 television stations. In addition to its magazines, the church had 13 different booklets in print. World events, as they relate to Bible prophecy, were a regular theme of church literature. The catastrophic terrorist attacks of September 11, 2001 received good coverage. In November, Gerald Weston was appointed Regional Director for the fledgling Canadian Work.

During 2002, Mr. Meredith was able to visit Australia, New Zealand and the Philippines. Among the many people he met were Mr. and Mrs. Rod King, who were considering becoming part of the Living Church of God. Dr. Meredith writes: "So it was a wonderful opportunity to meet with him and his dedicated wife. They were able to 'check us out' and ask all kinds of questions about the Living Church of God, what we believe, where we are headed, and so on." Mr. King became Regional Director for Britain in 2006, and later for Europe and Africa.

Living Moves to Charlotte

In 2003, the church moved its headquarters office facilities from California to Charlotte, North Carolina. The reasons for this move were mainly financial—as this move enabled the Living Church of God to purchase and own its headquarters office building for half the price it would have cost in San Diego. During this year, Dr. Meredith also wrote on the subject of health and healing. Members should strive for correct balance on this emotive issue. Although God can and does heal disease, and many members have experienced the blessing of divine healing, it is not a sin to seek medical help in appropriate situations.

In 2004, the church received a sad reminder that we are all human and will one day die. The May-June issue of the *Living Church News* carried a moving tribute to Mr. Carl McNair, a 66-year-old evangelist and the Director of Church Administration. Dr. Meredith writes:

> "... soon after I arrived home, I was awakened from a deep sleep to be told of the death of my friend and brother Mr. Carl McNair. I feel that I can rightly say most sincerely 'a mighty oak has fallen!' For Mr. McNair was one of the 'founding fathers' of the Global Church of God. He and Mrs. McNair came early on to devote their lives and their service to reviving the work of God after the massive apostasy had taken over our former association. It took faith and courage for both of them—sterling examples of love and service in this work of God—to step out as they did at that time."

The year 2005 saw terrible tragedy unfold, when on March 12 in Brookfield, Wisconsin, a member of the local Living Church of God congregation shot several people dead during a Sabbath service, including the local pastor, and then killed himself. The story was carried on several television news channels in various parts of the world. As Dr. Meredith explained, we do not always know why such terrible events take place or why God allows it.

Later that year Mr. John Ogwyn, a much-loved minister and prolific writer for Church publications, also died. Memorializing this dedicated servant of God, Dr. Meredith wrote in the July-August 2005 *Living Church News*:

> "He was one of the most capable, hard working and loved ministers anywhere on this earth. On a personal level, he was a much-loved pastor and confidant to hundreds of people ... For me personally, John Ogwyn was also a dear friend and confidant. He was one of the key individuals to whom I *always* turned for advice, counsel and prayer regarding the management of the entire Work. He was, of course, invaluable in his service to God's Work and God's people. He was a *vital* part of the

> leadership 'team' of this entire Work—a minister, teacher, writer, presenter on our television program, a member of the Board and of the Council of Elders. He was all of the above and more, while at the same time having the 'heart of a pastor' in continuing to *personally* serve, counsel, pray for and encourage hundreds of God's people."

The next year, 2006, saw real growth in the Work and several new opportunities in different parts of the world. One such area was the UK and Ireland. The *Tomorrow's World* telecast began to be shown on a British satellite television station that could be seen not only in the UK and Ireland, but also in Western Europe and Scandinavia. The Church continued to experience steady growth in membership. Hundreds of enquiries were received from new people interested in attending Sabbath services. Sadly, however, these new people did not always receive the welcome that they should have. Dr. Meredith, in a *Living Church News* article from the November-December 2006 issue, confronted the problem:

"Sadly, reports indicate that some of our members tend to be stiff and cold around new attendees. They 'stay apart.' They do not enthusiastically go forward to warmly welcome these new people who are—so to speak—'dipping their hand in the water' for the first time to see what we are like. Some of our brethren are a little bashful, and stay among their current friends because of a fear of meeting new people."

Living Bears Fruit

Early in 2007 the Work of God achieved an interesting "first!" For the first time ever the *Tomorrow's World* television program received more than 5,000 responses from a single program. It was titled "Armageddon and Beyond!" Publishing too, was moving ahead. Each issue of *Tomorrow's World* magazine was being sent to some 326,000 subscribers. Mr. Gerald Weston, Canadian Regional Director, was ordained an evangelist on May 1.

Plans were also announced for the start of *Living University,* which would provide educational opportunities not only for youth, but also for more mature students of the church. Dr. Michael Germano, formerly Dean of Faculty for Ambassador College, was appointed to direct this new initiative, assisted by Dr. Scott Winnail.

As world conditions continued to deteriorate during 2008 with the worldwide credit crunch, interest in Bible prophecy increased. Dr. Meredith felt compelled to urge the membership not to let down spiritually but to trust God and become fully involved in doing His Work.

During 2008, Mr. John Meakin, a long-serving British minister, left COGaIC and became part of the Living Church of God. Over a period of several months, and into 2009, more than 50 other people, mostly from other Church groups, joined the Living Church of God in Britain. The British Feast Site in North Wales at Llangollen quickly became filled to capacity.

In late 2008 Dr. Meredith's wife, Sheryl, suffered a reoccurrence of cancer. Dr. Meredith suffered a slight stroke, which thankfully did not impair his speech or mental faculties, although it did leave him with some impairment of motor functions.

Church magazine articles during 2010 covered some important topics such as "Seeing Other People as God Sees Them," "Knowing God," "Loneliness" and "What is the Holy Spirit?" On December 9, 2010, long-time French evangelist Dibar Apartian, who had raised up and supervised the Work of God in the French language for many decades, died at age 94. Dr. Meredith mourned the loss of "my oldest and longest personal friend" of 55 years. He went on to say:

> "His dedication to teaching *and practicing* the way of God became a hallmark of his life. His warmth, his loving personality and his enthusiasm for building the French Work—and for serving *all* of God's people—will be greatly missed. I will personally miss the advice and the encouragement of one of my best friends on this earth. Yes, a 'mighty oak' has fallen."

Richard Ames

Now more aware of his own mortality, Dr. Meredith appointed Mr. Richard Ames to succeed him in the event of his death or incapacity. Mr. Ames, brother-in-law to Dr. Meredith, came to Ambassador College in the early 1960s, and Mr. Herbert W. Armstrong had ordained him as an evangelist during the Days of Unleavened Bread in 1984. In the Worldwide Church of God he held a number of senior positions in the Work, including his service as a faculty member and administrator at Ambassador College in Pasadena and Big Sandy.

Richard Ames

Richard Ames and wife Kathryn. Mrs. Ames is the sister of evangelist Roderick C. Meredith. Mr. Ames is one of the presenters of the Tomorrow's World *television programme and Editorial Director of the magazine of the same name.*

After Mr. Armstrong's death, Mr. Ames served as a presenter on the *World Tomorrow* television program. In 1997, Dr. Meredith added Mr. Ames to Global's *World Ahead* telecast, and from the beginning of the Living Church of God Mr. Ames served as a presenter on the *Tomorrow's World* program. As Director of Media Operations, Mr. Ames was given the responsibility to oversee Living Church of God publications and television productions, and he has been appreciated by many as an outstanding example of loyalty to the Work and to the basic truths of God.

The Gospel to China

In 2010 there were exciting new developments in the production of television programs for the newly emerging Hong Kong market. It was clear that God was opening a major new door for the preaching of the gospel to China. The first telecast went out in June 2011 and received 78 responses in the first 24 hours. But it soon became apparent that a somewhat different format to *Tomorrow's World* was required. Dr. Meredith asked the Canadian Regional Director, evangelist Gerald Weston, to be the lead television presenter for these programs and asked him to set up new studio facilities in

Canada that came on stream in 2012. French-language programs, presented by French-Canadian minister Mr. Yvon Brochu, also began to be recorded in the Canadian television studios that year. In addition to maintaining a strong television initiative, throughout 2013 and 2014, Dr. Meredith and the leadership also continued to invest in Internet and Social Media strategies in English, French, Spanish, German, Russian and other languages. New Social Media projects were launched and enhancements were made to the multiple *Tomorrow's World* flagship Web sites, which are available in various languages. In 2013, new television programs and Internet initiatives were launched in Russian- and Spanish-speaking areas, and advance plans were under way to start television coverage in India.

Sixty Years an Evangelist

On December 20, 2012, Dr. Meredith celebrated the 60th anniversary of his ordination as an evangelist. During a simple yet profound ceremony in December 1952, Mr. Herbert W. Armstrong had ordained five pioneer students, the firstfruits of Ambassador College, as evangelists. Dr. Meredith was the last to be ordained. By this time he was writing articles for Church publications and had several other college-related duties.

Holding a position of leadership in the Church of God is often a difficult and challenging role. Such a man requires both humility and balance, along with strong and decisive leadership qualities. Unlike some political leaders, he cannot be a dictator, but must be willing to consider the views and input of others.

As this is a spiritual position, such a leader must fully grasp and apply God's system of government and understand the spiritual truths contained in the Bible. He must not be influenced by apostates or spiritual "wolves," but be able to protect his flock from such individuals. Those who apply the quality of servant leadership also need to understand how to be a team player or team leader. They need vision and the ability to plan ahead and make wise decisions. For any one person to have and apply all of these qualities or virtues seems an almost impossible task. Dr. Meredith, although he acknowledges that he is far from perfect, is certainly one of the best examples of these qualities in action. Most important, the "fruits" of the Living Church of God certainly indicate that—at this time—it is the foremost organization that is proclaiming the full Truth of the Bible and really doing the Work with increasing power.

Onwards to the Kingdom

The precise future history of the Church of God is not something we can know at this time. But what is certain is that there will always be trials and tests along the way on our journey towards the Kingdom of God. A prophesied time of even greater deception lies ahead (2 Thessalonians 2:1–12). But what is also sure is that the Church, the Bride of Christ, "will have made herself ready" to marry Jesus, the Lamb of God (Revelation 19:7), and reign with Him over the earth in the Kingdom of God.

We close with the words of Jesus ringing in our ears: "Then many false prophets will rise up and deceive many. And because lawlessness will abound, the love of many will grow cold. But he who *endures to the end* shall be saved" (Matthew 24:11–13).

Chapter Summary

The work and teachings of Mr. Armstrong revived. Various new groups set up to restore the truth. The life and work of Dr. Roderick C. Meredith. The rapid growth and success of the Living Church of God.

ACKNOWLEDGEMENTS

Ever since my wife and I began attending with the Living Church of God in 2009, I have been pleased and gratified to discover that many within the ministry and leadership of LCG had read my book and shared my desire to see a second edition. Dr. Roderick C. Meredith, Presiding Evangelist of the Living Church of God, personally encouraged me greatly in this regard.

I am also grateful to many who have made available their organizational, managerial, publishing and editorial experience to assist in this project. Most especially, I am indebted to Mr. John Meakin for his keen editorial eye and expert guidance. Messrs. Rod King and Wyatt Ciesielka faithfully guided and encouraged the publication of this second edition almost from its inception. Mr. John Robinson gave of his design and layout expertise, and Mr. Lehman Lyons helpfully coordinated the printing of this volume. I am grateful to them all for their part in helping this long-cherished hope of mine become a reality.

The Author with Dr. Roderick C. Meredith
In May, 2010, Ivor Fletcher met Dr. Meredith in London to discuss the idea of republishing his authoritative work on the history of the true Church of God. This updated book is the result.

BIBLIOGRAPHY

Andrews, J.N., *History of the Sabbath*

Armstrong, Herbert W., *Autobiography,* 1973, Ambassador College Press

Anglo-Saxon Chronicles

Acts of Pastor and Timotheus

Ante Nicean Fathers

Authentic Details of the Valdenses, 1827

Annals of Clonmacnoise

Bacchiocchi, S., *From Sabbath to Sunday,* 1977

Bailey, J., *History of the Origin and Growth of Sabbath-keeping in America*

Bale, *Old Chronicle of London*

Bampfield, Francis, *The Life of Shem Acher,* 1677

Baronius, (Cardinal), *The Ecclesiastical Annals*

Barrett, David A., *The Fragmentation of a Sect: Schism in the Worldwide Church of God,* Oxford University Press, 2013

Bede, *Ecclesiastical History of England*

Benedict, D., *History of the Baptist Denomination,* 1848

Bosanquet, J., *Synchronous History*

Burges, T., *The Ancient British Church,* 1815

Caesar, J., *The Gallic War*

Camden, William, *Remains of Britain,* 1674

Cave, William, *Antiquities of the Apostles, Lives of the Apostles, Chronicles of Eri*

Chronicles of the Kings of Briton

Chrysostom, *Epist. Contra Judaces*

Clement, *The Recognitions*

Clement, *Epistle to the Corinthians,* A.D. 95–96

Clementine Homilies

Collier, *The Ecclesiastical History of Great Britain,* 1707

Connon, F.W., *London Through the Ages,* Covenant Books Ltd.

Constitutions of the Holy Apostles

Cox, R., *Literature of the Sabbath Question*

Creasy, *History of England*

Davies, E., *Celtic Researches*

Davis, J., *The Autobiography*

The Incredible History of God's True Church

Denison, F., *Westerly and its Witnesses*
Elder, I.H., *Celt, Druid and Culdee,* Covenant Books Ltd.
Epistle of Barnabas
Eusebius, *The Ecclesiastical History, Evangelical Demonstrations, Life of Constantine*
Faber, G.S., *The Ancient Vallenses and Albigenses,* 1843
Fuller, *Church History of Britain*
Gildas, *De Excidio Britanniae,* 542
Godwin, *Catalogue of Bishops*
Good News magazine, Ambassador College Press
Gordon, E.O., *Prehistoric London*
Grunther, Professor, *The Racial Element of European History*
Guest, E., *Origines Celticae*
Hardinge, L., *The Celtic Church in Britain,* 1972, S.P.C.K.
Heath, A., *The "Painted Savages" of England,* Covenant Books Ltd.
Henry, Dr., *History of Great Britain*
Herodotus, *The History*
Hislop, Alexander, *The Two Babylons,* S.W. Partridge and Co.
Hoeh, Herman L., *A True History of the True Church,* 1959, Ambassador College Press
John of Lincoln, *The Writings and Opinions of Justin Martyr,* 1836
Jones, *Church History,* 1837
Josephus, *The Antiquities*
Justin Martyr, *The Apology*
Keating, G., *The History of Ireland*
Kiesz, J., *History of the Church of God (Seventh Day),* 1965, Published in *The Bible Advocate*
Latham, R.G. Dr., *Ethnology of Europe*
Lightfoot, J.B., *The Apostolic Fathers*
Lingard, *History of England*
Lysons, S. M.A., *Claudia and Pudens, Our British Ancestors*
Macmillan, D.H., *The True Ecclesia,* 1955
McGeachy, James, *The Times of Stephen Mumford,* 1964, The Seventh Day Baptist Historical Society
McNair, Raymond F., *The Key to Northwest European Origins,* 1963
Margouliouth, M., *History of the Jews*

298

Martial, *The Epigrams*
Milton, *History of England*
Moore, *The History of Ireland*
Morgan, R.W., *St. Paul in Britain,* 1860
Monastier, *The Vaudois Church,* 1846
Mosheim, *The Ecclesiastical History*
Muston, A., , *Israel of the Alps,* 1852
National Message magazine
Newell, E.J., *A History of the Welsh Church*
Nickels, Richard C., *Six Papers on the History of the Church of God,* 1977
O'Halleron, *History of Ireland*
Painter, K.S., *The Water Newton Early Christian Silver,* 1977, British Museum Publications Ltd.
Parsons, Robert, *The Three Conversions of England*
Phillips, Sir Richard, *Millions of Facts,* 1835
Phlegon, *Chronology of the Olympiads*
Pitsaeus, *Relationes Historicae de Rebus Angficis,* 1619
Plain Truth magazine
Polwhele, *History of Cornwall*
Pryce, Dr., *Archaeologia Comu-Britannica,* 1790
Prynne, *Dissertation on the Lord's Day,* 1633
Randolph, *History of the Seventh Day Baptists, History of the Seventh Day Baptists in West Virginia*
Rawlinson, *History of Herodotus*
Robinson, *Ecclesiastical Researches*
Rogers, A.N., *One People Bound Together,* 1965
Scott, B., *The Catacombs at Rome*
Scottish Declaration of Independence, 1320
Seventh Day Baptists in Europe and America
Seventh Day Baptist Memorial
Smith's Religion of Ancient Britain, 1846
Spelman, Sir Henry, *Concilia*
Stillingfleet, *Antiquities of the British Churches*
Stillman, K., *Seventh Day Baptists in New England,* 1671–1971
Tacitus, *Annals of Tacitus, Life of Agricola*

Taylor, G., *The Celtic Influence,* 1972, *Division and Dispersion,* 1974,
    The Hidden Centuries, 1969, *The Magnet of the Isles,* 1971, *Our
    Neglected Heritage,* 1969, Covenant Books
Tertullian, *Apologia*
Townsend's *Abridgment,* 1816
Transactions of the Baptist Historical Society, 1912
Turner, S., *The History of the Anglo-Saxons*
Underwood, A., *A History of the English Baptists,* 1947
White, Bishop, *A Treatise of the Sabbath Day,* 1635
Whitley, W.T., *History of the British Baptists*
William of Malmesbury, *A Life of St. Dunstan, De Gestis Regum
    Angliae*
Williams, J., *Claudia and Pudens,* 1848
*Wilson's History of Dissenting Churches,*1808
Wylie, Dr., *History of the Scottish Nation*

FOOTNOTES

Chapter 1: The Setting
1. *Do Excidio Britannico* p. 25
2. Caesar, *Gallic Wars* Book 6, Chapter 14
3. *Epist Contra Judaeos*
4. *A History of the Welsh Church*, E.J. Newell

Chapter 2: Land of the Celts
1. *Tac. Ann. Lib.* v. c. 28
2. *Ecclesiastical History of England*, Bede, p. 7
3. *Antiquities of the British Church*, Stillingfleet
4. *The History of the Anglo-Saxons*, S. Turner, vol. 1, p. 57
5. *ibid.,* p. 87
6. *History of England*, Milton, Book 3, p. 406–407
7. See Bede's *Ecclesiastical History*, chapter 1
8. Smith's *Religion of Ancient Britain*, p. 22
9. *ibid.,* p. 6
10. *ibid.,* p. 10
11. *Celtic Researches*, E. Davies
12. Smith's *Religion of Ancient Britain*, p. 5
13. *Key to Northwest European Origins*, Raymond F. McNair, p. 72
14. *ibid.,* p. 76
15. *Ant.* XI., V., Sec. 2
16. *Key to Northwest European Origins*, McNair, p. 88
17. *ibid.,* p. 91
18. Rawlinson, *History of Herodotus*, Bk. 4, Appendix, Note 1
19. *Our British Ancestors*, Lysons, p. 23
20. *ibid.,* p. 27
21. *History of the Anglo-Saxons*, S. Turner, vol. 1, p. 23
22. *Our British Ancestors*, Lysons, p. 27
23. *ibid.,* p. 265
24. *Our British Ancestors*, Lysons, p. 93
25. *Division and Dispersion*, G. Taylor, p. 45
26. *ibid*
27. See *The History of Ireland*, Geoffrey Keating and *The History of Ireland*, Moore, vol. 1, p. 59
28. *ibid.,* p. 60
29. *Ethnology of Europe*, p. 137
30. Keating's *History of Ireland*, p. 40
31. *The History of Ireland*, Moore, p. 60
32. *I Maccabees*, chap. 12 and Josephus, *Antiquities of the Jews*, chap. 12 and 13
33. *National Message* magazine, September 1976, p. 268
34. *ibid.,* p. 268
35. *Ethnology of Europe*
36. Josephus, *Ant.,* 3:4 and 1 Kings 7:14
37. Smith's *Religion of Ancient Britain*, p. 3
38. *The History of Ireland*, Moore, pp. 86–88

39. Cambrensis Eversus, Lynch, written 1662
40. Chronicles of Eri., vol. 2, pp. 98–103
41. Key to Northwest Europe Origins, Raymond F. McNair, introduction
42. ibid., p. 45
43. The Magnet of the Isles, G. Taylor, p. 14
44. ibid., p. 13
45. The Celtic Influence, G. Taylor, p. 19
46. The National Message magazine, September 1978, p. 246
47. Synchronous History, vol. 3, J. Bosanquet
48. The Celtic Influence, G. Taylor, p. 13
49. Our British Ancestors, S. Lysons, pp. 93–94
50. Smith's *Religion of Ancient Britain*, pp. 41–42
51. ibid., p. 36
52. ibid., p. 36
53. ibid., p. 40
54. The Two Babylons, Hislop, p. 45
55. St. Paul in Britain, R. Morgan, p. 12
56. Gallic War, vi. 13, 14
57. The "Painted Savages" of England, A. Heath, p. 16
58. Celt, Druid and Culdee, I.H. Elder, pp. 57–58
59. ibid., p. 59
60. The Two Babylons, Hislop, pp. 103, 116, 232

Chapter 3: Did Jesus Visit Britain?
1. *The Ecclesiastical History*, Eusebius Pamphilius, Book 1, chapter 13
2. *ibid.*, Book 2, chapter 2
3. *Chronology of the Olympiads*, Phlegon, Book 13
4. *St. Paul in Britain*, R.W. Morgan, chapter 1, p. 9
5. Tertunian, *Apologia c. 21*
6. *Archaeologia Cornu-Britannica*
7. Hecant. ab. Diod Sicul, Lib III Avienus

Chapter 4: The Glastonbury Story
1. Vol. 1, p. 15
2. *Ecclesiastical History of England*, Bede
3. *Remains of Britain*, p. 5
4. *Antiquities of the British Churches*, p. 1
5. *De Gestis Regum Angliae*, second edition
6. *Antiquities of the British Churches*, Stillingfleet
7. *Concilia*, Sir Henry Spelman
8. *Antiquities of the British Churches*, Stillingfleet
9. *St. Paul in Britain*, R.W. Morgan, p. 64
10. *Antiquities of the British Churches*, Stillingfleet
11. *Greek Men.*, ad 15 March
12. *Isidorus Hispalensis*, vol. vii, 392
13. *ibid.*, vol. v, 184

14. *Polwhele's History of Cornwall*

Chapter 5: The Utmost Bounds of The West
1. *The Ancient British Church*, p. 21
2. *Mosheim's Ecclesiastical History*
3. *Lives of the Apostles*, William Cave, vol. 1, p. 290
4. Theodoret, *De Civ. Graec.* off, lib. i.x
5. *Epistle of Clement to the Corinthians*, 3:12–14
6. *The Apostolic Fathers*, J.B. Lightfoot, vol. i
7. *The Ancient British Church*, T. Burges, pp. 48, 117–118
8. *Origines Celticao*, E. Guest, p. 121
9. *The Apostolic Fathers*, J.B. Lightfoot, Vol. 2, p. 31
10. Tertullian, *Def. Fidei*, p. 179
11. See the marginal notes, p. 7 in *Bede's Ecclesiastical History of England*
12. *The Ancient British Church*, Burges, p. 26
13. *London Through the Ages*, p. 13, Covenant Books
14. *Our Neglected Heritage*, p. 67, G. Taylor
15. The manuscript was reproduced by kind permission of The Covenant Publishing Co. Ltd., of London
16. *The Ecclesiastical History*, Eusebius, Book 2
17. *ibid.,* Book 3
18. *Life of Agricola*, chapter 17
19. *Annals of Tacitus*, 13:32
20. *The Apostolic Fathers*, Lightfoot, vol. 1, p. 30
21. *ibid.*, p. 128
22. *Antiquities of the British Churches*, Stillingfleet, p. 43
23. *The Apostolic Fathers*, J.B. Lightfoot, p. 30
24. *Origines Celticae*, E. Guest, p. 124
25. *Claudia and Pudens*, Samuel Lysons, M.A
26. *Lingard's History of England*, vol. i, Chap. 1, p. 65
27. *Dr. Henry's History of Great Britain*, p. 187
28. *St. Paul in Britain*, R.W. Morgan, pp. 83–84
29. Iolo M.S.S. p. 7
30. *Gwehelyth Iestyn ap Gwrgant*
31. *St. Paul in Britain*, R.W. Morgan, p. 118
32. Epig 6 v. 58
33. Epig 11–53
34. *Claudia and Pudens*, Samuel Lysons, M.A
35. *Sir Richard Phillips' Million of Facts*, pp. 872, 1835
36. *Fuller's Church History of Britain*, p. 9
37. *Antiquities of the British Churches*, Stillingfleet
38. Epigram 4:32
39. Epithalamium 4:13
40. Epigram 11:53
41. *Claudia and Pudens*, J. Williams, p. 35
42. *Origines Celticae*, E. Guest, p. 124

43. *Claudia and Pudens*, J. Williams, p. 9
44. *ibid.*, p. 24
45. *Our Neglected Heritage*, G. Taylor, p. 24
46. *Annales Ecclesias*
47. *Evangelical Demonstrations*, book 3, chapter 7
48. Page 203 of *Cave's Antiq. Apost*
49. *Synopsis de Apostol*
50. *Our Neglected Heritage*, G. Taylor, p. 48
51. *Cave's Antiq. Apost.* p. 148

Chapter 6: The Great Conspiracy
1. *The Ecclesiastical History*, Eusebius
2. *Bede's Ecclesiastical History of the English Nation*
3. Eusebius, *Hist. Eccl.,* book 3, chapter 39
4. Herodotus' *History*, bk. 2, p. 109
5. *Mosheim's Ecclesiastical History*, Vol. 1
6. *Antiquities Apostolicae*, William Cave
7. *The Ecclesiastical History*, Eusebius, book 2, chap. 13
8. *The Clementine Homilies*, chap. 11
9. *The Catacombs at Rome*, B. Scott, p. 84
10. *The Ecclesiastical History*, Eusebius; book 2, chap. 3
11. *ibid.,* book 2
12. *Mosheim's Ecclesiastical History*, p. 121
13. *Ante-Nicene Fathers*, vol. 7, p. 379
14. *The Epistle of Clement to the Corinthians*
15. *The Two Babylons*, p. 103
16. *ibid.,* p. 104
17. Tertullian, part 2, Anti-Marcion, *The Prescription Against Heretics*, chap. 32, 229
18. *Ecclesiastical History of Eusebius*, book 5, chapter 24
19. *History of the Sabbath*, Andrews
20. *ibid*
21. *The Constitutions of the Holy Apostles*, book 5
22. *The Apostolic Fathers*, J.B. Lightfoot, vol. i, p. 74
23. H.E. 11, 25, 6, 7
24. *Our Neglected Heritage*, G. Taylor, p. 45, Covenant Books
25. Adv. Haer. iii, 3
26. *The Apostolic Fathers*, J.B. Lightfoot, vol. 1
27. *Cave's Antiquities Apostolicas*, p. 138
28. *The Ancient British Church*, T. Burges, p. 43
29. *Ecclesiastical History of Eusebius*, book 5
30. *The Apostolic Fathers*, J.B. Lightfoot, pp. 68–70
31. *Robinson's Ecclesiastical Researches*, chap. 6, p. 5 1
32. *The Apology of Justin Martyr*
33. See the writings and opinions of Justin Martyr, by John, Bishop of Lincoln, 1836
34. *Eusebius's Life of Constantine*, book 3
35. *Dissertation on the Lord's Day*, 1633, p. 163

Footnotes

Chapter 7: A Light in the Dark Ages
1. *Antiquities of the British Churches*, Stillingfleet, p. 55
2. *Ecclesiastical History of Great Britain*, Collier, vol. 1, p. 27
3. *Ecclesiastical History, Mosheim*, p. 135
4. *The Hidden Centuries*, G. Taylor, p. 21
5. *Antiquities of the British Churches*, Stillingfleet
6. *Townsend's Abridgment*, p. 110. Ed. 1816
7. Tertullian, *Def. Fidei*, p. 179
8. Origen, *In Psalm CXLIX*
9. *Bede's Ecclesiastical History of England*, chapter 7
10. *The Water Newton Early Christian Silver*, K. S. Painter, p. 7
11. *ibid.*, pp. 20–21
12. *ibid.*, pp. 22–23
13. *ibid.*, p. 16
14. *ibid.*, p. 24
15. *Our Neglected Heritage*, G. Taylor, pp. 60–61
16. *Jones' Church History*, p. 208, ed. 1837
17. *From Sabbath to Sunday*, Samuele Bacchiocchi, p. 80
18. *ibid.*, p. 173
19. *ibid.*, p. 212
20. *ibid.*, pp. 232–233
21. *Bede's Ecclesiastical History of England*, chapter 15
22. *The Celtic Church in Britain*, Leslie Hardinge, p. 32
23. *ibid.*, p. 48
24. *ibid.*, p. 82
25. *ibid.*, p. 84
26. *Eccl. History* ii, 19
27. *History of the Sabbath*, J.N. Andrews
28. *The Celtic Church in Britain*, Leslie Hardinge, p. 80
29. *ibid.*, p. 78
30. *ibid.*, p. 79
31. *ibid.*, p. 58
32. *Six Papers on the History of the Church of God*, Richard C. Nickels, part i, p. 4
33. *The True Ecclesia*, D.H. Macmillan, p. 21
34. *The Celtic Church*, Leslie Hardinge, p. 186
35. *The History of the Welsh Church*, E.J. Newell
36. *Six Papers on the History of the Church of God*, R. Nickels, p. 3
37. *ibid.*, p. 4
38. *ibid.*, p. 5
39. *History of the Sabbath*, J.N. Andrews
40. *Townsend's Abridgment*, p. 361

Chapter 8: The Church In The Wilderness
1. *Jones' Church History*, p. 238
2. *ibid.*, p. 187
3. *ibid.*

4. *History of the Sabbath*, J.N. Andrews
5. *The True Ecclesia*, D.H. Macmillan, p. 23
6. *Jones' Church History*, p. 380, ed. 1837
7. *ibid.*, p. 355, ed. 1837
8. *idem.*, p. 259
9. See *The Ancient Vallenses and Albigenses*, p. 163, G.S. Faber
10. *idem.*, p. 163
11. *ibid.*, pp. 169–172
12. *ibid.*, p. 181
13. *The Vaudois Church*, Monastier, p. 40
14. *ibid.*, p. 45
15. *The Vaudois Church*, Monastier, p. 38
16. *The Ancient Vallenses and Albigenses*, G.S. Faber, pp. 204–205
17. *ibid.*, p. 208
18. *ibid.*, p. 374
19. *Townsend's Abridgment*, pp. 405–409
20. *Israel of the Alps*, A. Muston, p. 3
21. *ibid.*, p. 4
22. *ibid.*, pp. 4–7
23. *The Vaudois Church*, Monastier, p. 93
24. *Jones' Church History*, p. 260
25. *ibid.*, p. 259
26. *Authentic Details of the Valdenses*, ed. 1827
27. *The Vaudois Church*, Monastier, p. 146
28. *The Vaudois Church*, Monastier, pp. 270–1
29. *Israel of the Alps*, A. Muston, p. 20
30. *ibid.*, p. 45
31. *ibid.*, p. 34
32. *ibid.*, p. 74
33. *ibid.*, p. 141
34. *ibid.*, p. 204

Chapter 9: The Man Who Wrote to a King

1. *History of the Sabbath*, Andrews
2. *A Treatise of the Sabbath Day*, Francis White, 1635
3. *History of the Sabbath*, Andrews
4. *ibid.*

Chapter 10: The Persecuted Church

1. *History of the Sabbath*, Andrews
2. *ibid.*
3. *ibid.*

Chapter 11: The Amazing Life of Shem Acher

1. *History of the Sabbath, Andrews, and Wilson's History of Dissenting Churches*, Vol. 2
2. *The Life of Shem Acher*, Francis Bampfield

3. *Transactions of the Baptist Historical Society*, p. 12
4. *A History of the English Baptists*, A. Underwood, p. 115
5. *History of the British Baptists*, W. T. Whitley, p. 86

Chapter 12: Sardis in Decline
1. *A History of the English Baptists*, Underwood, p. 112
2. *The Seventh Day Baptists in Europe and America*, p. 1264
3. *ibid.*, p. 87
4. *A History of English Baptists*, Underwood, p. 99
5. *The Last Legacy, or the Autobiography and Religious Profession of Joseph Davis, Snr*, pp. 28–47
6. *History of the Sabbath*, J.N. Andrews
7. *Literature of the Sabbath Question*, R. Cox
8. *Six Papers on the History of the Church of God*, R.C. Nickels, part 1, p. 16
9. See *Seventh Day Baptists in Europe and America*, pp. 53–54
10. *Six Papers on the History of the Church of God*, R.C. Nickels, part 1, p. 18
11. *Wilson's History of Dissenting Churches*, vol. 2, pp. 603–604
12. *Six Papers on the History of the Church of God*, R.C. Nickels, part 1, p. 18
13. *Transactions of the Baptist Historical Society*, p. 12
14. *History of the Sabbath*, Andrews
15. *History of Ireland*, O'Halleron
16. *Six Papers on the History of the Church of God*, R.C. Nickels, part 1, p. 12
17. *History of the Baptist Denomination*, D. Benedict, p. 920
18. *Wilson's History of Dissenting Churches*, vol. 2, pp. 585–6
19. *A History of English Baptists*, Underwood, p. 147
20. *History of the Baptist Denomination*, D. Benedict, p. 921
21. *Six Papers on the History of the Church of God*, R.C. Nickels, pp. 22–23

Chapter 13: The New World
1. *Sabbatarian Baptists in America*, R.C. Nickels, p. 1
2. *History of the Sabbath*, J.N. Andrews
3. *The Times of Stephen Mumford*, James McGeachy, p. 1
4. *ibid.*, p. 2
5. *Sabbatarian Baptists in America*, R.C. Nickels, p. 3
6. *History of the Sabbath*, J.N. Andrews
7. *The Times of Stephen Mumford*, James McGeachy, p. 5
8. *History of the Baptist Denomination*, D. Benedict, p. 921
9. *ibid.*, p. 921
10. *Seventh Day Baptist Memorial*, p. 160, vol. 2, no. 4; Randolph, *A History of the Seventh Day Baptists in West Virginia*, pp. 19–20
11. *History of the Sabbath*, J. N. Andrews
12. *Seventh Day Baptists in Europe and America*, Plainfield, New Jersey, pp. 600, 608
13. See *Westerly and its Witnesses*, F. Denison, pp. 59–60
14. *Sabbatarian Baptists in America*, R.C. Nickels, p. 7
15. *Seventh Day Baptists in New England*, 1671–1971, Karl G. Stillman, p. 2
16. *ibid.*, p. 5

17. *Seventh Day Baptists in Europe and America*, pp. 602–3, 613
18. *Sabbatarian Baptists in America*, R.C. Nickels, pp. 8–9
19. *Seventh-Day Baptist Memorial*, vol. 2, no. 3, pp. 120–121
20. *ibid.*, pp. 101–108
21. *Seventh Day Baptists in Europe and America*, p. 674
22. *Sabbatarian Baptists in America*, R.C. Nickels, p. 20
23. *Seventh Day Baptists in New England*, 1671–1971, K.G. Stillman, p. 7
24. *ibid.*, pp. 7–8
25. *ibid.*, p. 10
26. *History of the Origin and Growth of Sabbath-keeping in America,* James Bailey, pp. 25–26, 20–23
27. *Sabbatarian Baptists in America*, Richard C. Nickels, pp. 49–51
28. *Randolph's History of the Seventh Day Baptists*, p. 15
29. *ibid.*, pp. 20–24
30. See *Seventh Day Baptists in Europe and America*, p. 639
31. *Sabbatarian Baptists in America*, R.C. Nickels, p. 23
32. *A True History of the True Church*, Herman L. Hoeh, p. 23
33. *Our People Bound Together*, Albert N. Rogers, pp. 4–5
34. *See A History of English Baptists*, Underwood
35. See *Seventh Day Baptists in Europe and America*, pp. 153–209
36. *ibid.*, pp. 855–59, 887–88, 854–64, 1367
37. *Sabbatarian Baptists in America*, Richard C. Nickels, pp. 57, 59
38. *ibid.*, p. 60
39. *ibid.*, p. 66
40. *A True History of the True Church*, Herman L. Hoeh, p. 23
41. Sabbath Adventists, 1844–1863, R.C. Nickels, p. 40
42. *A True History of the True Church*, Herman L. Hoeh, p. 23
43. *ibid.*, p. 24
44. *History of the Church of* God (Seventh Day), John Kiesz, p. 12
45. *ibid.*, pp. 13–14

Chapter 14: Go You into All the World
1. *The Autobiography of Herbert W. Armstrong*, p. 10
2. *ibid.*, pp. 76–77
3. *The Autobiography of Herbert W. Armstrong*, Volume 1, 1986 hardback ed. p. 220
4. *The Autobiography of Herbert W. Armstrong, 1973 ed.* p. 210
5. *ibid.*, p. 221
6. *ibid.*, p. 261
7. *ibid.*, p. 263
8. *ibid.*, pp. 276–277
9. *ibid.*, p. 286
10. *ibid.*, p. 294
11. *ibid.*, p. 309
12. *ibid.*, p. 344
13. *ibid.*, p. 360
14. *ibid.*, p. 449

15. *ibid.*, p. 451
16. *ibid.*, p. 455
17. *ibid.*, p. 499
18. *ibid.*, p. 527
19. *The Autobiography of Herbert W. Armstrong*, Installment 55
20. *ibid.*, Installment 56
21. See *The Good News* magazine, January 1979

Chapter 15: A Plot Is Thwarted
1. *Fearless Love*, Anne Sanderson, p. 238
2. *Mystery of the Ages*, Herbert W. Armstrong, pp. 50–51
3. *Where is the True Church*, Herbert W. Armstrong, p. 24
4. *The Plain Truth about Christmas,* Herbert W. Armstrong, pp. 11–12
5. *The Plain Truth about Easter*, Herbert W. Armstrong, pp. 10–11

Chapter 16: The Spearpoint
1. *The Global Church News*, Global Church of God
2. *The Living Church News*, Living Church of God

KEY SCRIPTURES

The Incredible History of God's True Church

INDEX